Praise for *Rough Sleepers*

"Excellent . . . a detailed portrait of the lives of homeless Americans . . . Kidder, to his credit, never gives short shrift to the larger context. He just asks us—correctly, I think—to consider that in a world of far too much cruelty, the compassionate person standing at the bottom of the cliff is part of the story too."

—*The Washington Post*

"Excellent and immersive . . . sure-handed."

—*The Wall Street Journal*

"To read *Rough Sleepers* is to confront not only the consequences of homelessness, but to wrestle with knowing that, as terrible as the problem is now, it would so be much worse if not for the sacrifices of people like O'Connell."

—*Los Angeles Times*

"O'Connell is a fascinating protagonist. . . . The picture that emerges over the course of the absorbing, inspiring Rough Sleepers is that O'Connell is not only one of the good guys but a good guy who is vigorous, self-critical and even funny."

—Minneapolis *Star Tribune*

"[An] uneasy portrait of the United States . . . Kidder turns his meticulous but generous eye on Jim O'Connell."

—*Harper's Magazine*

"A book that celebrates the great good that one man and his program have done in the face of grueling, unimaginable odds. Kidder has humanized a sprawling, thorny subject by focusing on people, not policy."

—*Portland Press Herald*

"What does it mean, in our time of inequality, to care for the vulnerable in ways that strengthen the better angels of our common humanity? Tracy Kidder's book, and the work of Dr. Jim O'Connell, connect us to unforgettable individuals who allow us to get closer to the suffering that is only one part of what we need to see."

—ADRIAN NICOLE LeBLANC,
author of *Random Family*

"I couldn't put *Rough Sleepers* down till the last page. Kidder's writing sidesteps labels like 'homeless' to reveal the humanity of those who live on the streets. As with *Mountains Beyond Mountains,* I am left in awe of the human spirit and inspired to do better. That is Kidder's genius."

—ABRAHAM VERGHESE,
author of *The Covenant of Water*

"*Rough Sleepers* will do for homelessness what *Mountains Beyond Mountains* did for public health. I'm in awe of this book. I'm in awe of Jim O'Connell. What a compellingly beautiful, inspiring read."

—ALEX KOTLOWITZ,
bestselling author of *There Are No Children Here*

"The nightmare of homelessness can seem both overwhelming and slightly abstract to the safely housed. That abstraction vanishes in the pages of *Rough Sleepers*. Tracy Kidder has reported the hell out of important stories before, but never more finely and relentlessly. It's a story full of hard questions, a story with many heroes."

—WILLIAM FINNEGAN,
author of *Barbarian Days*

"The estimable Tracy Kidder has found another unsung saint—this time not in the backcountry of Haiti or in genocide-ravaged Burundi but on the streets of a major American city. And once again, he has crafted a story that sheds light on a larger landscape of injustice."

—ADAM HOCHSCHILD,
author of *American Midnight: The Great War, a Violent Peace, and Democracy's Forgotten Crisis*

"Tracy Kidder, a master of narrative nonfiction, is drawn to self-effacing, unsung heroes who work tirelessly to make the world a better place. Kidder delves deeply into his subjects, deftly weaving the fruits of his research into a strong narrative line that keeps readers turning pages. He doesn't hide his admiration for his subjects. . . . *Rough Sleepers* is yet another enlightening reminder from Kidder that we should, and can, do better."

—*The Christian Science Monitor*

"A searching, troubling look at the terrible actualities of homelessness."
—*Kirkus Reviews* (starred review)

"With a straightforward scrutiny that reveals without judging, Pulitzer Prize winner Tracy Kidder offers a long, hard look at the lives of homeless people. . . . Intensely immersive."

—*BookPage* (starred review)

"Poignant . . . Drawing on five years' worth of reporting, Kidder vividly portrays life on the streets. . . . Keenly observed and fluidly written, this is a compassionate report from the front lines of one of America's most intractable social problems."

—*Publishers Weekly*

By Tracy Kidder

ROUGH SLEEPERS

ROUGH
SLEEPERS

TRACY KIDDER

RANDOM HOUSE
NEW YORK

Published in the United States by Random House, an imprint and division of
Penguin Random House LLC, New York.

Random House and the House colophon are registered trademarks of
Penguin Random House LLC.

Originally published in hardcover in the United States by Random House,
an imprint and division of Penguin Random House LLC, in 2023.

Grateful acknowledgment is made to the following for permission
to reprint previously published material:
Jim O'Connell, M.D.: "Prescription for Housing" by Jim O'Connell, M.D.
Reprinted by permission of Jim O'Connell, M.D.
Ben Tousley: Excerpt from "A Song for Barbara" by Ben Tousley.
Reprinted by permission of Ben Tousley.

Library of Congress Cataloging-in-Publication Data

Names: Kidder, Tracy, author.
Title: Rough sleepers: Dr. Jim O'Connell and his quest to create a community of
care / Tracy Kidder.
Description: New York: Random House, [2023]
Identifiers: LCCN 2022017445 (print) | LCCN 2022017446 (ebook) |
ISBN 9781984801456 (trade paperback) | ISBN 9781984801449 (ebook)
Subjects: LCSH: O'Connell, James J. (James Joseph), 1948– | Homeless persons—
Services for—Massachusetts—Boston. | Homeless persons—Care—Massachusetts—
Boston. | Homelessness—Massachusetts—Boston.
Classification: LCC HV4506.B67 K54 2023 (print) | LCC HV4506.B67 (ebook) |
DDC 362.5/920974461—dc23/eng/20220420

LC record available at lccn.loc.gov/2022017445
LC ebook record available at lccn.loc.gov/2022017446

Printed in the United States of America on acid-free paper

randomhousebooks.com

2 4 6 8 9 7 5 3 1

Book design by Susan Turner

In Memoriam

Richard Todd

Keep watch, dear Lord, with those who watch or work or weep this night, and give your angels charge over those who sleep.

—Attributed to Saint Augustine

I Am

I am sometimes upfront
I am sometimes off-centered
I am sometimes concealed by myself
I am sometimes not even friggin' there
I am strong as an oak and weak as an acorn
I am a child, love me
I am a boy, take my hand
I am a soldier, so please understand
I am peaceful and proud, humble yet arrogant
I am calm, yet violent
I am quiet, yet thunderous
So if we should meet for a moment on my life's journey
Smile at me, talk to me, or simply be still
And know that I am.

—MICHAEL FRADA,
U.S. Army veteran and for many years
a patient of the Street Team

Contents

CONTENTS

Author's Note

I have changed the names of many patients.

The following names are pseudonyms, listed under the headings of chapters in which they first appear:

The Van: Johnny, Charlie, Nick, Sandy, Jerry, Jane, Manny, Lou Anne, Allegra, Arnold, Caroline, Jacqueline, Jack
Foot Soaking: Mr. Carr
Disaster Medicine: Bill, Gary, Santo
A New Face: Tony Columbo
The Street Team Meeting: Bo, Mack, Joe Z
Angels Without Wings: Johnny Smith, Harrison, David
No Loud Voices: Art
Death by Housing: BJ
A History of Tony: Isaac
The Social Director: Sally, Timmy, Andy, Jackie, Jane
Winter Comes: Rocky, Angie
The Beauty of Human Connection: Harmony, Jake
Sisyphus: Ronnie, Rabbit, Leon
The Gala: Rebecca
The Hug: John Jones
The Portrait Gallery: Kay, Lena, James Smith, Jimmy Dagget, Jonah Daniel, Bob, Jack, Nat, Dawn, Phyllis, Matthew, Gretel

I

The Van

Around ten on a warm September night, the outreach van stopped in the kind of South Boston neighborhood said to be "in transition." On one side of the street was a new apartment building, its windows glowing, its sidewalk lit by artful imitations of old-fashioned streetlamps. On the other side, in murky light, stood an abandoned loading dock. A heap of blankets lay on the concrete platform. Someone passing by wouldn't have known they were anything but discarded blankets. But when the driver of the van walked up the steps and spoke to them, saying he was doing a wellness check, a muffled voice came back from underneath: "Fuck you. Get the fuck outa here."

The driver turned away and shrugged to Dr. Jim O'Connell, who was standing at the bottom of the steps. "Let me try," the doctor said, and he climbed up to the platform and knelt by the gray mound. "Hey, Johnny. It's Jim O'Connell. I haven't seen you in a long time. I just want to make sure you're all right."

An earthquake in the blankets, then an eruption: Tangled hair and a bright red face and a loud voice, saying in a Boston accent, "Doctah Jim! How the fuck are ya!"

For the next half hour, Johnny reminisced—about the alcohol-fueled adventures of his past, about mutual old friends, mostly dead. The doctor listened, laughing now and then. He reminded Johnny that the Street Clinic was still open on Thursdays at Mass General. Johnny should come. That is, if he wanted to come.

Dr. Jim—James Joseph O'Connell—had been riding on the outreach van for three decades. During those years he had built, with many friends and colleagues, a large medical organization, which he called "the Program," short for the Boston Health Care for the Home-less Program. It now had four hundred employees and looked after about eleven thousand homeless people a year. Jim was its president, and also captain of the Street Team, a small piece of the Program, with eight members serving several hundred homeless people who shunned the city's many shelters and lived mainly outside or in make-shift quarters. About half of Jim's administrative work now lay in managing the Street Team, and all of his clinical work went to doctor-ing its patients, Boston's "rough sleepers," as Jim liked to call them, borrowing the British term from the nineteenth century.

The van was a crucial tool for reaching those patients. It was fi-nanced in part by the state and managed by the Pine Street Inn—Boston's largest homeless shelter. Nowadays two vans went out from the Inn each night. They had become an institution, which Jim had helped to foster in the late 1980s. Back then he used to ride three nights a week, usually until dawn. Now he went out only on Monday nights and got off around midnight.

When Jim had begun these tours on the van through Boston's nighttime streets, he had imagined the world of rough sleepers as a chaos. But it turned out that most of them had territories where they hung around and panhandled during the day—"stemming" was the street term, its etymology obscure. For sleeping, they had favorite doorways, park benches, alleys, understories of bridges, ATM parlors. Rough sleepers were like homebodies without homes. At the start of a ride, Jim and the driver and the driver's assistant would trade the names of people they were worried about, and they could usually find each of them within an hour or two. Jim was like a 1950s doctor mak-ing house calls, though the van rarely dispensed more than minor medicine. Rather, it was meant for bringing food and blankets and socks and underwear to rough sleepers, and, more urgently, for find-ing people in distress and bringing them in, if they would come—to hospital emergency rooms or the city's homeless shelters. The van was also a tool for keeping in touch with patients and their ailments and collecting the unpublished news of the streets.

Like all members of his Street Team, Jim carried a small knapsack, his doctor's bag, its contents refined and miniaturized over the years. It consisted mostly of basic first aid gear and diagnostic equipment—a blood pressure cuff that wrapped around the wrist, a little pulse oximeter, an ear thermometer, a simple blood glucose meter, a stethoscope. Among the losses he regretted was the pint bottle of whiskey he once carried for the times when a patient was in alcohol withdrawal and on the verge of seizure. "You couldn't do that now. It's become a moral issue."

He wore his cellphone in a holster on his hip, and he carried a small flashlight, thin enough to hold in his teeth if he needed both hands to examine a patient. A flashlight remained one of the Street Team's essential tools for checking on rough sleepers. Some years back, one patient had asked how Dr. Jim would feel if *his* doctor came to *his* bedroom in the middle of the night and woke him up by shining a flashlight in his face. Jim took the issue to the Program's board of directors, a group of about sixteen, which included experts in health and medicine and finance, and several formerly homeless people. The board convened a meeting of about thirty rough sleepers who issued this advice, long since become policy: The wellness checks should continue, but when they woke people up late at night, Jim and his Street Team should first shine their flashlights on their own faces so as not to startle the patients.

· · ·

The van stops under streetlights on Bromfield Street not far from Boston Common. It's like a small bus, with several rows of seats, mostly occupied by boxes of blankets, underwear, and socks. In the rear there's a small canteen, with boxes of sandwiches and condiments, vats of hot chocolate, coffee, and soup. Jim gets out, opens the back doors, and looks around for customers. He has a ruddy face and silver hair that falls almost to his collar and over the tops of his ears. He wears light-colored corduroy pants, a collared shirt, and clogs. He's six feet tall and trim and moves with an athlete's self-assurance that makes a task look easy, and his voice is full of energy and cheer as he waits on the customers at the back of the van.

A thin Black man comes wandering into the light, out of an alley.

"You got soup?" he asks.

"Yes!" says Jim, grabbing a Styrofoam cup and filling it from one of the vats.

"You got crackers to go with it?"

"Sure!"

"Isn't there a doctor who goes with you guys?"

"I'm a doctor," says Jim. Then he introduces himself, offering his hand.

"I want to change my doctor," says the man. "I hear good things about you."

"We'd be happy to take care of you. We'd be thrilled." The man should come to Street Clinic this Thursday, Jim says, adding that it's held at "Mass General"—the gigantic Massachusetts General Hospital, not far away, near the banks of the Charles River.

The van makes many stops. It encounters a mixture of people. There seem to be about half as many women as men, and lone women are rare, almost certainly because the streets at night are especially dangerous for them. There are many Black faces, but far fewer than white ones, and this is surprising. Homelessness afflicts Black and Latino people disproportionately both in the United States and in Boston, and one might expect that the same would be true of the city's rough sleepers. Jim has long worried that the van and other outreach efforts have consistently missed rough sleepers of color, and yet most of the van's drivers and their helpers are themselves Black and Latino. Over the years they have often searched for their own in the nighttime city. Maybe, Jim thinks, the Black and Latino communities are more willing than Boston's white world to harbor their homeless. In any case, once people have fallen to living on the streets, they have reached a certain horrible equality.

A young-looking white woman comes into the light on Washington Street, hopping on one foot and then the other, running her hands through matted, strawberry blond hair, all the while feverishly scratching her arms and neck and face. "That's what people will do on K2," Jim says softly, as the woman approaches. K2 is synthetic marijuana, which has notoriously unpredictable effects.

Her voice is loud and high: "Holy shit! I got lice! I was exposed to *lice* and I'm freaking out. I already got all the treatment and somebody stole it."

"Where did you get the treatment?" Jim asks.

"I bought the shit at CVS, and somebody stole a hundred dollars' worth of frigging lice removal shit, I got court tomorrow, my mother's sick in the hospital, dying, and I need to go see her but I'm not gonna go there and expose people. A lot of chicks have 'em and don't tell."

He moves closer to her, glancing at her collar as she speaks, looking for lice. ("Scabies get under your skin," he'll explain later. "Lice feed on your skin but live in your clothing. If she had lice, they'd have been on her collar.") He doesn't see any bugs there, but he never argues in cases like this, where the patient seems delusional. Instead he makes her an offer, phrasing it provisionally, in an evenhanded tone: "Do you want to go to one of the shelters where they can do the treatment? Or no?"

She says she has to see about something else first, but adds, "Thank you, sir."

"My name is Jim O'Connell. I'm a doctor, actually. So nice to meet you. Let us know if you want to come in." He smiles. "How 'bout some nice hot soup?"

"No."

"How 'bout some hot chocolate?"

"Yes! Hey, what kinda sandwiches do you guys have?"

His voice and attentions seem to have calmed her. She begins to tell him some of her life story. It includes an attempted rape, which has left her with a damaged shoulder. "Mind if I have a look?" She does not, and holding her shoulder with one hand, he gently moves her upper arm in several directions. It isn't dislocated or separated, he tells her, but if she wants a better evaluation, she should come to the

Mass General Street Clinic this Thursday. He writes down the phone number of the van, in case she decides to go to the shelter tonight.

"The pull of the streets" is a phrase that Jim and his team have used to explain to themselves why many of their patients leave detoxes and hospitals before their course of treatment is finished—leave "AMA," Against Medical Advice. Jim says he still feels drawn to these rides partly because of the relative simplicity of the city's nighttime streets—"When everything else has gone away, and it's just you and the people there." The van moves on. Jim stares out the window, at the woman sitting on cardboard under a streetlight, drinking her hot chocolate, eating her sandwich. He adds, "There's something about the van that keeps you riding on it. It's never quite the same, it's always a little different."

• • •

I first met Jim in 2014. A friend, a Boston entrepreneur, had wanted to learn about homelessness in the city, and Boston Health Care for the Homeless had offered him a van ride with Jim. I tagged along. I was struck by the relationships between this Harvard-educated "Doctor Jim" and the people the van encountered on the nighttime streets. His patients, and prospective patients, were sleeping in doorways, arguing drunkenly with statues in parks. I had rarely spoken to such people— and congratulated myself when I had. For me, the night's tour was a glimpse of a world hidden in plain sight. I was left with a memory of vivid faces and voices, and with a general impression of harsh survival, leavened by affection between a doctor and his patients. Afterward, I wondered if I'd misunderstood, or misremembered what I'd seen. Some months later, I contacted Jim and asked for another van ride.

Off and on for the next five years, I followed him with a notebook. Of all the various settings of his work, he seemed most comfortable on his weekly nighttime rounds, out in the city and on the move. The streets were a place, I came to think, where he could be just a doctor, where a stranger could watch him work and never guess that he was president of anything.

Julie Bogdanski, Jim's assistant, says that whenever she rides with Jim in his car, he asks what route they should take. She doesn't answer anymore—"He's better than Google Maps"—and yet he still asks, out of courtesy, she thinks. He learned the city's geography from riding the van. He never seems disoriented. But after dozens of rides I still find myself asking where we are from time to time. I don't recognize places where I'd been walking only that morning. When I step out of the van, the buildings feel much taller, the light around some of them much brighter, and all the alleys very much darker, the rough sleepers emerging from them onto the empty, late-night streets as if onto a spotlit stage.

Near the Haymarket, a muscular young man in apparent good health sits at the door of an ATM parlor, his current bedroom, telling Jim how he lost his college career and fiancée to what he calls "OC"— Oxycontin, that is. He speaks about his descent to the streets without self-pity or regret but as just a matter of fact. Then for a time he expounds like a pharmacist on the history of opiates, the physiology of addiction. Jim listens, leaning toward the young man. He shows Jim the knuckle of his right index finger. He abraded it last night. A friend, he explains, had overdosed on the potent, often deadly opiate fentanyl, and he had managed to revive him by performing a "sternum rub," a standard procedure among EMTs. Jim studies the injured knuckle, flashlight in his teeth. The cut looks infected. The young man should go to Mass General tomorrow, where Katy, the Street Team's nurse practitioner, will prescribe an antibiotic.

When the van moves on, Jim says, "That kid who's addicted, take away a little twist of fate, and maybe he could be playing for the Patriots. A big kid, with lots of potential . . ." Jim often catches himself speculating in this way about people he encounters on the streets. Usually, he reminds himself that he doesn't know the whole story and pulls the thought back before he utters it.

A tall, thin, handsome boy, perhaps Latino, catches up with Jim outside the 7-Eleven on Causeway Street, and in a reedy voice pleads to be sent back to the psychiatric ward from which he was just released. There's panic in his voice: He's afraid he's going to kill himself! Jim calls the emergency department at Mass General. A tedious negotiation and finally the okay. The hospital isn't far. The young man heads there on the run, disappearing into the dark beyond the streetlights, running from death, as Jim turns to another petitioner.

· · ·

From night to night many things don't change. There's the visual irony of Newbury Street, with its art galleries, boutiques, and cafés, where at night the usual people sleep in cardboard boxes and under the gray government-surplus blankets that the van distributes. The sleepers are variously positioned—inside the Gothic doorway of the Church of the Covenant, and on the pavement beside the windows of the public radio station, and under the display windows of Brooks Brothers clothiers. The grate in the Brooks Brothers alley emits hot air and always draws tenants in the cold seasons. Three men from Guatemala and two from Mexico one night, and on another a longtime patient of Jim's who looks and speaks like the headmistress of a boarding school.

There's an old man all alone in a park near Mass General, his elbows on his knees, unmoving, answering Jim's questions with shakes of his head. And a gray-haired woman in a cloth coat who says, "I kind of gave up on life for a while"—in a voice that suggests she hasn't yet finished giving up. And a longtime patient with a broken leg in a plastic cast who starts clomping across Newbury Street toward Jim, calling after the speeding car that has just narrowly missed him: "Go ahead and hit me! Like I really give a fuck!"

Jim recalls a night full of such moments, when every rough sleeper made him think of the phrase "the living dead" and of a rare psychiatric malady that actually defines the idea—Cotard's delusion, the belief that one is already dead, or doesn't exist, or is putrefying, or has lost one's blood and inner organs.

He says he remembers a time when he felt he knew everyone on the streets, and now he probably knows only half. But at each of the van's usual stops there's at least one of his patients waiting.

Partway down the block from a noisy crowd on the corner of Friend and Causeway Streets, a man stands alone in a darkened doorway. He has furrowed cheeks, as gray as boiled beef. His face looks inanimate. And then his eyes slowly widen, a smile blossoms. Jim is standing in front of him.

"Charlie!" says Jim.

"Doctor Jim," the man murmurs.

They talk briefly. In parting, Jim quickly slips a folded twenty-dollar bill into Charlie's pocket.

At some stops, several of his patients surround him. Waiting his turn, one of these, Nick, says to me: "This always happens. To get five minutes with him—it's impossible." And when Jim finally turns to him, Nick says with a touch of reproach in his voice, "You're like a celebrity."

Jim disregards this. "Nick! How are *you*?"

And Nick begins. "Lots of pain, Dr. Jim . . ."

Over near the corner of Mass Ave and Newbury Street, a thin woman with a weathered face comes flying out of the dark like an apparition. She rushes up behind Jim and throws her arms around him, almost knocking him over. "Sandy! How are *you*!" She is one of Jim's special favorites. "A legendary *charactah*," he says, with a trace of a southern Rhode Island accent. Sandy and her boyfriend lived for years deep in the tunnels under Copley Square. Now she's about to move into an apartment. She announces this triumphantly. Housing is a big goal for the Street Team and most of its patients, and for some— only some—it has meant salvation.

"It has big bay windows, Jim."

"Did you leave the tunnel?"

She laughs. "I'm going to school, Jim. I'm getting my GED."

"Sandy, I'm really glad to see you."

"You're coming by when I get in my apartment. I'm going to serve you cheese and tomatoes. You have to write the number down."

"I'll write the number down. But *you* have to come see us at the clinic on Thursday. Promise? You call me when you get there." He

moves toward the open van door, then turns back. Like every rough
sleeper, she has chronic medical problems. He'd like to see her again
and give her a checkup. "Wow, Sandy! Congratulations. *So nice* to see
you. You just made my night. Made my *day*. I'll see you Thursday, all
right?"

As the van heads toward the next stop, he tells me, "Sometimes
I'm not sure people remember what we've done. Getting a big hug
from Sandy just felt really nice. It felt like it was a hug stretching across
years. There were nights I was nervous she was going to die, and we
would never get through to her."

Clearly he got through in her case, but not all encounters are so
affirming. As the van rolls on through the mottled light and dark of
the city, he speaks about the difficulty and danger of applying measurable standards to the treatment of rough sleepers. "There are some
things you just do because it's the right thing to do. And the outcome
is out of my hands or in somebody else's hands. I want to believe
there's value in that. You're doing everything you can for the patient,
but you're not deluding yourself into thinking that what you do isn't
worth doing because the person is going to die anyway."

• • •

Jim remembered a time in the early days of the Program, back in the
mid-1980s, when he and his colleagues had practiced a version of
disaster medicine, a time when everyone they met on the streets was
in desperate need of help. There were bodies on the pavement, elderly people with skin cancers that had gone untreated for decades,
illnesses that American doctors knew only from textbooks—including
wounds full of maggots and even a case of scurvy. Both wet and dry
frostbite had been common, often followed by gangrene. "We used to
see maggots and frostbite four times a day. Now it's mostly diabetes
and hypertension. I think it's something to celebrate."

He remembered a very cold night some years ago when a rough
sleeper, in the throes of hypothermia, began dancing on a sidewalk,

taking off his clothes. Boston weather still held dangers for rough sleepers, especially in the spring and fall, when cold nights often follow warm days—as in a recent case, when a longtime patient, another of his "charactahs," drank too much in an alley on a warm March afternoon and woke the next morning with frostbitten toes.

On an evening in early January, a blizzard looming, Jim and a social worker headed out to find rough sleepers. But the van driver and his helper had neglected to bring a shovel, and Jim and the social worker hadn't worn boots. They ended up trudging across a field, wading through knee-deep snow, to rescue a pair of homeless men living in a patch of marshy urban wilderness known as the Fens. The men's makeshift tent had collapsed in the storm. Jim and his companion had to dig it out with their hands. Only one of the men inside was willing to leave.

They took him back through the snow to the van and eventually to South Station, one of the city's two principal train and bus terminals. For some years it had served as a favorite informal wintertime shelter for many rough sleepers. Jim's van rides, now confined to Monday nights, usually made their last and longest stop there—in the station's waiting room. By then, the last trains would have departed and the drugstore and kiosks and the restaurants would be shuttered, and yet the place would be rush-hour crowded, the men and women at the tables next to Starbucks like stranded travelers, staking out sleeping spots for the night. One woman in her eighties never left; she bought a bus ticket every month, and because she was a ticketed passenger, the station security let her stay there in all seasons. She suffered from heart disease but would not agree to go to a hospital. All efforts to persuade and even to force her had failed, and for several years the Street Team had treated her heart in the station, the bent-backed, elderly woman seated on one of the old wooden benches as one of the team knelt in front of her, dispensing out of a knapsack.

She was gone now, to a nursing home, and the old forbearing rules had changed. A private corporation now held the lease for South

Station's concourse, and the mayor had been obliged to work out a deal with the owners. Homeless people would be allowed to stay there after midnight only on what were defined as cold nights—that is, only when the temperature fell below thirty-two degrees. This rule had come into effect by the time of the blizzard, when Jim helped to dig the men out of their tent in the Fens.

Four nights later, the weather abruptly changed. Rising temperatures were predicted. People from the Department of Mental Health and social workers from various shelters gathered at South Station so they could offer the rough sleepers rides to the city's shelters in case the outside temperature climbed above freezing. Jim got to the station much earlier than usual, around nine. He counted 127 homeless people in the cavernous waiting room. Evidently, they'd been drawn there by a false rumor of free food, maybe even cots. But nothing was provided, except some blankets. Moreover, the station's security guards had herded all 127 into a barren section of the concourse.

When Jim arrived, a light freezing rain was falling outside. It was windy. But as predicted, the temperature was rising—"soaring to 34 degrees," Jim wrote mordantly in the notes he made that night. And once it had risen, at ten o'clock, a squad of Transit Police came in and started escorting all the homeless people out, a cop on each arm of the difficult ones.

A representative from the mayor's office was on hand, and he protested the eviction. The officer in charge rebuffed him: The cop didn't have time to argue, he had his orders, he had to get everyone out before midnight.

Some rough sleepers protested loudly. "I'm not leavin'! You don't have any right to kick me outa here!"

"Yes, we do, sir. You're coming with us."

Jerry, a patient of Jim's, was sleeping on the waiting room's stone floor surrounded by the four garbage bags that constituted all his worldly possessions. Jim watched helplessly as a Transit cop bent down and said loudly in Jerry's ear: "We're taking your stuff now and putting it outside!" Jerry woke up shouting. When he jumped to his feet, two Transit policemen grabbed him, one on each arm, and walked him to the doors. Another officer followed with the garbage bags.

Later, some city officials defended the operation. The Transit Police hadn't roughed up anyone. Every homeless person had been offered a ride to a shelter, and if rough sleepers didn't want to sleep in shelters, that wasn't the fault of the cops or the station's owners or the city. Some rough sleepers routinely got into fistfights at the station, some drank there, some took drugs. Occasionally, or so the story went, they broke into the restaurants late at night and cooked up meals for themselves. They often left the floor of the men's bathroom littered with food wrappers, toilet paper, plastic bottles. The owners of the station could say with some justice that the traveling public shouldn't have to put up with that kind of behavior.

Jim agreed with some of those arguments. "Rough sleepers aren't generally good houseguests." But the mass eviction left him sick at heart. He had thought the days were gone when an event like that would have been called regrettable but necessary. "I brag about the city being much kinder in general. And now I don't know why." In his notes that night, he wrote: "Felt like return to yesteryear and was very discouraging and upsetting to witness."

Among the evicted were many of the Street Team's patients. The list included Jane, sober five years and now trying to quit again. Manny was just getting over pneumonia. Lou Anne left the station fuming: "They gave us the bum's rush." Jack had asthma and was running a fever when he was put outside. Allegra had an abscess on her right hand; she had departed Tufts Medical Center AMA and without antibiotics. "Promises to go to MGH today (doubtful)," Jim wrote. Elderly, incontinent Arnold left dressed in a hospital johnny. Caroline left quietly, in her Santa Claus hat, with her grocery cart of possessions and her cardboard sign that spoke of a family home that she dreamed was still hers: I NEED A RIDE TO MY HOUSE. IT'S ONLY EIGHT MILES AWAY FROM HERE.

Jacqueline, another elderly woman, put up a fight when the Transit Police told her she had to leave. "I won't bother anybody. I haven't had sex for thirty-seven years. I don't drink, I don't smoke, I don't do drugs. I'm clean inside out." But they took her by the arms and led her away, her shrill, piercing voice wailing, "Please! Don't do this to me! I'm an old lady. I have no place to go. Don't you think if I had someplace to go, I wouldn't be here?"

II

The Art of Healing

1

~~~~~~~~~~

Conscripted

Jim was sometimes asked how he came to be a doctor to homeless people, and what kept him going. At one public lecture, he answered the question this way: "Most of the patients I've been close to over these thirty-two years are dead. So there's a certain sadness and moral outrage that I can't get rid of. But when you work with people who've had so little chance in life, there's a lot you can do. You try to take care of people, meet them where they are, figure out who they are, figure out what they need, how you can ease their suffering. I was drafted into this job, I didn't pick it, but I lucked into the best job I can imagine."

Jim had started Harvard Medical School later than most—at thirty, after a decade of adventure and quest. He had grown up in the Irish American working class of Newport, Rhode Island. He went on to Notre Dame, where he majored in philosophy and graduated as salutatorian of his class, a young man with many possible futures before him.

He tried out philosophy first, continuing his studies for two years at the University of Cambridge in England. But he quit that field soon afterward. "I don't think I had a mind for philosophy," he later said. What he did have was a mind for ideas connected to action. He went to Hawaii and spent two years teaching literature and coaching basketball at a high school. "I left to keep looking," he remembered. He returned to Newport and tended bar for a time with a college friend. With their earnings they bought an old barn in northern Vermont and turned it into a dwelling of sorts. He decided to become a New England country lawyer, and then, by happenstance, he finally discovered his life's work.

It was on a vacation trip with Cambridge friends in England. He had gone with them to the Isle of Man during the week of the Tourist Trophy motorcycle race, the island's festive, noisy phase. They were out for a drive when a spectator's motorcycle crashed on the road ahead. Jim's friends went off for help, while Jim sat with the biker. The man's leg had been cracked in half, a compound fracture, one end of the bone sticking out through the skin. Jim looked at the injured leg once and didn't dare look again for fear of vomiting. Mostly he listened, a bartender's art, while the man, a tough guy from Manchester in obvious agony and trying not to show it, told about the mistakes he'd made as a kid and how he'd ruined his marriage and earned his children's enduring anger.

Listening to the man's story, Jim felt he'd been granted a privilege. This was intimate contact with life, the very thing he had missed during all those years of reading philosophy. A doctor dealt with what all human beings have in common. A doctor could make a vital connection with anyone. "You didn't have to believe God sent you. You were on hand just because a man fell off his motorcycle and got a compound fracture." What Jim remembered thinking as he sat listening by the roadside, not looking at the broken leg, was wishful: "This would be perfect, if I knew how to take care of that leg."

Back in Vermont, Jim resolved to become a country doctor. He applied to the University of Vermont's medical school, but was told that at thirty he surely lacked the "superhuman endurance" that medical training required. So he settled for Harvard.

The year was 1978, when tuition didn't yet cost half a lifetime of debt. He managed to pay most of his own way by tending bar on the side. He loved his four years at Harvard, mostly because he was learning how to actually do something. As usual, he excelled in his studies, and the venerable Massachusetts General Hospital accepted him for one of its scarce, prestigious residencies in internal medicine.

On match day, fourth-year medical students receive a letter telling them where they will serve their internships and residencies. Mass General had also chosen two of Jim's best medical school friends. They went out that night to the Black Rose pub, both to celebrate and also to worry over the many warnings they'd heard about internship— the impossible hours, the scoldings one got from doctors and nurses. It was the Sunday of St. Patrick's Day weekend, so the pub was packed and rowdy. Just then, the crowd was cheering for a man dressed all in green who was hopping from table to table, dancing a jig. He was small and agile, a leprechaun. When he jumped onto their table, he looked down at Jim and his friends, then paused in his dance, crouched down on his haunches, and said, "What's wrong with you guys? You look like you just heard you're dyin'."

They were medical students, they explained, and today was match day. Soon they would become interns and never sleep again.

"Oh my God!" cried the man. He had a rich Boston accent. "You poor sons of bitches! Don't do it! Life is too shawht! Don't do it!" Then he rose and danced off.

Three months later, in an auditorium at Mass General, Jim sat amid a crowd of new doctors in crisp white coats, and at the lectern welcoming them stood that same man, the dancing leprechaun, transformed into the hospital's assistant director. When the ceremony ended, he walked up to Jim, wearing a smile of recognition. "I warned you," he said.

This was Dr. Tom Durant, an important figure at Mass General, informally its chief liaison officer to the regional powers. Friend of the Kennedys and Massachusetts governors and legislators, of Boston mayors and city councilors, and of many powerful women, many of whom were his patients. He played rugby for recreation. He also belonged to a school of medicine that conceives of physicians as doctors to society, many societies in his case. He managed to spend a lot of time in troubled countries, helping to create clinics in places like wartime Vietnam and refugee camps for survivors of the Cambodian slaughter.

During his three years inside the hospital, Jim got to know Durant only as an extravagant and admirable presence. In retrospect, he felt sure that Durant must had been keeping tabs on him during residency. Jim never confirmed this impression before Durant died, in 2001. But the man had seemed to know Jim's background—that Jim came from the Irish working class and that he had tended bar. And Durant must have heard about Jim's enthusiasm for working with a motley group of patients in Mass General's community clinics and its emergency department, where one served impoverished people, AIDS patients, ailing prostitutes.

By the spring of 1985, Jim had all but completed his residency and seemed on his way to a brilliant career in mainstream medicine. For the past several months, he had been the senior resident in the ICU, where very sick people arrived at all hours from all over the world. And he had just been awarded a prestigious fellowship—in oncology, at Memorial Sloan Kettering in New York City. He was walking down Mass General's long central corridor, flanked by glass and steel, feeling freshly accomplished, when Durant came up beside him, and said: "Hey, Jim, how about we go up and pay a call on John Potts?"

Potts was the hospital's chief of medicine. Jim remembered feeling a touch of schoolboy anxiety, as if he were walking with Durant to the principal's office. The chief's office itself was decidedly—indeed deliberately, ostentatiously—lacking in ostentation, small with a big metal desk and metal chairs with the usual ersatz-leather upholstery. Potts and Durant must have planned the occasion. They took turns explaining their case to Jim.

Homelessness had risen alarmingly all over the country as well as in Boston. Emergency departments were jammed with unfortunate people who didn't have homes or doctors. In response, the Robert Wood Johnson Foundation and Pew Charitable Trust had invited cities to compete for grants to build something called Health Care for the Homeless programs, which would integrate these poorest of the poor into a city's mainstream medical care. Boston had applied for a grant. The terms required a doctor, but Durant's friend Mayor Flynn couldn't find one. Would Jim sign up to fill that slot for a year, just one year?

It was Potts who made the request. Durant lightened the mood. He recalled the bantering advice he'd given Jim and his friends three years before, from the tabletop at the Black Rose pub. "I always told you not to be a doctor. You remember. But you went and did it, and this is what you've gotta do now."

Jim was thirty-seven, and he felt he didn't have time for a detour in his career. After three years of 110-hour weeks inside Mass General, he had absorbed both its general code—to pursue excellence in medicine—and also a corollary, which was not to mistake yourself for an ordinary doctor. It was one thing to treat the excluded and despised inside the great hospital, another to imagine treating them in dreary clinics elsewhere.

But these were his distinguished elders. They carried the weight of the institution. Jim felt he'd been "conscripted," but he couldn't think of a way to refuse. He remembered saying that the project sounded interesting, then added, "The one thing I fear is, I'll be marginalized in my own profession. So, you guys, if I do this, you've got to make sure you won't just cut me loose."

"No, no," Potts said to Jim. "Mass General wants to be part of this. We will send you as a full member of this hospital."

This at least was reassuring. Potts was both a scientist—his field was calcium—and a physician, and as chief, a fatherly figure of the comforting sort. He conceived of his role as "enabling," he told me years later. Durant had made the pitch, but Potts owned the desk in that office and with it the authority to make promises and to see that they were kept.

It was only a year, Jim remembered telling himself. It would be his year of "giving back." Then he would go on with his life.

2

~~~~~~~~

Foot Soaking

O n July 1, 1985, the day after Jim finished residency, he boarded
a train on Boston's old elevated Orange Line and headed
toward the South End. It was a hot day in the city. He wore a
collared shirt and necktie and pressed slacks. He had his stethoscope
in a back pocket and no idea of what awaited him. He'd been told to
go to the Pine Street Inn homeless shelter and report to the nurses'
clinic, whatever that was. A woman colleague who knew Jim back
then remembered him as a trim athletic guy with brown hair and keen
blue eyes. "Handsome, of course," she said. "And cheery, glad to see
you." He wasn't cocky, she insisted, indeed quite the opposite—
diffident, self-effacing. He was self-assured about medicine, though.
At that moment in his life he would have said, if pressed, that he
didn't know much about a lot of things, but he did know medicine.

Mass General had taken such good care of him, he told me, that he never suffered a lapse of confidence during his residency. And as he rode the train into the South End, he still felt enfolded by that grand institution. He was resigned to this year of service, even looking forward to it now. It would be a break from the pressures of residency, he figured. The only thing that looked difficult was budgeting a life on the salary, which was $40,000 a year, at that time less than half the median salary of an M.D. in internal medicine. As for doctoring, he was anxious to show the people in this nurses' clinic how well he could do the job. Only a few days earlier, he'd been part of a team running Mass General's ICU. The role of doctor in a clinic in a homeless shelter couldn't possibly be as challenging. An old friend of his told me: "I can imagine him thinking, 'They'll probably be glad to see me.'"

He had lived in Boston for seven years, but you didn't get to see a lot of the city through the windows of Harvard Medical School and Mass General. So this short trip felt like an adventure, the train bisecting increasingly ramshackle neighborhoods, which he could observe with an explorer's fascination, not yet being implicated in their squalor.

Out of the jumble of memory, these scenes remained: The orange-brick Pine Street Inn, seen from the train, its Tuscan bell tower rising over acres of industrial buildings and dilapidated flophouses. A short walk through a neighborhood of abandoned aspirations, of vacant lots, sagging chain-link fences, dark-faced bars. Then, as he turned onto Harrison Avenue, a very long line of men snaking down the sidewalk and into the alley toward the Pine Street Inn's front door— hundreds of men, all looking for beds, some carrying backpacks or garbage bags, some staggering, a few falling-down drunk. And finally the shelter's lobby, a big room with a ceiling of pipes and heating ducts, the air full of odors and the clamor of voices. It felt like a train station, people milling about with no one clearly in charge. He had to look around for the door to the nurses' clinic, a swinging double door. He could have been entering a saloon in a movie, unwarned and unarmed.

In the world of nursing, this clinic inside the Pine Street Inn shelter was a significant organization, the country's first clinic run entirely by nurses and independent of other medical institutions. It was in part the byproduct of a change in nursing that had begun with the feminist movement of the 1960s. One keeper of that history is a retired nurse and nurse manager named Barbara Blakeney. She had organized and run one of Boston's homeless shelters. Later, she'd served as president of the American Nurses Association, which represents the interests of America's four million registered nurses. She told me: "By the 1980s, nurses were starting to say, We have an area of practice that's independent from physicians. Yes, we can partner with physicians, we can take orders from physicians, but in addition there's the whole practice of nursing. It has a component that medicine does not attend to— that's the human being and the context in which patients find themselves."

In Blakeney's experience, the general treatment of homeless people in the city's teaching hospitals had set an example of callousness. "At the teaching hospitals, homeless people had very few advocates, and the homeless were often assigned to residents and interns to practice and learn on." She remembered a case where a homeless patient of hers went to Mass General's cardiology department for a 9:00 A.M. appointment, was made to wait for hours until all the other patients had been seen, then was asked why he hadn't bothered to take a shower that morning, and was finally seen by a medical student. The nurses at Pine Street could all tell such stories. Various state agencies now financed their clinic, but the nurses had founded it with donations, in a spirit of flight from hospitals and mainstream doctors and the dismissive treatment of homeless people.

Blakeney knew many of those nurses and had heard them talk about the prospect of their clinic being invaded by physicians. "Some were cynical enough to say, 'Yeah, medicine shows up when they can get reimbursed for it. We've been doing this for years without being paid.'"

Many of the nurses at the clinic were in fact volunteers, working there in exchange for the chance to practice their art. "Caring for homeless people is one department of nursing where you get to spend as much time as you need with a patient," Blakeney explained. "You *have* to spend a lot of time. Otherwise you won't have any patients. That's what attracted so many nurses to the Pine Street model. It didn't matter how often Joe Smith came in. He could come every night, and you could take care of him. There was no insurance company saying, 'You can only have six visits.' We could give him what he needed. So the idea of moving to a medicalized model where there were fees for service—it would mean losing nursing independence. And the nurses felt threatened: 'We don't need medicine coming in here and changing what we do'."

Blakeney concluded: "So Jim walking into Pine Street represented all those bad things to the nurses."

• • •

The morning when Jim arrived, the clinic was closed for lunch break, but half a dozen nurses were already inside, awaiting him. In the cramped space near the clinic's front desk, chairs were arranged in a semicircle, with one chair facing the nurses, the chair meant for him. In his memory, he sat there surrounded by nurses. Their faces were stern. They said they weren't interested in investing their time to train a doctor who planned to leave in a year. And if that was what he planned to do—to play doctor to a bunch of homeless men, earn their trust, have them learn to rely on him, and then desert them—it would be better if he didn't come at all. He was probably looking for an interesting experience, they said. He probably thought he was doing a good deed.

They were warning him, in a way that made him feel accused of having committed that crime already—as he had, inwardly. He felt shocked, too shocked to feel offended.

When they finished with him, one of the nurses took his arm and led him outside to the lobby. This was Barbara McInnis. She was a nurse at the Pine Street clinic, technically employed by the state's public health department to watch for outbreaks of tuberculosis. A

number of people had told Jim that she was *the* person to know in the
world of Boston homeless health care. He had imagined someone
prepossessing, but the real Barbara McInnis was short and, to his doctor's eye, a bit too heavy for good health. She was dressed not in a
nurse's uniform—she never wore one—but in a shapeless shift and
sandals. He noticed that she had a turquoise cross tattooed on the inside of her wrist. He learned later that she was a lay Franciscan. That
is, she believed in service and simplicity and in kindness to all crea-
tures. She actually fed the mice in the alleys outside the shelter.

Her voice, though high and small, sounded gentle. The nurses
had seemed hostile, but he shouldn't take that to heart, Barbara said.
Nurses had created this clinic, and they were proud of it, and many of
them would be happy never to see a doctor on the premises. She disagreed. Homeless people ought to have the benefit of doctors' skills.
"I really think we want doctors," she said. "But you've been trained all
wrong."

She later gave him a piece of paper, a copy of a page from a book
with something like a poem printed on it, a message to "healers," an
injunction against insisting that anyone *had* to be healed. "Just give
love," it read in part. "The soul will take that love / and put it where
it can best be used." This came from *Emmanuel's Book: A Manual for Living Comfortably in the Cosmos*. The words, it was said, came from the
spirit of Emmanuel, channeled through one of the authors. Jim
thanked Barbara for the gift.

At the time he thought the words were sappy, but he had kept the
page for many years and now it sat in a frame on a shelf in his office.
It was, he eventually realized, another way of telling him what she
had told him there, in a corner of the raucous lobby: That most if not
all of the Pine Street clinic's patients had experienced severe trauma,
and that the typical doctor's approach often terrified them. So it would
take time and patience and a lot of listening before he'd even have the
chance to act clinically. He remembered Barbara saying: "You have to
let us retrain you. If you come in with your doctor questions, you
won't learn anything. You have to learn to listen to these patients."

And then he heard her say, "Come on in now, and you're going to soak feet. I'll show you how."

She led him back into the clinic. He hooked his stethoscope around his neck on the way. Then he saw Barbara shaking her head at him emphatically. She pointed at a drawer in a nearby table. He dutifully deposited the instrument there. Why did he submit to all this? I asked him decades later. He told me, "I don't know if it's a weakness or not, but I've always had a hard time saying no. I remember wishing that I could say something like 'This is probably not appropriate.' And then it was overwhelming. I was spellbound."

The clinic had opened, therapies were in progress. Along the walls of the little clinic sat elderly, disheveled-looking men, their feet in plastic buckets, while nurses bent over them, speaking softly. This was strange enough, but especially strange because Jim recognized many of these homeless men. Over the past three years, he'd seen them in the Mass General emergency room, sullen, angry, snarling, resisting all treatment. Here they seemed so docile they might have been drugged, via foot soaking.

Barbara showed him the technique. It was simple enough. You filled a plastic tub halfway up with Betadine and put the patient's feet in it. And, in keeping with an old rule left by the founder of the Pine Street Inn, you always addressed the patient by his surname and an honorific—"Mr. Jones."

· · ·

The Pine Street clinic was one of the principal sites where Jim worked during the Program's first year. He spent three afternoons and evenings there each week, soaking feet and not doing much else for more than a month. Among the regulars was a very large man usually dressed in three layers of coats, with wary eyes and a salt-and-pepper beard and a great wave of white-and-gray hair that seemed to be in flight—Mr. Carr. Jim knew him from Mass General's emergency room. The police had brought him there repeatedly because they didn't know what else to do with him. He was classified as a paranoid schizophrenic, and his chart was thick, phone-book-size, a record of twenty-five years of what is known in medicine as "noncompliance"— those habitually guilty of this are "treatment-resistant." Jim had tried to tend Mr. Carr's ailments many times in the Mass General ER, but the man had always refused to take medications or to be admitted to the hospital. No matter how sick Mr. Carr appeared to be, Jim and his colleagues would have to let him return, untreated, to the streets.

At times Jim felt frustrated in the Pine Street Inn's clinic, kneeling in front of patients, beginning to form silent diagnoses, and not being allowed to act. But having already failed to get medicine into Mr. Carr so many times before at Mass General, he felt a certain resigned contentment in merely soaking the man's feet. They were so huge and swollen that Jim had to prepare a separate tub for each.

Mr. Carr didn't speak to him for weeks. Finally, one evening, as Jim knelt on the floor filling the tubs, he heard Mr. Carr say, "Hey, I thought you were s'posed to be a doctor." He was looking down at Jim with the suggestion of a smile around his lips, and amusement in his eyes.

In the last month no one here had called Jim "doctor." Yes! he said, looking up at Mr. Carr. Yes, he was indeed a doctor!

"So what the hell you doin' soakin' feet?"

Jim glanced around and saw Barbara and other nurses nearby, obviously eavesdropping. He looked back up at Mr. Carr. "You know what? I do whatever the nurses tell me."

Mr. Carr nodded. "Smart man. That's what I do."

About a week later, the old man put his feet in the buckets and said to Jim, "Hey, Doc. Can you give me something to help me sleep?" He never slept for more than an hour, he said. Within about a month, Jim had Mr. Carr taking a variety of medicines for his many ailments. Foot soaking in a homeless shelter—the biblical connotations were obvious. But for Jim, what counted most were the practical lessons, the way this simple therapy reversed the usual order—placing the doctor at the feet of the people he was trying to serve. As a doctor in training, he'd spent most of his time telling patients what *he* thought, saying, "We need to get that blood pressure down," or "I'm concerned about the results of your kidney tests." This new approach was entirely different, and, he began to realize, it was much more effective clinically, at least with homeless people. And foot soaking was the perfect way to begin.

These were, after all, men who wandered around all day on concrete and stood in lines for hours to get a bed or a meal. When they came into the clinic, they were usually exhausted, and their feet were sore. They'd let you look at their feet before they'd let you examine any other part of them. Cases of athlete's foot, corns, toenails that had gone uncut for years and were coiled around and around themselves, all were uncomfortable and easily fixed, as was trench foot. A nurse at another shelter taught him her honey-based treatment for the fungus. After he applied it, patients were always grateful for relief from the incessant itching, and many were willing then to talk about invisible things that were bothering them. Moreover, feet were often diagnostic in themselves. They revealed important internal problems, such as neuropathies from drinking and vitamin B_{12} deficiencies. Loss of feeling in the feet was an alarm telling him he'd better try to coax the patient to a hospital. You could also read a patient's likely future in the signs that frostbite leaves on toes. Jim and a colleague made a small study of death records. It suggested that patients with a history of frostbite—or of trench foot—had a death rate *seven times* higher than other homeless people of the same age group.

But that study was conducted more than a decade later. Around the time of his success with Mr. Carr, Jim's internship at the Pine Street clinic ended, and Barbara let him use his stethoscope again.

3

Disaster Medicine

Nineteen cities received grants from the Robert Wood Johnson Foundation and Pew Memorial Trust to build Health Care for the Homeless programs. Each city got $300,000 a year for four years; Massachusetts gave Boston's Program an additional $250,000. The financing was small, the ambitions large. At the outset, in the early 1980s, Jim heard some of the administrators speak as if they were tackling an isolated, manageable problem—as if homeless people would surely be receiving mainstream health care within the allotted four years. Jim had assumed they must be right.

In Boston, a mayoral committee drew up the Program's founding charter, during two years of rather contentious meetings. One camp represented the city's hospitals. The other was a group of "advocates" for the interests of homeless people—founders and managers of shelters and shelter clinics and a few medical professionals such as Barbara Blakeney. The other Barbara, Barbara McInnis, was also on the committee but rarely attended. "She wasn't fond of meetings," Blakeney remembered. "It was, 'Thank you very much. I'd rather not.'"

The mayoral committee drew up a charter, largely a set of rules about what the Program must and must not do. Jim wasn't aware of these rules until he started the job, in the summer of 1985. By then he had rounded up half a dozen Mass General residents to donate some of their time to the project, and he was astonished to learn that the charter forbade the use of any volunteers, except for nurses, of course. No doctors in training allowed, and no mental health treatment either. When Jim asked around for a reason, he was told that the state was being sued for failing to provide adequate mental health services to homeless people, and the committee's advocate wing didn't want the Program to ease the state's burden or undercut the lawsuit. On top of that, the Program would not be allowed to do research—mainly, Jim gathered, because the Reagan administration had used a study of mental health problems among homeless mothers to argue against housing subsidies—to say in effect that families were homeless because of mental illness, not a lack of housing.

These quixotic prohibitions expressed profound distrust of the medical and political establishments. At the insistence of the advocates, the committee hired a prominent law firm to enshrine the rules in a legally binding document, to ensure those rules could not be broken with impunity by the people who managed the Program—by people such as Jim. He got a taste of the advocates' passion during a prejob interview, when he was ambushed by a woman named Kip Tiernan, a former advertising executive who had founded a local shelter for homeless women. She wore a brown cargo shirt and a fedora; a cigarette usually dangled from her lower lip. In the midst of the interview, she reached across the table, grabbed Jim's necktie below the knot, and snarled, "Charity is scraps from the table, social justice is a seat at the table, and remember, we want a *seat*." Jim could imagine that sort of righteous anger without feeling it himself, but as a practical matter, the prohibitions felt like important handicaps. Volunteers, mental health, research—to Jim, these were vital components of a small, modestly funded, fledgling attempt to bring medicine to the poorest of the city's poor.

The charter also contained requirements. These made better sense to Jim. As he saw it, they all came wrapped in the phrase *continuity of care*—a prescription for ending the fragmented state of medicine for homeless people, who, if they ever saw a doctor at all, rarely saw the same one twice. The Program was required to seek out homeless patients wherever they lived in Boston, and to follow their treatment consistently. The Program would have to be integrated with the city's medical system so that Jim and his colleagues could send patients to hospitals and specialists, and make sure they were cared for properly. And the staff was to work in teams, so that if one doctor or physician assistant or nurse practitioner quit or got sick, homeless patients would still get treated by someone they knew and trusted.

Much of the budget went for salaries, set by the founding planners' decree. They were skimpy. Jim earned only a thousand dollars more than the Program's first two nurse practitioners and its registered nurse. The planning committee had selected the first seven medical personnel and left Jim to figure out how to deploy them. He put one pair to work with homeless families living in subsidized rooms at various motels. Another pair set up a clinic inside a two-stall bathroom at a day shelter called St. Francis House. Jim's own team included a case manager and nurse practitioner. He worked with them at five different sites—at three large homeless shelters and two new clinics they'd created. The teams were often rushed, sometimes fretful and unsure, but within a few months Jim felt they had made a start on what he envisioned—a citywide clinical practice, mainly situated in clinics inside homeless shelters and integrated with two major hospitals, all tailored to suit homeless people.

And then, rather suddenly, the enterprise became more complex. The change began at the Pine Street Inn on a night in August 1985.

Two of the staff who worked on the floors of the shelter brought a middle-aged homeless man into the clinic. He was a longtime resident at Pine Street, a cheerful, heavy-drinking fellow—in Jim's lexicon, one of the "old crusties." The workers said he didn't look right.

Those workers dealt with a lot of men who were grizzled and dirty and hungover. When they picked out someone from that background as a candidate for worry, Jim should have paid attention. But he hadn't yet learned that lesson. He took the man's vitals and listened to his heart and lungs. He didn't hear anything alarming through his stethoscope. But two nights later, the workers returned, insisting that the man was now clearly sick. Barbara McInnis ordered a chest X-ray. The clinic had an ancient machine, like an apparatus in an old Frankenstein movie, with a conelike protrusion and braided metal cables. When the technician turned it on, the lights in the clinic would dim. Like all but one of Boston's shelters, Pine Street was "wet"—it admitted people who were drunk, and there were many of those. So a nurse or aide often had to prop up a patient in front of the machine. Jim's "old crustie" was sober enough that night to stand without help for the X-ray.

Jim and a doctor from the health department read the film. It was dramatic-looking. One of the man's lungs was completely white—probably overrun by TB bacilli, as the state lab soon confirmed. Jim rarely used profanity, but when he saw the picture, he cried out, "Holy shit! This guy's been living at Pine Street for months!"

During Jim's first weeks at the Pine Street clinic, Barbara had remarked that while the clinic was an oasis of order, the shelter itself was not, and he should tour it. It dampened his spirits to see the Inn's barracks-like dormitories during the day, with their institutional green walls and rows of beds, a number stenciled on the gray concrete floor at the head of each. At night those sleeping halls were spooky. A guest at the Inn heading for bed was obliged to take off his clothes. These were returned later, but first they went into a basket and passed through a heater hot enough to kill vermin. Then the guest walked naked down a corridor of shower nozzles, which drenched him as he passed. After drying off, the guest was given a large white nightshirt, joining the ghostly figures of men in flowing white shirts moving toward their beds under "black lights"—lights that reduce but don't halt TB transmission. Jim imagined men with TB lying in their beds in those huge communal chambers, coughing and coughing, infusing the air around them with bacilli, scores of other men lying nearby, breathing in the pathogens. How many were now infected? And how many of Boston's citizens were being infected when, as required every morning, guests left the Inn for the day?

Jim's fears were outsized. He hadn't been taught much about the pathogenesis of TB. As he soon learned, the outbreak didn't greatly endanger the general public. However, it did put the Inn's residents at risk. For them, the news got worse. The elderly patient, Jim's "old crusty," had been spreading a mutated, drug-resistant form of TB.

During the next several months, sixty men with active cases were identified, all heavy drinkers, none with AIDS. Those men would need to take four different antibiotics daily for eighteen months. Pine Street's clinic could have managed this, but after learning that they'd caught the disease at the Inn, many men left and wouldn't come back. They had to be found and persuaded to take the necessary pills.

Nurses from city and state agencies did most of the work, finding the men, teaching them about the disease, and coaxing them to take the drugs. Jim's small team joined in, on foot and bicycle, and so did some citizens. Early on, the Pine Street clinic received a call from the bartender at J. J. Foley's, saying that one of his regular patrons seemed very sick and asking if anyone could help. Jim walked over to the bar. Maybe it was a matter of veteran bartenders recognizing each other. In any case, the two men became fast friends. It turned out that eight of the bar's regulars were among the sixty with active cases of the drug-resistant strain. Jim arranged to have their medications delivered to the bartender, who made the homeless men take their pills before he'd pour their beer. Through some other patients, Jim also got acquainted with a barber in Southie who kept a little coffeehouse in his shop that three other TB patients frequented. The barber, like the bartender, insisted the men take their medicine before he served their beverage.

. . .

In America, lengths of hospital stays had greatly diminished. Patients were sent home to recuperate after procedures that once would have meant a week or more in a hospital bed. But for people without homes this change meant recuperating in the shelters or on the streets. Mainly for this reason, the founding rules of the Boston Health Care for the Homeless Program required that it create a "respite facility." The charter defined this as a "home-like" place. It would differ from the shelters in that patients would have their own beds and wouldn't be obliged to leave every morning and to stand in line for a bed every night. It would be a place where patients would receive proper nutrition and medical care. The founding committee had rented twenty-five beds to create a facsimile of such a respite facility. It was situated in a corner of a homeless shelter at the Shattuck Hospital.

They opened the facility in a hectic time, in the early days of the TB outbreak. A week later, the Program's first AIDS patient arrived, another beginning of sorts. AIDS hit Boston's homeless population later than the relatively well-to-do, but when it came, it formed a dreadful synergy with the special miseries of homelessness. Among painful early cases, one of Pine Street's stood out for Jim. Just months after the onset of the TB outbreak, a homeless middle-aged man came to the nurses' clinic with an odd complaint. He told Jim that he didn't quite know where his hand was, and that he couldn't move it. In medical lingo, he had a "paretic hand," a possible symptom of a rare and fatal neurological infection called PML. In his three years at Mass General, Jim had learned that AIDS could show up in the guise of almost any illness, any infection that a damaged immune system couldn't deter. As he'd been taught, he assumed that this homeless man had AIDS.

Jim had sent him to the emergency room at Boston City Hospital, where the man pleaded for a bed. He was rebuffed. "THIS PATIENT IS MALINGERING! PLEASE DISCHARGE," a neurology resident wrote in capital letters in the clinical notes. It was winter in Boston. Evidently the young man left the hospital looking for a place to sleep and found an unlocked car outside a South End flophouse. He died there in the night, of AIDS. Jim copied the offensive note from Boston City and put it away. Thirty years later, he couldn't find it, but he knew it still lay in his filing cabinets somewhere, like a memento mori.

At the Shattuck respite, the number of homeless AIDS patients grew from one to two, from two to eight and then to ten, and finally to twenty, which meant that the respite had become an AIDS treatment center. On his daily visits there, Jim found the staff scrambling to treat whatever opportunistic infection came next—pneumonias they'd never seen before, cryptococcal meningitis, toxoplasmosis, Kaposi sarcoma. No matter what they did, everyone died. The respite was the worst site imaginable for treating people with AIDS, because its patients shared the same huge, crowded room of 180 shelter beds, where homeless men with all sorts of maladies lay breathing and coughing. Jim tried to persuade hospital administrators to take in the respite's homeless AIDS patients. He wrote letters to various hospitals, begging them not to discharge people with AIDS to the shelters or, even worse, to the streets. All to no avail. "The truth is we have nothing, no tools," Jim remembered thinking. "It's like we're putting our fingers in the dike, but the dike is going to cave in soon. We just can't stop it."

Fear came with the illness. Early on, the Pine Street Inn received a gay man who had been kicked out of his apartment by his partner. Innocent of the protocols of shelter life, the man told others he'd been diagnosed with AIDS. General alarm followed. Barbara McInnis summoned Jim to a midnight meeting of the staff. They wanted a medical opinion on a host of questions: Could the man with AIDS use the same bathrooms as everyone else? Could he sleep in the same dorm? Did he need special shaving equipment? Jim didn't blame them for asking. Knowledge of how the disease was transmitted still wasn't common, and no test was yet available to certify infection. He told the staff that for now they should assume everyone had the disease and take the same precautions with everyone, ostracizing no one. Barbara took his side on this. He wasn't sure most others did. Above all, he wanted them to understand the essential irony of the situation—that the dying man everyone feared was the person in greatest danger.

The days and nights ran together. Before he knew it, most of his one-year commitment had passed. Jim wrote to Sloan Kettering in New York, asking that they defer his fellowship for another year.

• • •

The TB outbreak had obliged Jim's team to take to the streets, in search of patients with active TB. They also found many others who were sick and dying from other ailments. One man had frozen to death only two blocks away from the Pine Street Inn. Jim remembered Barbara saying, "Oh my God, Jim. We need to get to them." What they needed, she said, was a vehicle to find and help the homeless people who weren't coming regularly to the shelters and clinics. In 1986, the state financed what became the first of the outreach vans—"The Overnight Rescue Van"—which went out every night offering food and blankets and medical help. In the beginning, it operated only during the three coldest winter months, the time when, it was assumed, people who stayed outside were most likely to die. Barbara told Jim that they should keep track of deaths among rough sleepers, to find out in what seasons most were dying.

Wouldn't that be research? Jim asked. One of the activities that she and the Program's other founders had banned?

"No, this is different," she said. "We'll call it *a report.*"

During the next year, fifty-six deaths were documented among rough sleepers, and just as many had died in spring, summer, and fall as in winter. Jim wrote up a brief report, which he and Barbara took to the State House on Beacon Hill. The legislature's public health committee agreed to finance the van year-round. Afterward, hoping this victory might begin to undo the taboo against research, Jim submitted his mortality report to the *Journal of the American Medical Association*. They accepted it but asked for revisions. He intended to comply but he never found the time.

He had worked at the two largest shelter clinics for over a year, and for a while he had imagined that he knew most of the city's homeless population. But once he began riding the van three nights a week, he realized that he'd never met most of the city's rough sleepers. They didn't use the shelters or even the shelter clinics, which had seemed to Jim like models of accessibility—so easy to get to, so welcoming. Why weren't they coming in? And what were they doing to stay alive out there? What was it like to live under a bridge? To answer those questions, he had to win the trust of this other part of the homeless population. He worried that this task would be more difficult than in the shelter clinics, where homeless patients typically felt safe and where he could trade on some of Barbara's and the other nurses' popularity. But the crews that ran the vans soon became popular, too, and the food and clothes and blankets they provided never failed to draw rough sleepers from their hiding spots to the back of the van, where Jim met them, as I saw him do several decades later, with a bartender's patience and a student's sincere interest. "It was just a privilege to be there. I loved it," he said.

Once they got used to seeing Jim at their encampments, many rough sleepers would chat. He often asked why they preferred to sleep outside rather than in the shelters. The most common answer began with a question. Had Dr. Jim ever tried to sleep in a shelter, with a hundred other people in the same room? Well, they just couldn't do it. Almost always, they would add that he shouldn't think they *chose* to live outside. Offer them someplace else besides a shelter and they'd gladly move in.

The most striking explanation came from a man who slept under one of the Storrow Drive bridges—a sweet, soft-spoken fellow who suffered from schizophrenia. Jim had met him half a dozen times and given him coffee and blankets and socks and treated him for a few minor ailments. In the middle of a very cold night, afraid the man might die of hypothermia, Jim begged him to come back in the van to the Pine Street shelter. But the man demurred. "Look, Doc, if I'm at Pine Street, I can't tell which voices are mine and which are some-body else's," he said. "When I stay out here, I know the voices are mine, and I can control them a little."

In the shelter clinics and on the van, Jim came face-to-face with dozens of people who hadn't seen a doctor in years, let alone a psy-chiatrist or dentist. He saw many with rotted teeth and many cases of scabies and lice. He came across people with AIDS who had been discharged from emergency rooms with no platelets, including a few who appeared in the lights of the outreach van with blood flowing from their ears and noses. Jim met an elderly man who looked fairly normal until he took off his hat at Jim's request, revealing a grotesque-looking cancer that had invaded his head, paralyzing the left side of his face. That patient had been a professor at MIT, had suffered a psychotic break, and had been living on the streets for years, no one noticing or caring to notice what must have started as a small, easily treated basal cell carcinoma, now metastasized into an overspreading, fatal growth, which had reached his spine. Another man, eighty years old, was afflicted with a hernia the likes of which Jim had seen only in a medical textbook, a hernia that, like the professor's cancer, had gone untreated for decades and now hung down below the old man's knees. At times Jim imagined that he and his colleagues were practicing something like wartime or post-earthquake medicine. It was as if he had been parachuted into another world that modern technologies had never reached. The situation was appalling, the work overwhelm-ing. And, if he was honest with himself, utterly fascinating.

. . .

When Jim had planned to go to Sloan Kettering and specialize in oncology, one of his close friends assumed that he imagined himself finding cures for cancer. Perhaps the friend had ambitions for Jim that were grander than Jim had for himself—at least by then. A temporary job among homeless people, at the other end of the prestige scale in medicine, didn't inspire dreams of glory. During a meeting at the Robert Wood Johnson Foundation, Jim met several people who still seemed to believe that when the grants ran out in 1989, the numbers of homeless people would have shrunk and mainstream medicine would have taken over the care of the remaining few. He heard voices saying, "We're working our way out of this job." But these were administrators, not practitioners in the field. He wished he could share their confidence, but by then he had seen too much in the shelters and on the streets.

It was obvious that he and his colleagues weren't addressing the many root causes of their patients' misery. But they were trying to figure out how to ameliorate some of the deepest suffering that lurked in the city, and that job seemed challenging enough. How do you treat HIV in a person who has no place to live? How do you treat diabetes in patients who can't even find their next meals? How do you treat physical illnesses in mentally ill patients and patients whose days and nights are ruled by the consumption of alcohol, the search for narcotics? At medical school, questions like those hadn't come up. He was discovering the role of homelessness doctor, with a lot of help from Barbara McInnis.

What did "continuity of care" actually mean in doctoring homeless people? Around the time when Barbara let him use his stethoscope again, he found himself in an exam room at the Pine Street shelter's clinic with a patient seemingly in crisis. The man—Bill—was weeping, saying, "I'm going to kill myself." He pulled a knife out of a pocket.

The guy seemed genuinely desperate. Jim would have known what to do at Mass General, but he didn't here. He hurried out of the room to find Barbara, and asked her, "What's the process when you think someone's really suicidal?" She led Jim back to the exam room.

"What's going on?" she asked Bill.

"Bill's thinking of hurting himself," said Jim.

Then Barbara sat down and leveled her gaze at the patient. "Bill. You know we don't use talk like that around here. If you're going to use that kind of language, I need you to go outside and talk in the alleyway. When you come in here, you're not suicidal."

Jim was astonished. He couldn't imagine talking to a patient that way, especially one threatening suicide.

And then Bill cleared up the whole matter. "Oh, okay, Barbara. I'm sorry. I'll be okay."

The explanation was plain. The clinic did, of course, have a protocol for managing suicide threats. Indeed, Barbara was known for sniffing out the real cases, including those who made no threats. But she had known Bill for a long time, and she knew he talked this way periodically, and she understood that he didn't intend to harm himself this time either. Continuity of care in this context was a transaction. It was important that homeless patients know their physicians well enough to trust them, and it was vital that the physicians and nurses spend the time it took to know each patient.

Jim was taught the same general lesson more than once, and one time at much greater cost to the patient. The man, Gary, was old for the streets. He had served as a fighter pilot in World War II. Jim didn't yet know him well, when, one summer morning, a call came from the minister of the Old South Church, near Copley Square. The minister told Jim that Gary was sleeping on the grass in front of the church, and he had a terrible wound in his leg. Jim stopped by soon afterward. Gary's wound was deep and wide, and it was full of maggots. An unsettling sight. Jim talked Gary into going with him to Mass General, promising to rid him of the maggots, and there at the ER, Jim was shown how to do this—one drew them out by packing the wound with beef and then, when the maggots had swarmed the meat, anesthetizing them with ether.

The wound was not infected. That was the great thing about maggots—they kept wounds clean by consuming the dead tissue. Now that they were gone, the wound itself needed urgent treatment. But when Jim told him he should stay in the hospital for a while, Gary said, "Nah. Thanks for gettin' rid of the maggots. I'm fine now." He would not relent.

Jim tried to keep an eye on him, but the next time he located Gary on the streets, the leg was severely infected, and when Gary finally agreed to go back to the hospital, his leg had to be amputated. His problems belonged to Jim then. The only remaining intervention was to find Gary a decent nursing home.

In this fledgling practice, patients also taught Jim and his colleagues what the term "patient-centered" ought to mean. For instance, Santo. He was small and thin, a perennial boarder at the Pine Street Inn. Jim first met him at the shelter's clinic. Santo said he couldn't swallow his food, but up until recently he'd been able to manage liquids. Now he couldn't swallow his vodka. A person sleeping in a shelter, trying to survive out on the streets each day, tended not to pay attention to aches and pains or even hunger, not until some essential function was impaired—in this case, swallowing vodka.

It turned out that Santo had a very large cancer of the esophagus, long-standing and untreatable. Jim arranged for him to have a tube inserted in his stomach, so he could take liquids. Jim also resolved that this poor fellow, having lived for years in a shelter barracks, shouldn't have to die in the strident chaos of the Pine Street Inn. He spent a long Friday evening writing up applications, insisting that Santo must be admitted to a nursing home. The effort paid off. On the following Monday, Jim picked him up at Pine Street and drove him to a first-class nursing facility, and went home that night feeling pleased with himself.

About a week later, as Jim was walking down the alley to the Pine Street Inn's front door, he heard from up ahead a cacophony of men's voices, laughter and shouting of a high alcoholic content. Among the voices he thought he recognized Santo's, and when the drinking men came into view, there he was, Santo indeed, holding a bottle of vodka and pouring its contents down the tube in his stomach.

Jim approached him. What was he doing here?

Santo said he appreciated what Jim had tried to do for him. "*But*. I was in that nursing home and everybody was sittin' in a chair, lookin' out the window, starin' into space, and drooling or watchin' TV, but nobody's talkin'." He gestured at the drinking crew. "These are my people, okay?"

This was Jim's summary of the case: "Santo had lived in the Pine Street shelter for forty years. It was the world he knew. And if he was dying, he wanted to be around the people he knew. So I realized, you know, more power to him, because he was going to continue to drink his vodka and be with his friends. What I did for him didn't seem right from the perspective of the person we were trying to serve."

• • •

Jim's work consumed virtually all his waking hours. Two days a week at the Boston City Hospital clinic and two at the Mass General clinic. Three nights a week at the Pine Street nurses' clinic—doctoring, no longer soaking feet—and two nights at another large shelter. Three overnights on the outreach van, starting when the Pine Street clinic closed. Also frequent visits to the little bathroom-based clinic at St. Francis House and to the respite that had turned into an AIDS treatment center at the Shattuck. He did some of the paperwork, too.

He was then in his late thirties. He figured he was working about a hundred hours a week, and he recalled thinking, "Well, this is easier than residency anyway." He wasn't married, unlike most of his peers. Besides, many colleagues in the Program and at Pine Street—Barbara, for one—were working similar hours. He was making about eight dollars an hour, and he found it hard to manage on that. He took an extra job—as medical director at one of the local detoxes—and added about $500 a month to his pay. That role required mostly phone calls, which he could handle on the side. And he reasoned that this role extended the Program's reach, since many people in detox were current or potential patients.

This was Jim's first job as a full-fledged doctor. He wanted to do it

well. The hours were just what it required. As for managing the emotional side of the work, he could fall back on his medical school training in "compartmentalization"—you're in a hospital and you go into
a room where the patient is very sick and failing, and then, when you
enter the next room, you forget the tragedy unfolding in the previous
one, and concentrate on the person in front of you. Eventually,
though, he couldn't shut out any of the rooms. The problems in each
would accumulate all week, and on Friday nights when the Pine Street
clinic closed, many of the staff would drive out to Jamaica Plain and
crowd into Doyle's Cafe, and they'd drink and talk about how mad-
dening it felt to witness deaths that could have been prevented, and
how if you fixed one problem for a patient, that same patient was
there again the next week, afflicted with a dozen additional problems.
By midnight, the effect of the talk and the beer was cathartic.

In graduate school, Jim had studied Albert Camus' essay *The Myth
of Sisyphus*. (Camus begins: "The gods had condemned Sisyphus to
ceaselessly rolling a rock to the top of a mountain, whence the stone
would fall back of its own weight. They had thought with some reason
that there is no more dreadful punishment than futile and hopeless
labor." At the end of the essay, Camus refutes its beginning: "The
struggle itself toward the heights is enough to fill a man's heart. One
must imagine Sisyphus happy.") Jim often thought about the myth
during those early days of homelessness medicine, but he never mentioned it to the crew drinking at Doyle's. Alluding to Greek mythology
would seem pretentious, he thought, in that practical and burdened
company. He could talk to Barbara about anything, though, and on
occasion he did speak to her about the Sisyphean nature of the work—
carefully, so as not to offend her with existentialist notions about the
absurdity of life. She was a radical Catholic in the Dorothy Day mold,
but still Catholic. She told him once that she had the turquoise tau
cross tattooed on her wrist because she wanted something beautiful to
look at when she was dying.

Barbara always came along to Doyle's on Friday nights. Jim would
sit beside her at the bar and drive her home afterward. On the way

sometimes, he'd take her and a few of the staff to his place, so that she could watch her favorite TV show, *Miami Vice*. He never quite figured out what she saw in it, but he enjoyed watching her enjoy it. Some nights at Doyle's, he would rebel against his normal practice and rant a little to her. How could this country treat people this way? How could any Americans, homeless or not, never have had their own doctor? Never even have seen one? Never have been given a screening? Never have been given *anything*? How for that matter could a *hospital* send people out onto the streets with *no platelets in their blood*?

Barbara would listen, and in her high but somehow calming voice would tell him, "Jim, you're a doctor. You're not God. There are things you can't fix. You just have to do your work." It was always the same general message, and it had corollaries. One that became like a proverb for him concerned new hiring for the Program: "We don't want saints and zealots. We want flawed human beings who do their jobs. Just make this an ordinary job that people like to do."

He had bought into that notion. He told himself that he was just going to dig in and work, and not look beyond that. He recalled saying to himself, "This is what I was trained for. I wanted to take care of people who were sick. And, oh my God, have I landed in a world where people are sick."

Jim called Sloan Kettering, to say that he wouldn't be coming after all.

III

The Pantheon

1

Numbers

The modern era of American homelessness began in the 1980s, when the size and visibility of the problem began to rise dramatically. Driving south on I-93, Jim tried to draw me a picture of what had gone wrong in Boston. Coming out of the tunnel beneath the center of the city, he gestured to a portion of the South End. "Just look at this. Look at these new buildings, all along here. All those are apartments and all the ones behind them. There's got to be, by my calculation, at least four thousand new units there, right next to the Pine Street Inn. But not a single one for homeless people." From the car, it seemed as if the glassy new apartment buildings were pressing in from all sides upon the Inn's tall, orange-brick tower, once a fire station's lookout, now a Boston landmark. A giant ad for the latest

Apple iPhone hung on the tower's face. The explanation was obvious. "They need revenue," Jim said.

The thickets of luxury housing, both new and renovated, had replaced a mostly bleak landscape of industrial warehouses and factories and vacant lots, of bars and boardinghouses and Victorian brownstones chopped up into single-room-occupancy units. Back in the 1920s, Boston had 35,000 of those SROs for rent. They had served as homes for immigrants and low-wage workers, elderly people on fixed incomes, and, more recently, for struggling Vietnam veterans and former residents of mental hospitals. In 1965, the city and South End residents had overwhelmingly approved a plan to turn the neighborhood into "an economically, socially and racially integrated community," with rental housing for "all displaced low-income residents wishing to remain." The destruction of the old buildings, with their inexpensive, often shabby rooms, was widely praised as an act of civic virtue, and it might have been, if anything like that plan had followed. But when the old buildings were razed or renovated into condominiums, the people who once lived in those SROs were turned out, onto the streets by day and into the Pine Street Inn at night. They came to the shelter in such large numbers that in order to provide breakfast and dinner and beds for all, the original Inn was forced to relocate to a larger building, its current headquarters with the tall Sienese lookout tower.

A severe recession in 1980 had inaugurated the era of rising homelessness. But the problem was driven and sustained by many long-brewing problems: the shabby treatment of Vietnam veterans; the grossly inadequate provisions that had been made for mentally ill people since the nation began to close its psychiatric hospitals; the decline in jobs and wages for unskilled workers; the continuation of racist housing policies such as redlining and racially disproportionate evictions; the AIDS epidemic and the drug epidemics that fed it. Also the arcana of applying for Social Security disability—a process so complex that anyone who could figure out how to get assistance probably didn't need it.

Many commentators and scholars have written that the Reagan administration fostered the rise in homelessness, with its deep cuts in programs for the poor and policies that led to declines in the supply of inexpensive housing. Some responsibility for those cuts and policies also belonged to Democrats, who had controlled the House for all eight years of Reagan's term and the Senate during the last two. Homelessness grew rapidly during Reagan's time, and it continued to grow with every presidency that followed. Given the problem's complex etiology, no single group can be blamed for all its constituent parts.

In an interview at the end of his presidency—with David Brinkley on ABC-TV—Reagan defended his record, blaming rising homelessness on homeless people themselves. Some, he said, were "mentally impaired," consigned to wander the streets because left-wing lawyers had shut down mental hospitals. Some were too poor to buy or rent homes, because they didn't want to work and ignored the "hundreds of ads" offering jobs. Others simply chose to live outside, even though there were shelters all over the country. "They make it their own choice for staying out there," the president said.

These notions, and his administration's attacks on Black welfare mothers, had deep roots in Western attitudes toward poor people generally and especially poor Black people. Reagan simply carried on the tradition of justifying inequality while also propagating enduring misconceptions. The shuttering of mental hospitals and the failure to create adequate replacements for them contributed to the size and complexity of modern homelessness. But homelessness afflicted many other Americans, along with the mentally ill. The president's claim that a lot of unemployed people didn't want to work was at best simplistic—most ads for jobs were aimed at skilled workers. And in asserting that many people preferred the streets to shelters and were therefore homeless by choice, Reagan in effect conflated homeless shelters with homes.

· · ·

Homelessness exists in virtually every country. According to a 2020 report from the United Nations Human Rights Council, more than 1.8 billion people worldwide lacked "adequate housing," and about 150 million were homeless. There was no reliable way to compare the extent of homelessness among most Western nations, but rough estimates made it obvious that the United States had a problem similar to some of western Europe, a bigger problem than the Scandinavian countries, and a much bigger problem than Japan or South Korea.

One heard on the news—and also read in some scholarly articles—that between 500,000 and 600,000 Americans were homeless. Those numbers came from yearly counts of people who, on a single winter night, were found sleeping in homeless shelters or transitional housing, or in "unsheltered" locations—in what the Department of Housing and Urban Development (HUD) defined as "a public or private place not designated for, or ordinarily used as, a regular sleeping accommodation for people." Those one-night figures gave the illusion of precision—580,466 in 2020, for example—but they didn't include all the homeless people who happened to be in a hospital, detox, or jail on the night of the count, or the unsheltered people who for their own safety slept in well-hidden spots, or those who slept on floors and sofas in the houses and apartments of friends and relatives. One member of the Program's board of directors spent his homeless years that way, and he knew that many other homeless Black Americans in Boston did likewise.

A more accurate one-night count would still have vastly understated the size of the problem, in part because homelessness was a fluid predicament—some people used shelters intermittently, and a much larger number stayed briefly and never returned. Another study from HUD tried to remedy this flaw by estimating the total number who stayed in shelters at any point during a given year. The official estimate for 2018 (published by HUD in 2020) was 1.446 million. But this number left out rough sleepers and couch surfers and many others. Counting only public school students—no parents or siblings, just the students—the federal Department of Education found that about 1.4 million suffered homelessness during the 2018–19 school year. Many nongovernmental estimates placed the yearly total of homeless people at 3 to 3.5 million, but those figures were based on a single study made by the Urban League in 2001—a study that, twenty years later, had been referenced at least 597 times, a case of references referencing one another, all based on one estimate.

When Jim began his work in Boston, national attempts to enumerate homelessness were sporadic and wildly inconsistent. The methodology for counting had improved since then, but there were still no certainties in this arena, except for the fact that homelessness was much larger than usually asserted, and no one knew its real dimensions.

Many Americans also lived in a state known as "housing insecurity"—at risk of being evicted or unable to pay their rent. One estimate, from the National Alliance to End Homelessness, found that 10 million American households were suffering such insecurity in 2019—6.3 million because they were spending more than half their income on housing, and 3.7 million because they were "sharing the housing of others for economic reasons."

Looming evictions and rising costs for housing all but guaranteed that the ranks of homeless people would continue to grow, a threat already manifest in many places, such as New York City and Los Angeles. The problem in Massachusetts was small by comparison, but between 2012 and 2017—according to official state estimates— homelessness had risen by nearly a third, and the number of homeless families had doubled. Boston had a population of about 700,000, and according to one loose calculation from Jim and a colleague, between 24,000 and 36,000 "experienced homelessness" at one time or another during 2017.

· · ·

Homelessness had a complex taxonomy. It included families and also many lone individuals, generally divided into four categories. There were the "hidden," such as the Street Team patient who slept in a rented storage locker. The "transitional," by far the most numerous, fell into homelessness only briefly, while the "episodic" did so a few times a year. A smaller number—about 10 percent in 2018—belonged to the "chronic" category, living in constant or near-constant homelessness. That chronic group had two main subgroups—those who spent most of their nights in homeless shelters and those who slept rough, on pavement and park benches, in doorways, ATM parlors, tents on the outskirts of towns.

In 2018, according to a federal estimate, about a third of "the chronically homeless" usually slept outside of shelters. In Boston, by contrast, less than 5 percent slept in the rough. This was partly because of Boston's harsh winters, and also because for the past thirty years every Boston mayor had promised a bed for anyone who chose to come inside. Shelters were abundant, and all but one admitted people who were drunk.

The Program now treated people stuck in every form of homelessness. The Street Team, still a very small part of the whole, had narrowed its clientele to include only the hardcore rough sleepers, the people who stayed outside through the cold months—300 to 400 in all. These patients were an anomalous group demographically: Two-thirds were white, 70 percent were men, all were adults, about half of them between eighteen and forty-four years old.

Some rough sleepers claimed their own distinction, labeling as "snowbirds" those who slept out only in the warm months and retreated to shelters in the winter. In fact, the difference was important. In Massachusetts, the people who lived mostly in shelters suffered a death rate about four times higher than that of the state's general adult population. But the people who stayed outside year-round—the Street Team's special patients, whom Jim had once imagined as "hardy survivors"—died at about ten times the normal rate.

By 2017, Jim had long since retreated from the day-to-day management of the Program. He still had an important role in overseeing the whole operation, but he spent at least as much time serving as captain of the Street Team, and he did all of his actual doctoring with rough sleepers. Behind their appalling death rate and other harsh statistics lay many challenges and many faces. It was the challenges, I came to think, that drew Jim to this work. The faces held him there.

2

A New Face

According to a doctor who had worked for the Program in its early years, Jim had a knack for "pre-admiration." The doctor explained: "Even the average extrovert is not super excited about meeting somebody who smells bad, who's wearing tattered clothes, is lying on the ground and asking for money. But it's possible to do, and Jim was the most powerful example I'd ever seen in *my* life of somebody who was doing that naturally." Pre-admiration was something like the opposite of prejudice, a quality the doctor had tried to emulate: "I think that Jim has an attitude of pre-admiration for the people he doesn't yet know. His presumption is, 'Oh, I'm eventually going to like this person. I will probably find some reason over time to like them. I just happen not to know it *yet*.'"

· · ·

It was a Thursday, Street Clinic day in a corner of the Massachusetts General Hospital. Like the van, this clinic had become an institution. When it had started, in 2002, homeless patients and their knapsacks and bags of belongings had shared the waiting room of the hospital's Walk-In Clinic with more proper citizens of Boston. It had been an uncomfortable arrangement for both parties, "traditional" patients disturbed by drunken yelling, and homeless patients humiliated when all the people around them got up and moved away. After six months, Street Clinic was allotted its own waiting area, a floor below the Walk-In, in a lightly trafficked corner of the hospital. The waiting room was small and windowless, but the team stocked it each Thursday with coffee and donuts, bagels and sandwiches. Patients could get passes for the subway and meal tickets for the hospital's restaurants, and they could sit on the long row of attached chairs in the hallway outside as long as they liked, talking to their friends. The usual atmosphere was mixed chaos and order, shopping carts filled with gear crowding the hallway, slumped figures dozing in the chairs, slurred voices of patients raised in argument with others and sometimes themselves, while off to the side other patients sat in quiet conversation with Street Team staff and volunteers who were helping them fill out forms, listening to their stories, offering advice and consolation, mediating squabbles. Once in a while a patient threatened the charge nurse, on occasion there were fisticuffs among patients, but, Jim insisted, there hadn't been a truly dangerous incident in more than fifteen years.

On these Thursdays, Jim became something like a traditional physician again, seeing patients in an office upstairs—a small exam room at the rear of the Walk-In Clinic, one of two tiny exam rooms that the hospital had rented to the Program for the past thirty years. He once told me that about three-quarters of his job had more to do with social work than medicine. And, he would say, it wasn't medical school that had trained him for that, but rather the bartending he'd done to put himself through medical school. "If you're not willing to listen to lots of people talking at you, not all of them coherently, you'll go crazy tending bar." Most Street Team patients required lengthy visits, sometimes for medical reasons, more often for moral support. Typically, he'd see five, rarely six, in the course of a clinic, and finish up by late afternoon. This Thursday, in September 2016, had passed in relative serenity. He was getting ready to head home when his assistant, Julie, called from the waiting room downstairs. A brand-new patient had arrived, asking to see "Dr. Jim." The man seemed "pretty wild," Julie said. She gave Jim the name and date of birth: Anthony Columbo. December 19, 1968.

Jim told her to bring the man upstairs to the exam room. He did this with misgivings. He had promised to head for home by four, at the latest five. His wife, Jill, was at home alone with their infant daughter, Gabriella, and would be in need of relief by now. Maybe he could keep this visit short—simply meet this new patient and arrange to see him on another day.

Jim always stood to greet his patients. He would put on a listening smile for the talkative ones, all the while observing them carefully. The exam room wasn't much bigger than a janitor's closet and crammed with basic medical equipment. When this new patient walked in, he made the room seem even smaller. He was taller than Jim, tall enough that Jim had to look up to meet his eyes. He introduced himself as Tony. He had a powerful handshake. Even when he sat down, in the chair beside the doctor's gray metal desk, he looked outsized. He wore several layers of shirts, but it was clear that he was lean and muscular, much fitter-looking than most rough sleepers who were pushing fifty. He brought an odor of sweat and slightly rotten fruit. Several days' growth of black beard charred his face. He was balding, his hair close-cropped with a few strands stippling his high forehead, which he mopped now and then with a wad of paper towel—sweating either because of all his clothing, Jim thought, or else withdrawal from gaba-pentin, an anticonvulsive widely used as an ingredient in euphoria-inducing drug cocktails. The man's face was classically proportioned, with a slightly hooked Roman nose and dark brown eyes, which moved observantly around the room.

Jim asked Tony what brought him here. A torrent of words poured out. His voice was slightly hoarse, with a baritone timbre and a North End variant of the Boston accent. When he said, "Make a long story shawt," he tended to do the opposite. He said he'd spent twenty years in prison, had been living on the streets ever since, and had been buying the drug Suboxone for a long time, both in prison and outside. Jim often prescribed this rather new drug to help patients wean themselves from heroin. It was in itself only mildly addictive. Tony said he was using it mostly for the pain in his back and knees, and now he was feeling sick from withdrawal—"Subo sick." He needed some Suboxone now.

Did he use other drugs? Jim asked.

"I do, I do," said Tony. "I smoke a lot of K2, stuff like that, and coke sometimes."

On his computer, Jim had located Tony's medical record, which revealed that he'd been seen sporadically at one of the Program's clinics, and that he had been prescribed Suboxone for opiate withdrawal. Giving him a prescription was justifiable, but Jim wasn't sure he ought to do that. Tony might be using Suboxone as a base for a drug cocktail. Jim told him that he could take a urine sample from him now, and then give him a script next week.

Tony's eyes narrowed. The effect was dramatic. It turned his face dark, like north wind on the ocean. "Well, that was the whole thing," he said. "That's why I don't come to these places." He moved forward in his chair, about to rise.

"Wait a minute," Jim said. "Sit down for a minute. Talk to me."

And Tony sat back down, telling Jim how hard it was to live on the streets, how much pain he was in right now.

There was no mistaking the man's desperation. Still listening, Jim turned to the computer screen and looked again at Tony's medical record. The file was scanty, but it confirmed the outlines of what Tony was saying. Jim thought, "If I don't take the time now to get him his meds, I probably won't ever see him again."

If he gave Tony a week's prescription for Suboxone, Jim asked, would he promise to come back next Thursday?

"Damn right!" said Tony. "That's what I'm heah for!"

Jim typed the script and handed it to Tony. If Jim had left then, he would have been only an hour late getting home. But Tony said he had another problem. "I don't have an ID right now." The reason was a fight, Tony said. He'd beaten up a fellow homeless man in Pi Alley a few weeks ago, a guy who had money of his own but was stealing from other homeless people. Tony said he'd given the man not an ordinary but a *very bad* beating, and afterward, fearing it had been caught on the surveillance camera there, he had thrown away his state ID and his Social Security, Medicaid, and bank cards. "I didn't want to have IDs on me, in case the cops were looking for me," he explained.

Jim's pager went off, interrupting Tony. The ring tone Jim had chosen reproduced the blaring bicycle horn of Clarence the Clown. He often apologized for it to patients. "Awful sound, isn't it?" he'd say. "The reason I have it is, it's the only sound that can wake me at night." It was Jill. He phoned her. He said he was with a patient, could he call her right back?

"You supposed to leave, Doc?" asked Tony.

Actually, Jim said, he was supposed to have left by four. "But let's finish this." He told Tony he would go with him to the CVS pharmacy on Cambridge Street and vouch for Tony's identity.

It was after six by the time they got to the store. The pharmacist accepted the script. But when he came back, he said there was something wrong with Tony's Medicaid insurance policy. They wouldn't pay.

Jim asked the pharmacist how much the script would cost. The pharmacist said $120.

Tony erupted. "Dude! On the street? *Five* bucks."

Jim pulled out his wallet and laid his credit card on the counter. "Use this."

"Whoa! No, no, Doc." Tony grabbed the card and handed it back to Jim.

Then the pharmacist looked at Jim. "Wait a minute, you're the doctor? Let me make another call."

And then finally it was over. Medicaid would cover Tony's Suboxone after all. As they left the store, Jim asked Tony if he had any money. He didn't. Had he eaten today?

"Pretty much," said Tony.

Jim went back inside and bought a sandwich from the cooler, then slipped a twenty-dollar bill into the bag, and handed the package to Tony, who protested. Not strenuously, but for form's sake, it seemed.

Many people disapproved of such gifts, including some members of Jim's own Street Team—not the sandwich but the cash. Would Tony buy alcohol or drugs with the money?

Jim had resolved that issue for himself years ago, with help from Barbara McInnis. He had told her he was thinking of donating a hundred dollars to the Pine Street Inn, and Barbara had said, "Why don't you just give it to the people you take care of? You won't get a tax break, but at least you won't be giving it to the military-industrial complex." Not long afterward he'd found himself working with homeless people who were sheltering in a facility on the outskirts of the city, far from places where they could cadge money. So when the food trucks came to the site, the patients would hang back. He imagined them like kids at a candy store window. Jim used the food trucks himself but felt callous when he did. He thought about buying food for the patients, but then decided he should give those small sums freely and privately, so that patients had the power to buy what they wanted, and not what he thought they should buy.

He had been giving money away ever since—a dollar at a time at first and now usually a ten or a twenty. For the past few years, the Program had paid him a handsome salary, and the money he slipped into patients' hands amounted to only a few thousand dollars a year.

Jim and Tony parted at a little after seven o'clock, the big man shambling away down Cambridge Street. Jim later told me that the twenty he'd given Tony was potentially therapeutic, another incentive to return.

3

~~~~~~~~

The Street Team Meeting

Since the Street Team's beginning, faces had changed and changed again. One of Jim's favorites, a nurse practitioner, had left the team reluctantly after eight years, when her second child was born. She told me: "It was so much clinical work and so much after hours. Put the kids to bed, log on, finish your notes. It was doable with one kid. I couldn't do it with two." She also said, "The good days are *so* good and the bad days are *so* bad. It has to be almost a calling."

The current team, a core group of eight, included an assistant to Jim, a team manager, a "recovery coach" who helped the patients deal with addictions, two half-time psychiatrists, a nurse practitioner, and two doctors. They met twice a week, on Monday afternoons, in an unhurried session, and again for less than an hour on Thursdays, right before the weekly Street Clinic began.

The chaos of rough sleepers' lives made it hard for them to keep track of appointments, so they were welcome to arrive for Thursday clinic at any time between 7:00 A.M. and late afternoon. During a blizzard, or at the start of a month when Social Security checks arrived, as few as twenty or thirty rough sleepers might show up, but sixty to eighty was usual. They'd come inside Mass General's Wang Center and walk or stumble with their gear to the waiting area laid out for them. Most wanted only to have breakfast or lunch and hang around with friends in the hall outside the waiting room. Some would have their vital signs checked by the charge nurse, a tall man named Davis who worked for the team once a week. As a rule, about twenty patients would ask for a visit with one of the team's providers, and at 9:00, Davis would take the roster upstairs to one of the team's exam rooms at the back of the hospital's Walk-In Clinic.

By then, the Street Team would be assembling in one of the little rooms, along with various interns and volunteers and sometimes a visitor or two, and the place would feel like a subway car filling up at rush hour. Seventeen was the record attendance, ten or eleven the average. Team members stood in the corners, leaned against the filing cabinets, or sat side by side on the exam table. Once the meeting began, they had to keep the door shut—otherwise the Walk-In Clinic nurses would complain that the team was making too much noise.

Jim was usually the last to arrive. He'd close the door and lean back against it, facing the room. He always wore a collared shirt and necktie—his office uniform ever since Barbara McInnis had told him that patients expected him to look like a doctor and not a homeless person. His expressions were lively throughout. He'd smile at a piece of good news, then he'd grow wide-eyed and exclaim "Yikes!" at some startling report, his dark eyebrows flying up. To me, he seemed like a composite portrait of the ages of man, youthfulness topped off with silver hair.

"So, Davis, drive," Jim would say, and the tall charge nurse would begin to read the names of patients on his roster, and then the talk would begin.

• • •

When Beckie Tachick, the case manager, went to her first Street Team meeting, she felt as if the names of patients came at her like a fast-moving crowd. It was indoctrination by confusion, and then one day she realized that the roster of patients had become just part of what she knew, along with faces, personalities, problems.

Part of a meeting dealt with patients' medical issues: high blood pressure, emphysema, diabetes slipping out of control, broken bones from falls, occasionally frostbite or frost nip, cirrhosis, cancer. But mostly the team talked about what might be called psychosocial matters. This man, now housed after years on the street, was so lonely the other night that he hired a prostitute to come over just to talk. Meanwhile, this other patient, a woman, had been attacked, dragged by her hair down the concrete stairs at the Charles Street T station by her boyfriend. How to keep them away from each other? A usually mild-mannered patient had put his arm through a liquor store window the day before yesterday and explained afterward that he was feeling frustrated and just wanted something to drink, and the team agreed that they needed a plan for him. A woman patient had once again gone from one member of the team to another, trying to get them to prescribe benzodiazepines, and threatening to kill herself or start shooting heroin if they didn't. They had tried any number of solutions before. What should they try next?

As the listing of names and commentary went on, the air in the room growing humid, it was possible to imagine that this was a faculty meeting at a small but good private school. Every team member knew the patients in many dimensions—their ailments, temperaments, drugs of choice; whose boyfriend was whose, who hated whom, who was in imminent danger.

Although every member was a generalist in knowledge of their patients, each had a specialty. Beckie Tachick had several. She was in her thirties, cheerful, uncomplaining, hardworking. She'd been with the team for only two years but had proved so adept with paperwork and patients as to seem indispensable to Jim. He'd realized that she might have to leave them for a job with better pay, and he'd doubled her small salary. He justified the raise by enlarging her job description to fit what she was already doing. Finding housing for their patients wasn't one of the Street Team's prescribed roles, but Beckie had taken it on, because nearly all the patients wanted help finding a subsidized place to live and none of the agencies assigned that job seemed to be doing enough. She kept track of all the many shrinking lists of housing opportunities in both Boston and surrounding towns and the tangles of rules that limited those dwindling opportunities. She'd also learned the paths through the Social Security and state welfare mazes to get patients some income and benefits such as food stamps: "I'm applying for SSI for Mack, and it won't work," she tells the team. "But just to buy time for EAEDC benefits." (In the room, I'm the only one who doesn't know what she is saying: That this patient, Mack, isn't going to get Supplemental Security Income, but that applying for it will extend his benefits under a different program, the state's Emergency Aid to the Elderly, Disabled and Children.) Jim had also made Beckie the official team manager, another role she'd already assumed.

For authority on addictions and their possible treatments, there was Mike Jellison, the recovery coach. When the names of certain patients came up, it was usually Mike who gave a pharmaceutical accounting—"He's usin' a lot of cocaine. He's huffing, too. Electronic cleaner." Mike was tall, bald on top with close-cropped hair on the sides. He'd served in the navy, where he'd acquired an addiction to alcohol and whatever drugs he could get his hands on—a fierce addiction that lasted almost twenty years before he finally fought it off, with help from Alcoholics Anonymous. He was in his early fifties now and had been sober for the past decade. Sometimes he shared a bit of his story with the team. Once, they were talking about a patient who seemed to be giving up on the activities of daily living. Mike said, "I think passive suicide is normal. It was for me. It's not that you don't want to live, but you don't know *how* to live."

The room went silent. Then Beckie said softly, "It's good to have that perspective."

Mike had strong views, and he expressed them bluntly, which delighted Jim, even when he disagreed. When Mike's discourse got
heated, Jim would threaten to squirt him with "Valium spray," just as
Barbara McInnis had once threatened to do to Jim. And then he'd
thank Mike for speaking out. During one conversation about needle
exchange and harm reduction, Mike said he was tired of "thinkin'
outside the box." Maybe, he said, it was time to go back inside it.
Then he declared: "You know what most alcoholics would tell you?
The one thing that works? *Abstinence.*"

Mike held a weekly meeting for male patients who wanted to
come and talk about whatever was on their minds. He could wax mili-
tant about patients. He called them "our folks." He'd go to court and
argue with judges on their behalf. When Beckie mentioned that one
of their folks was having trouble getting his bed up the stairs into his
new apartment, Mike rolled his shoulders like a boxer getting ready
for the fight, and, softly laughing, declared, "I'll strap the bed to my
back. I've carried some beds up to these places."

Jim was the institutional memory in the room. He had presided at
hundreds of these preclinic meetings, and although he tended to listen more than he spoke, he was at pains to hand down lore and prin-
ciples from Street Teams past. First among these was the imperative
for continuity of care. When visitors came to the meeting, Jim would
use the occasion to explain what this meant: "So Barbara McInnis
was against a person seeing only one clinician. She hated the idea that
a doctor would come and leave, and the patient who had opened up
to them would be devastated. She was dead set against having only
one doctor for any given patient." Accordingly, all the team's providers should see each patient from time to time. But, Jim added, there
were "old classics" who had seen only him for "five hundred years."
And if they insisted on that wrongheaded tradition, an exception
should be made.

Jim liked to say that the team's work was hard and measurable success infrequent. But continuity of care could benefit them as well as
patients. One day the team's new nurse practitioner, Katy Swanson,

told him after a patient's visit, "I sometimes feel like I'm spinning, and I don't know quite what to do."

"Katy, I think you'll find over time that it's more important sticking with people than knowing what to do right now," Jim said. "Because if you feel bad after a visit, they'll be back next week, and you can fix it."

Complexity was another of Jim's themes. The patient who flushed pieces of her clothing down the toilet of the Walk-In Clinic and clogged up the plumbing—her diagnosis and resolving the trouble she'd caused were both "complicated." And a patient could be both "complicated" and "delightful," sometimes simultaneously, at least to Jim.

He tells the team, "Frankie called me at four-thirty this morning. Just to wake me up, he said." Jim adds, "You want to get angry at him, but he's just too funny and charming when you finally get to talk to him."

Not everyone agreed about Frankie's charm. Indeed, not many complicated people were delightful to every member, and everyone was allowed, even invited, to admit this. "Joe Z. I love him," says one of the team.

"He drives me nuts," Jim replies. "That's why we have a team."

It was a congenial group, all in all, but there was some tension between Jim and the team's younger doctor, Kevin Sullivan. It rarely surfaced, and then only subtly. The problem had nothing to do with Kevin's abilities or diligence. He had trained at one of the country's most prestigious residencies, at the Brigham and Women's Hospital in Boston. Like everyone on the team, he worked long hours. They all went out on street rounds and on visits to housed and hospitalized patients, and they all worked at the Thursday clinic. Kevin also saw patients on Tuesdays and Wednesdays at Mass General. He was deeply engaged in the mission. His credentials would have gotten him many other jobs with shorter hours and higher pay. When I asked why he'd chosen to work with homeless people, Kevin declared, "Because it's the right thing to do!"

Patients tended to be wary of the team's newcomers, and Kevin was still a recent arrival, but many of the rough sleepers told me they liked and trusted him. On the other hand, some of the Program's nurses disliked him, for the way he talked to them—"over his bow tie," as one nurse put it. Kevin was about six feet tall and fit. He rode a bicycle to work in all seasons. He wore a bow tie often, and for a sound reason—it's a far less germ-laden ornament than a standard necktie, which inevitably grazes contaminated surfaces. Now and then his way of speaking became oddly formal—an approach should be "proactive," a patient might be "desirous of treatment." I once heard him say, "There was also a random guy on Washington Street who would not arouse for us." Nurses can be sensitive about their status vis-à-vis doctors. For some nurses, Kevin seemed too sure of himself, too authoritative—in a word, too superior.

Kevin was Jim's junior by decades, in both age and experience, and, to Jim, too fresh from residency for comfort. For a long time, Jim had been at odds with what he called "the drive to be certain," which he believed was inculcated in doctors during residency and which took time to wear off. He favored something nearer to what the poet Keats called negative capability. "I like it when people on our team say, 'It's so complicated, I'm not sure what's going on.'"

It was in this spirit, I think, that on occasion Jim offered the team what seemed like his golden rule of street medicine. During one team meeting, he offered it especially to Kevin. A discussion about a difficult patient named Bo had seemed to come to an end, when Jim said, "Kevin, can I finish up on Bo? I tend to be overly nice to him, because inside I have this awful feeling about him. My feeling is we need to spread him out among us."

"The funny thing is, I care a lot about him," said Kevin.

"Oh, me too," said Jim. "I care a lot about him. I just dislike him. So let me give you permission to feel that way."

. . .

"My turn?" a voice would ask about halfway through the Thursday team meeting. "Can I get in a few?" The question came from a small man with white hair and a white mustache, seated as always in a chair lodged near the sink in the crowded exam room. This was Dr. Jim Bonnar, the older of the team's two psychiatrists. He had gone to both Harvard College and Harvard Medical School—"Preparation H," he called it—and he had spent most of his life getting away from the world of prestige and privilege that he felt Harvard represented. He'd worked for a couple of years with the Program, then he'd gone to New Zealand and later to the Dakotas to work in the Indian Health Service. When he was in his late sixties, near despair over the regimentation of medicine and the denigration of psychotherapy, he returned to the Program. "The spirit of the organization, I have loved it," he told me. "Because I haven't been on the factory floor being ordered by an insurance company to do an intake in forty-five minutes."

Dr. Bonnar had stayed on the team for most of a decade and would be retiring in another year. In the meantime, he still had several dozen patients among the team's rough sleepers. He would conduct talk-therapy sessions with some of them on Wednesday evenings, and with others early on Thursday mornings, and he would deliver his reports at the team meeting. He didn't usually generalize about patients, but he had some lore to impart, often of a cautionary sort. "She's very bright," he said of a patient long troubled by memories of childhood trauma and addicted to the relief of alcohol. "So she raises all kinds of false hope in us. Over and over and over again, we mental health people tend to really like smart people, and we think that they are much better off than what they really are. We underestimate the struggle they have. I've seen this now for a long time."

The memories of patients that Dr. Bonnar and Jim carried were a crucial background to the dreadful stories that were told in the crowded Thursday meetings. Dr. Bonnar had made rough estimates about the homeless patients he had known. Ninety percent, he told me, had been afflicted by substance abuse or mental illness or both. And at least 75 percent had suffered the physical and psychological effects of severe childhood trauma.

Over the years, Jim had learned the worst parts of many patients' biographies, and he'd been astonished at how many had suffered abuse as children. He thought Dr. Bonnar's estimate of 75 percent was credible, maybe even low. A colleague of Bonnar's, a psychiatrist who worked at various sites, shared this view. "I never heard such stories of childhood trauma in my life. Neighbors and stepfathers who raped them. Mothers who beat them with pots. It gives you the impression of a feral society."

Of course the Street Team worked downstream from childhoods, where it was too late for prevention. But sometimes repairs were possible.

4

~~~~~~~~~~

Angels Without Wings

I t was a Thursday morning in late March 2017, Street Clinic day at Mass General. Jim ended the team meeting a few minutes early. "I'm a little nervous," he explained. "Because when I came in, I saw all the heavy hitters out there." I wasn't sure what he meant by the term, but as I soon learned, it included Tony Columbo.

Tony came upstairs for his office visit around midmorning. Soon after the session began, Jim was called away, and I was left alone with Tony for a little while. He spent the time exalting "Dr. Jim," calling him the "cawnahstone" of the Program. When Jim reappeared, Tony turned to him and said, "Braggin' about you, saying you created an army of good people. Let me tell you something about you, Doc . . ."

"It's a nightmare downstairs," Jim said, as he sat down at the desk. He put a little chuckle in his voice. It sounded forced.

But Tony wasn't going to let him change the subject. He went on praising Jim. Floridly. All of the Street Team were "angels wit'out wings," but Jim was "the cawnahstone," the archangel of the homeless, "creatin' an army to catch 'em once they fall."

Jim tried again. "Sweet of you to say that. I wish it were true."

But Tony shouted him down. "It's the truth! I mean, come on! You don't discriminate, you don't just treat me, you do this for everybody!"

Some members of Boston's medical and philanthropic establishments had described Jim to me as "a saint." Invariably they remarked on his modesty. In fact, Jim practiced self-effacement as if it were a creed. He seemed reflexively uncomfortable with praise, and especially with beatification. He'd quote Barbara McInnis, who had once told him: "This work is way too interesting to be looked at as saintly." But the problem with denying you're a saint is that, in many eyes, it improves your qualifications.

The first few times I had talked to Tony he seemed infinitely distractible. Now, as he continued to extol Jim, it was clear there were subjects on which he would perseverate. I wasn't sure what had inspired this outpouring. People living on the street are apt to absorb the disapproval that walks by them every day. Tony's extravagant tribute seemed half-mad in execution, but maybe it was his way of preempting disapproval, from us and from himself—a case of his making himself feel better at the risk of his doctor's discomfort.

When Tony launched into the story of their first meeting, Jim gave up protesting. As he listened, he began to smile. At one point in Tony's high-speed narration, Jim shook his head, remarking, "I can't believe you remember all this."

Having finished the story, Tony said to Jim: "I feel like I'll let you down if I don't come in clean. Here you are helping me, I gotta do the other half and stuff. If I had a bottle or I was smokin', I'd hide it from you. If a cop came, I wouldn't give a fuck. I'd drink it right in front of his face. *You* I would hide it from." Evidently, Tony's moral code wasn't simple. You hid the bottle from Jim out of respect, and then told him you hid it to make sure he knew how deeply you respected him.

Finally, Jim turned to the computer screen hovering over the desk. He stared up at Tony's medical record. "Tell me how you're doing. Your blood pressure's up a littelllll," Jim elongated the last word, as he often did, as if holding a note.

During Tony's appointment the previous week, Jim had commented in a completely matter-of-fact tone that there were marijuana and cocaine in Tony's urine. Today was different. "Your urine's great, by the way," Jim said, still staring at the numbers on his computer screen. "Good job." He put the blood pressure cuff on Tony's arm and said, "Think good thoughts for a second." Tony's pressure had been towering—172 over 101—two hours ago, when he first arrived in the waiting room downstairs and the charge nurse had measured it. Now it had fallen to perfection, to 123 over 77. "Tony, you made my day. You made my day."

"I made his day," said Tony. "Listen to him. He's worried about my health more than *I'm* worried about it."

"A doctor cares about your health," said Jim. "What are you talking about here?"

And Tony was off once again, saying that I should grab ten random homeless people and ask them about Dr. Jim. "They'd all be stories about how the guy has compassion, *cares*. More than a doctor and more than human."

"Now you're gonna give me a big head," said Jim. "But your urine was great. So what did I miss here? Are you okay with—did you get your wallet back?"

Tony's office visits had protracted denouements. Always there was the normal complexity of a life on the streets to sort out. Tony had lost all his IDs again, this time when his wallet had been stolen as he slept. At the start of a month, Jim made up a budget for his cash gifts to patients, and he would come to Street Clinic with five-, ten-, and twenty-dollar bills pre-folded so he could pass them unobtrusively. Tony rarely asked for money. When he did, he promised to pay it back. He hadn't yet. But now he'd lost everything again, and when Jim handed him a folded twenty, he didn't even pretend to argue.

There was the ongoing quest to find him an apartment, which seemed near fruition at last. There was the weekly refilling of his prescriptions—weekly because an unhoused person has no place to keep medicines and is bound to lose them fairly often. One longtime patient used to hide her pills in her underwear. And there was also Tony's need for help with fundamental things. Patients often asked for meal tickets and taxi vouchers and five-dollar gift cards to places such as Dunkin' Donuts, which conferred both food and use of a bathroom—what a friend of Jim's called "the right to shit." Today for Tony, it was subway passes so he could get to the Social Security office to work on getting a new ID. "I hate sneaking on that train. I really do," he explained, as Jim reached into his doctoring backpack for the passes.

Finally, there was news of the street for Tony to pass on to Dr. Jim. Did Tony know anything, Jim wondered, about the rumor that people were using the anti-nausea drug Zofran in drug cocktails? Tony said he hadn't heard that, but he offered a brief tutorial, rapid-fire, less for Jim's benefit—he knew all of this already—than for mine: "Benzos are big out there. So are johnnies and pins, which are Klonopin. Suboxone *was* popular, now it's kryptonite. When you see people bend way forward, bending their knees? They do that on benzos."

"Yeah," said Jim. "It makes you loose in the knees."

"If they heard somebody died off of someone's heroin, everybody goes to that dealer. You ask them why, they'll say, 'That guy couldn't handle it, I can.'" By way of example, Tony told the story of a man he knew who had overdosed on heroin—probably mixed with fentanyl—and his girlfriend got scared and called for help and the EMTs arrived and gave him the antidote Narcan. "And afterwards he's screaming at his girlfriend. He says, 'You fucked up a sixty-dollar high.' She says, 'You were turning blue!' He says, 'Fuck it. Let me go.'"

Tony, who didn't observe transitions, went on: "You heard Johnny Smith died. With the white hair?"

"What? Oh, man. I had not heard that," said Jim. A long pause. Then he said to Tony, "You're like my eyes and ears out there."

"I enjoyed the visit," said Tony, all six feet four of him arising.

"See you later, Tony. Take care."

Jim lingered at his desk for a while afterward. He smiled. "Julie and I always take ten minutes to recover from Tony."

· · ·

In Jim's memory, there was a pantheon of vivid and mysterious patients from years past. Two former college professors stood out. Harrison and David. Both had been afflicted by mental illness, David most emphatically and strangely. What psychiatrists call a fixed delusion had warped his life. He believed that he had sired a two-headed child in Vermont and that he was still being pursued for this by people armed with what he called zappers. He could not be talked out of his bizarre fantasy, not by psychiatrists or Jim or a fellow professor friend who came and tried. And yet while living on the streets, David had become a member of a church choir and its social ministry, tutoring various people at the public library. He had doggedly visited a young Black man in jail and had helped to set him free.

As for the older professor—Harrison—he said he'd been the youngest person ever awarded tenure at Columbia University and also that he'd been a friend of Jack Kerouac and the beat poet Allen Ginsberg, among others. Jim had found a trove of evidence that all of this was true. When Jim had told Harrison that he loved Kerouac's book *On the Road*, the old ex-professor had said, "Jack was a dashing young man but a terribly shallow thinker."

Jim used to take Harrison and David to lunch once a month at the Union Oyster House. He would listen as they argued philosophical and literary issues—did postmodernism actually exist? The elder, Harrison, would clumsily spill clam chowder all over himself, and Jim would sit there feeling a bit nauseated. Now he'd say that he deeply regretted his squeamishness, that his time with those two men felt precious. Both had died, Harrison some years ago and David just recently, both from natural causes and at what constituted extremely old age for rough sleepers.

It was now almost a year since Tony had washed up on the Street Team's shore, and he seemed with his vividness to have become a candidate for Jim's pantheon. "I felt there would never be another David, and I felt the same about Harrison when he died," Jim told me. "I didn't think there'd be a new one, so Tony is sort of a surprise. He's *different*. Harrison and David stood apart from other patients. Not that they were aloof, but they just weren't part of the rough sleepers' community. Tony's in the middle of that vortex. In the time he's been out of prison he seems to know everyone on the streets."

In the exam room, awaiting his next patient, Jim offered a few final words about Tony. "He has a code. He's a bit of an enforcer out there. If you don't hurt people, you're okay, but not if you do."

Gradually, the room itself seemed to calm down—as if it too had a pulse, returning to normal. And then all that remained of Tony for now were a few feathers of down from the holes in his parka, white fluff on the office's pale green linoleum floor.

5

∼∿∿∿∿∿∼

The Memorial Service

Homeless people have one public power. If they gather in a place, other citizens tend to avoid it. Many of the people cared for by the Street Team had long ago appropriated their own agora, a small outdoor seating area made mostly of concrete. It lay on the grounds of Mass General, near the foot of the hospital's giant towers and adjacent to Cambridge Street, always busy, always loud with sirens.

This was the spot where on many days of the week, and especially on Thursdays, Street Team patients gathered and talked, sometimes fighting, often drinking, occasionally sleeping overnight. The place had no formal name, but the rough sleepers called it Mousey Park, in honor of a long-departed homeless man who used to hang out there. According to local lore, he had died years ago when someone doused him with gasoline in a parking garage and set him on fire.

For several years, the Street Team had held an annual memorial service in the park, a requiem for the rough sleepers who had died in Boston the previous year. It was convened this year in late March, on one of those days in the city's early spring when the weather mocks the calendar. The sunlight felt bright and cold. The only warm color came from three dozen daffodils arrayed around the trunk of a bare-limbed tree, a flower for each of the past year's dead—the list, I'd been told, was incomplete. Looking around, I found myself wondering, not for the first time, what it would be like to sleep outside in a place like this.

A sharp northwest wind off the Charles River reddened the faces of the small congregation. They were security guards and other personnel from Mass General, Jim and the other members of the Street Team, parishioners from the Episcopal Cathedral Church of St. Paul, and about twenty rough sleepers. In the mingled group, you could tell most of the unhoused people from the others not by clothing but by smiles—in the world's wealthiest country, the rich and poor are also starkly divided by their teeth. Jim was easy to spot in the crowd because he was the only one without a hat. And Tony of course stood out, being the tallest person in sight.

A homeless former fisherman—Karl, a longtime patient of Jim's—sat shivering in his wheelchair. A woman from the church rushed over, pulled off her gloves, and put them on Karl's windburned hands. The rites began without further delay. Tony stood near the director of the ceremony, the canon from St. Paul's, a bright-cheeked young woman—Reverend Tina. She said to him: "Tony, would you get us started, please?"

"Sure," said Tony. And then, turning to face the congregation, he bellowed, "Heidi!" Other voices followed, calling out names of last year's dead, the lifted cries muffled by the wind and the honking horns and blaring sirens of the traffic on Cambridge Street.

. . .

The ceremony lasted only half an hour. It was cold, and it was also a workday for many of the people there. As they began to leave, a small knot of men, rough sleepers clearly, gathered by the benches. Tony stood in front of the others. What he had said was true of them all: They didn't want Dr. Jim to see them drinking. Tony held a communal bottle of vodka behind his back. One of the men came up and grabbed it. Another hissed, "Where's Dr. Jim? Tony, keep an eye on Jim."

"I am!" Tony said over his shoulder. The bottle glinted in the sunlight as it passed from one gloved hand to another, while Tony stood like both sentry and shield in front of the drinking crew, staring toward the remnant of the crowd that was hurrying for the doorways of Mass General, Jim among them, his silver hair blowing like a bit of cirrus in the wind.

IV

Against Medical Advice

1

~~~~~~~~

No Loud Voices

Jim and his colleagues had begun to build the Boston Health Care for the Homeless Program without a place of their own. They had been guests everywhere they worked, a small group and unproven. They couldn't afford to offend their landlords and patrons, the people who ran the shelters, the hospitals, the state and city governments. Much later, describing the early years to a group of medical students, Jim said: "We chose not to be strident. Our tactic was to use the experience we gained to give us authority, which we could then use to advocate for our patients. People got to know that they could rely on us to give them good information, and that we weren't going to come through their doors screaming." And then, as if to demonstrate this tactic built on mild manners, he said, "And you can beat me up on that. I don't know if that's the right thing to do."

The need for diplomacy had been imposed. As a strategy, it suited Jim.

He addressed cab drivers as "sir." One of his laughs was sudden and high and clearly signified delight. Another was a nervous-sounding accompaniment to statements he was making, a laughter reminiscent of an old-fashioned hostess, which seemed to say, "I know this is a little forward of me," or "Please don't take offense, I can always take this back." Sometimes he expressed that message directly: "I'm talking with an eraser here."

Suzanne Armstrong, a veteran nurse, remembered a quarrel that she once had with a patient—a man named Art, a tough guy with severe septic arthritis. Jim had prescribed methadone for the pain, on condition that Art quit other opiates. But for two weeks running, Art's urine tests came back tainted with heroin. Suzanne and Jim confronted him, and Art began shouting at Suzanne. She was an idiot. She'd done the wrong test on purpose. Suddenly, Jim jabbed a finger at Art and yelled back at him, "You stop it! You stop it! You stop it!"

Art looked stunned. He stopped shouting and then defused the tension, saying, "Okay. But I know that urine can't be dirty, 'cause I got it from my fuckin' lawyer."

The occasion was memorable for Suzanne mainly because she'd never seen Jim angry before. "Jim *actually* yelled," she said years later. She sometimes wished he'd behave that way more often. "Where I come from, people yell and say what they think. With Jim, you say, 'How are you?' And you never really know. I also think it's hard for him to say no to people, and that comes out in different ways. Sometimes I think he *can't* be direct, he *can't* be straightforward and tell someone, 'Look, this is not okay.' It could be a marathon figuring out just what he meant. I felt like I had to become fluent in Jim."

Another long-serving member of the Program said, "I never knew where I stood with him, because he's so *fucking* nice."

More than once I watched Jim endure a siege of frustrations in his exam room without raising his voice. After one of those episodes, I asked him how he'd managed to keep his temper, and he said, "I felt like screaming, but I realized feeling that way interfered with what I was trying to do." Restraint was a knack he'd learned as an intern, he said. On another occasion, he offered an answer that seemed like a rumination, moving much further back in time. "When I was a kid and anxious before a ballgame, I just wanted to go to sleep."

Jim's father had never finished high school. He served in the navy through World War II, and afterward worked in maintenance at the naval yard and later the Naval War College in Newport, Rhode Island. At night, he stocked shelves in a liquor store. He never made more than $10,000 in a year, but according to Jim, the only essential thing that Jim and his siblings had lacked as children was their mother's presence.

She was brilliant and mischievous but beset by episodes of severe bipolar depression, which came on suddenly and could last a year. One night Jim and his two sisters might go to sleep listening to her read aloud to them, and the next day she would be gone—sometimes to her bedroom, sometimes to the hospital. Jim and his sisters knew that she loved them. So why didn't she want to leave her room or come home to see them? If they behaved better, maybe she wouldn't go away. He spent his early childhood on guard, careful not to do anything that might upset anyone. "There were *no* fights in the house," he remembered.

Jim's father came from a generation that conceived of mental illness as a failure of character, and of recovery as a matter of will. Jim remembered his father trying to cheer his mother up as if clinical depression were merely sadness or boredom, something diversions could cure. Jim never once heard his father complain, but they were difficult years for him. And difficult for the children, who also didn't complain.

The family's difficulties deepened around the time when Jim turned ten. A new wave of siblings began to arrive—one every year, two boys and a girl. After the last was born, Jim's father returned from the hospital, sat down at the kitchen table with the three eldest, and began trying to explain the new situation: There were six children now, he had to keep working his two jobs, they'd all have to pitch in. "Mother" wasn't coming home for a while, because the doctors said she needed professional care and medicine. Then the tough old navy man began to cry.

Jim knew his father to be warm but not demonstrative. It was surprising, even alarming, to see him in tears. But what his father had said about their mother was like an awakening, the answer to the anxious questions of their childhood. The doctors had said their mother needed medicine. She had a sickness. She had never wanted to get away from her children.

2

Upside-Down Medicine

In the early 1980s, the historian-sociologist of American medicine Paul Starr predicted the spread of "corporate management" in medical practices and with it "a profound loss of autonomy" for many physicians. "There will be more regulation of the pace and routines of work," Starr wrote. Many doctors would be required to meet "some standard of performance, whether measured in revenues generated or patients treated per hour." About a decade later, doctors remained the highest-paid professionals in the United States, and made about three times as much as their counterparts in Europe. But as Starr had predicted, many practiced under work rules aimed at increased productivity. And the time-limited, distracted doctor seemed more and more a commonplace.

The organization that Jim and his six colleagues had begun to

create in 1985 inverted that evolving norm. Not out of defiance, but
to serve their patients. Unlike their counterparts in mainstream medicine, they had ample time to spend with each patient, but first, as a
rule, they had to find the homeless people who needed care, and then
persuade them to receive it—for free.

This meant courting patients, such as the elderly former professor,
Harrison, homeless for many years after suffering a psychotic break.
He would simply walk away or pretend he was sleeping whenever Jim
and his colleagues approached his favorite park bench. And then one
night, Jim found him at South Station shivering in the cold. Jim fetched
him a coat from the van. A few days later, the professor came to the
Mass General clinic, and he kept coming back, maybe because Jim
could talk with him knowledgeably about philosophers and literary
critics whom the old professor claimed as his teachers, figures such as
Lionel Trilling and Carl Van Doren. He never allowed Jim to do so
much as measure his blood pressure, but he regularly returned, and
when his health began to fail some years later, Jim was positioned to
spot the alteration. In the event, Jim talked him into being admitted to
Mass General. When one of the staff asked if the old man's blood pressure had changed over the years, Jim could only smile and say, "I have
no idea." Embarrassing at the time, amusing in retrospect.

Once a patient was engaged, the first imperative wasn't measuring
vital signs, but rather enacting a saying of Barbara's: "You just have to
be there and be present and, if need be, stand with them in the darkness." Jim was reminded of the family doctor of his childhood, who
knew all the problems in their household and came when needed. A
country doctor approach for an urban population—this was the kind
of doctoring that could bring in suspicious patients. Most had been
bruised by hospitals and doctors, and if they were ushered in and out
of an exam room too quickly, most would stay away thereafter. This
happened to one of the doctors Jim hired during the Program's first
decade. He was a skillful and dedicated young man, but not long after
he started, he had to be counseled to spend more time with patients at
the clinic, because most of the people he saw refused to see him again.

Because they had routinely avoided doctors and hospitals, many homeless patients had problems that required complex, time-consuming interventions. This was true of every homeless person who had TB or AIDS, and of those with maladies grown dire from years of neglect, such as the old man with the hernia that hung below his knees—Jim spent hours in conferences with surgeons planning the successful repair. And virtually every patient had social problems: Women arriving at the shelter clinics with bruised faces, broken bones, whispering in tears about abusive boyfriends; men and women telling him they were sick of the drinking life and asking him to find a detox for them; dying patients who begged him to find their relatives and left him wishing the Program could afford to hire a detective.

It was what Jim once called "upside-down" medicine. He and his little band of providers were free to invent and practice it during the Program's first four years because they were financed by grants and received the same amount no matter how many patients they saw. When the grants ended, they were obliged to get their income from Medicaid, the state- and federally financed plan intended to bring low-income Americans into the mainstream of American health care. For Jim and the administrator he hired, this became a descent into complexity, into tomes full of syllogisms: *If this is a medically necessary visit, then you must determine the chief complaint, and if it is a complex and medically necessary visit as opposed to a simple one, then find on the following page how to generate the bill.* Jim hired a woman named Linda Brown, who had experience in finance. For six months she sat day after day inside a little windowless room in an annex of Boston City Hospital, studying the rules. In the end, she emerged with the news that just by continuing its current unconventional practice, the Program could bring in almost twice as much revenue as they'd received under the grants.

States have great latitude in determining how much money and care Medicaid provides their impoverished residents. Many states put up little more than the minimum, but Massachusetts funded its version of Medicaid generously. When Jim went looking for money and guidance at the State House, he found a ready audience in the president of the Massachusetts Senate, William Bolger, who expressed astonishment that an actual *doctor* was focusing on homeless people. He sent Jim to meet a man named Bruce Bullen, who later served as the state's director of Medicaid for a decade, under three different governors. Bullen became an ally, one with power, imagination, and longevity.

The increased income from Medicaid fueled growth, which brought more income. By 1996, in the Program's eleventh year, the annual budget had grown from $550,000 to about $7 million. At the start, in 1985, a handful of clinicians had seen 1,246 homeless patients. A decade later, dozens of clinicians saw more than six thousand patients, many of them on a regular basis. The rough sleepers represented a small percentage of all the patients, and there wasn't yet a full-fledged Street Team specifically devoted to them. But overall, patient care had broadened. It now included screening for cancers and treatment for TB and AIDS. The prohibitions of the founding charter had fallen away. They brought in volunteers and medical residents. They found money for research and for the beginnings of a mental health team.

By then, the landscape of their practice was like a subway map of the city. The staff worked mainly in clinics, more than two dozen. Some were large, such as one inside the Boston Medical Center. Others were small and provisional, such as the bedrooms converted into exam rooms inside the motels where the state lodged homeless families. For patients in need of specialty care—cardiology, say, or oncology—the map included both Mass General and the Boston Medical Center, whose chief of medicine had welcomed the Program as a partner and put its name on the department's stationery.

In the early 1990s, the Program had bought an old nursing home and made it over into a medical respite with more than one hundred beds. It was the Program's first real estate, the first work site for which they could make up the rules. Jim and his colleagues agreed that none would be best, because patients shouldn't be greeted with rules when they arrived. On the first night, though, one of the nurses walked into the recreation room and saw a couple—a man and woman, both homeless—having sex on the new pool table, which nurses at the Pine Street clinic had donated. "Mad sex," Jim remembered. The couple weren't sent away, but were told, in effect, "We understand this activity. Just not here." The next day the staff posted a sign in the recreation area: NO SEX ON THE POOL TABLE. It was the respite's first rule, the first of many.

By general agreement, the building was named the Barbara McInnis House, with her grudging consent. Her mother burst into tears at the news—"They only name buildings after dead people," she said. And Barbara lived to regret her consent when acquaintances started asking her for loans. "Don't let anyone name a building after you, Jim, because everyone will think you're rich."

. . .

Over the years Jim had heard, and more often overheard, objections to the Program's expanding practice: Many people who worked and paid taxes struggled to pay for health insurance. Why should their money go to providing what some would consider concierge medicine for these people who lived at public expense? For people who produced nothing except indecent public spectacles, and didn't even try to take care of themselves? Heard from inside a shelter clinic or McInnis House or out on the van, such protests seemed irrelevant. What was the alternative? Ignore chronically homeless people, as the city used to do, or imitate draconian regimes and imprison all rough sleepers in a stadium?

In fact, the Program lightened the burdens that homeless people placed on other medical organizations, and did so while providing good care at lower cost than in hospital emergency departments. Many of its patients were broken people, often damaged from infancy, and it was the Program's mission to mend what it could. Jim once told me he *wanted* to say something combative to the critics: "We're making up for what wasn't done for our patients. What *you* didn't provide— schools, jobs, safety." In truth, though, over the first ten years he and his colleagues rarely had occasion to question the worthiness of what they were doing, simply because they were so busy doing it.

By 1995 the Program had remained solvent for a decade while

growing rapidly. A recent Medicaid survey had ranked it among the best of the country's federally qualified health centers, both clinically and financially. But during that decade, both Jim's first marriage and a later relationship had failed, at least partly because he had let the work take precedence over everything. He was forty-seven now. For ten years he had served as senior doctor and executive director of the entire operation. It had become too large for him to do both jobs well. He chose to give up administration and return to doctoring, while still retaining some control of overall policy. Among other things, he hoped to gain the time and energy to build a more substantial Street Team and pursue his interest in rough sleepers.

About a year and a half after giving up his administrative chores, Jim came under attack from some of his colleagues. One young doctor called this episode "the time of the troubles." It was something like a family feud, involving personal issues, but it included an argument with real weight, about efficiency in medicine. Medicaid was altering its rules in ways that appeared to threaten the Program's operations, maybe even its existence. The Program's clinical productivity—the number of patients seen per year—was low by conventional standards. Embarrassingly low, according to some, and Jim was to blame. A prominent spokesperson for that view wrote to the board of directors that young clinicians were drawn to this job because they wanted to help needy people, but typically they didn't know or care much about productivity, efficiency, financial accountability. And Jim wasn't interested in teaching them the importance of that business side of medicine. In fact, he was adept at persuading them to ignore it.

This was true enough. Jim had counseled the practitioners not to rush through their sessions with patients. But he hadn't done this in disregard of financial realities, not in his opinion. He believed that he and his colleagues had already found a stream of funding large enough to sustain this practice—they'd even managed to put several million dollars in reserve.

One of Jim's critics thought that the practitioners should try to double their yearly patient visits. The young doctors didn't agree, nor did Jim, but it was the young doctors who took their case to the board, after they grew tired of waiting for Jim to act.

In the end, the threat from Medicaid changes didn't materialize, partly because Bruce Bullen protected the Program. And the board's ultimate solution to the family feud was to hire—at Jim's suggestion—a clinical psychologist named Bob Taube to serve as executive director.

Taube's credentials were substantial. Among other things, he had managed a community health center and had saved it from bankruptcy, and his experience as a clinical psychologist was also an asset. Although he didn't like to think of himself as "a bean counter," he felt, as he put it years later, "incredibly motivated" to make sure that the Program's payroll checks didn't bounce. This meant making some changes that the clinicians were bound to dislike. He dealt with the objections gently. One doctor remembered that when he complained—accusing Taube of trying to "regiment" their practice—Taube listened sympathetically and then enlisted the doctor's help. "Your desire to bitch was greatly reduced," the doctor later recalled. "Even though your problem wasn't fixed."

Jim was harder to manage. Taube told me, "My background is as a psychotherapist. I learned that you have to learn on multiple chan-nels. Jim's incredibly positive and supportive. He has real difficulty saying no. But it doesn't mean that he's not thinking no, or that he said yes. So if you actually have to work something through with him, you have to listen carefully. The first thing he would say was: 'Yes, we can do that.' But that was not meaningful. The second thing would be, 'The problem is . . . '" At one point, Taube almost quit because of a dispute with Jim about personnel. But he believed in the Program and he admired Jim. So instead of leaving, he instituted what he called "relationship counseling"—he and Jim tête-à-tête, overseen by a board member skilled in mediation.

This worked well enough. Taube stayed on for sixteen years, strengthening the Program's administration and finances. Jim told me, "I grew to totally love Bob. Because he knew how to manipulate me in the nicest human way, and it would take away all my anxiety and irritation." But Taube didn't change Jim's fundamental view of medicine and management: "Medicine is not efficient," I heard Jim say to a group of interns many years after Taube had retired. "It's not *supposed* to be efficient. It has *nothing to do* with efficiency."

3

Death by Housing

In 1999, one of the Program's patients, a woman who slept in the understory of the Longfellow Bridge, took a picture with a throwaway camera of some of her friends. In the photograph, it's a sunny summer's day in Mousey Park, next to the Massachusetts General Hospital. The little concrete place looks pastoral and festive, its three trees in leaf. The lone woman in the picture has covered her face with a coat, hiding from the camera. Eleven men sit in a semicircle around her, faces grinning at the viewer, as in a painting of a bacchanal. Their clothes are a little ragged, but most look vigorous, high-spirited. You wouldn't be surprised if afterward they all got a shave and started looking for a job.

Their average age was thirty-six. All were rough sleepers. All received primary care from the Program and specialty care at one of

the world's great hospitals. Six years later, when Jim first saw the photograph, all but one was dead. None from overdoses, a few from injuries, and the others from cancer, heart attacks, and cirrhosis of the
liver—that is, from diseases of alcohol and tobacco, which most had
begun consuming in their youth. The lone survivor, a man nicknamed
BJ, had by then begun a long passage, through vodka blackouts on
cold streets, to frostbite, to intractable infections.

"We knew them all," Jim said in a talk to a group of medical students. "They had these great stories. If you got to know 'em, they
would make you laugh. They would irritate you at the same time they
would make you laugh. And this is on the campus of Mass General,
which is our hospital. When we think of terrible outcomes in poor
countries, we should also think of the people we've neglected terribly,
right in the shadows of these great institutions."

When Jim saw the photograph in 2004, it crystallized what he and
others had discovered on the streets over the past decades. Histories
such as Nick's—his mother slit her wrists in front of him when he was
a child and said, "See what you've made me do?" And Nick's subsequent years in a foster home where, when he misbehaved, he got
beaten and put in a cage. Jim had witnessed firsthand the fatal sequels
of such histories in his patients—alcoholism, drug abuse, underlying
varieties of mental disorders such as clinical depression.

By the time Jim saw that photo of the incipient dead, he had found
the money to create the Street Team. They had extended special invitations for rough sleepers to come to the McInnis House respite, and
had created a special Thursday Street Clinic at Mass General, a clinic
tailored to the needs of rough sleepers. Those measures had been en-
thusiastically received. Many rough sleepers used McInnis as a virtual
hotel, and they flocked to the Thursday Street Clinic—often more of
them than could be seen that day. Together, the team had managed
to greatly improve their "process measures," raising the percentage of
rough sleepers who received preventive tests such as mammograms,
Pap smears, and colonoscopies, and the percentage whose blood

pressure or blood sugar or other vital measurements had been brought to acceptable levels. And in spite of all that, they had failed to reduce their patients' outsized death rates.

In 2005, the Street Team received what seemed like a possible solution—twenty-four housing vouchers for rough sleepers, part of a pilot project to test a new idea known as Housing First. One of its underpinnings came from a pair of sociologists who published a study of Philadelphia's and New York City's large shelter systems. For Jim, the study's findings had the force of revelation, of something long suspected but never brought to light before.

During the seven years studied, 80 percent of the people who used the two cities' shelters stayed briefly, and rarely if ever returned; 10 percent came and went episodically; and 10 percent used the shelters as "long-term housing," consuming more than half of all the resources spent on dealing with homelessness—and dealing with it inadequately. Many of that last 10 percent suffered from mental illness or substance abuse or both. In the old prescription, such people had to be treated and stabilized before they qualified for publicly financed housing, but they rarely got stabilized enough to qualify, and thus remained, in official lingo, "chronically homeless." Shelters were supposed to provide for emergencies, but for these people, shelters had become miserable substitutes for home. A mandate had grown out of this study: Get these chronically homeless people housed first, and help them get well once they're inside. That would improve their health and welfare, and save the public money.

If that argument held for chronic users of shelters, it seemed likely that the case for Boston's rough sleepers must be stronger. A recent study had shown that 119 of the Street Team's patients had made 18,384 visits to emergency rooms over five years, during which half of them had died. The cost of all those ER visits wasn't calculated, but it had to be significant. Jim focused mainly on the deaths. Maybe housing would prevent the slaughter. He wrote a prescription on his official Mass General Rx pad:

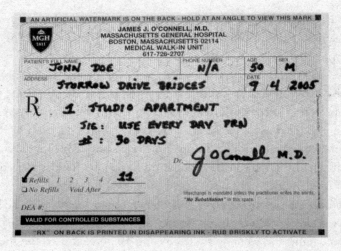

The team didn't try to decide which patients would do best in an apartment or which were the most deserving—every team member believed that dignified housing was a universal right. They simply offered the twenty-four vouchers to the patients who had been with them the longest. Only one refused—he said he didn't think he deserved the opportunity. By Medicaid rules, once patients were housed they no longer belonged to the Program, but one of the formerly homeless members of the board insisted that the Street Team continue to provide health care for these twenty-four patients and others who followed them into housing, whether the Program got paid for it or not.

As with all social service projects, a lexicon of terms accumulated around the Housing First movement. Permanent Supportive Housing (PSH) described the movement's general aim and means, and a model program conducted in the 1990s in New York had shown that housing for chronically homeless people could indeed be long-lasting and beneficial, provided they received adequate support. This trial—The Consumer Preference Supported Housing Model (CPSH)—had involved 242 people who suffered from either mental illness or substance abuse or both. The model had housed them, via various grants and public subsidies, in apartments situated in "affordable locations throughout the city's low-income neighborhoods." And they had been supported by Assertive Community Treatment (ACT) teams, somewhat modified from the general prototype, but substantial. These included nurses, social workers, drug counselors, administrative assistants, and "peer counselors," who directed the support services with the advice and consent of the tenants. Each team had access to psychiatrists and other professionals, and each stood ready to help the tenants every night and day of the week. After five years, 88 percent remained housed—a remarkable result.

The Street Team's project wasn't nearly as well endowed. Medicaid supplied the twenty-four housing vouchers and paid the salaries of two housing workers from a local organization called Home Start. The housing workers were supposed to find apartments for the twenty-four rough sleepers and to supply whatever support they might need, while the Street Team dealt with medical issues. Jim pitched in, but Jill Roncarati, the team's physician assistant and later Jim's wife, did most of the medical work.

Early on, Jill escorted a patient in his sixties to his new apartment only to find that the electricity hadn't been turned on. It was a Friday afternoon, the standard weekday over, and unlike the Street Team, which had someone on call at all times, the housing specialists kept regular hours. Jill couldn't find anyone to help. The apartment was in a town outside Boston, a foreign land to the new tenant. "He took off," Jill remembered, "and we couldn't find him for a week, because he was so spooked."

The vouchers supplied by Medicaid paid a landlord a fixed rent for a one-bedroom or studio apartment. The housing workers knew where to look for such places and which landlords would accept tenants with the blemished records rough sleepers usually carry. All of the first twenty-four got housed quickly, very quickly by the standards of the following decade. But many ended up in basement apartments with concrete walls, situated in parts of town where there wasn't a grocery store or train stop nearby, and where they didn't know anyone. In Jill and Jim's experience, rough sleepers with schizophrenia tended to keep their own company and tended to fare better than the gregarious patients, who would invite their friends to join them inside. Partying usually ensued, and evictions often followed.

In the model project in New York, modified ACT teams had helped the tenants master the basics of a settled life, providing lessons in "money management" and "vocational training" and "recreational activities." By contrast, neither Jill nor the workers from Home Start had any experience in teaching domestic arts to rough sleepers, whose finely honed skills for outdoor living didn't help them indoors. Jim remembered a patient who actually pitched a tent in his apartment. Industrial cleaning was needed sometimes, not just because of partying but because many new tenants didn't know how to clean a stove or a bathroom. Most didn't know how to pay bills or shop for groceries, let alone cook. One freshly housed man, unable to sleep for a few nights, went back out to the streets and made a tape recording of the sounds of traffic and sirens, which he used as his lullaby, his antidote to indoor insomnia. People who had adapted to the exigencies of street life had no idea how to fill their time indoors. Jill would get calls from housed patients who hadn't operated a TV for decades and couldn't figure out how to turn one on, and calls from people who would say, "I watched everything there is on TV. What do I do now?"

Jim remembered half a dozen occasions when he went with Jill to an apartment and found their patient dead. Some people had been very sick when they got housed, and the fact that they died in apartments of their own and not on the streets seemed like progress toward decency. But in many cases, patients who had looked like good candidates for success were evicted, or moved to other apartments to avoid evictions. Some others drank themselves to death. Finding their corpses left Jim and Jill wondering if they weren't violating the physician's oath, actually harming patients by putting them in apartments—abetting what Jill, on one very bad day, called "death by housing."

In the following years, several hundred Street Team patients were housed through other auspices, but the original twenty-four vouchers remained in effect. The team was still using and reusing them fourteen years later, when Jill took a scholarly look at the results of that first experiment. By this time, she and Jim had become a couple. She had long since left the Program and earned a doctorate at Harvard's School of Public Health. She titled her study "Housing Boston's Chronically Homeless Unsheltered Population: 14 Years Later." The overall results were disheartening—over ten years, seventy-three different people had used the twenty-four vouchers, 45 percent had died, and only 12 percent of the survivors had remained housed.

Jill's study didn't negate the moral imperatives behind the Housing First movement, but it did raise questions. Boston's rough sleepers made up the smallest part of the city's chronically homeless, but they were the most vulnerable and costly to the city. They fit a crucial category for the movement, which aimed to improve the health and general welfare of its beneficiaries while saving the public money. The study showed that for most of that especially vulnerable group, housing alone was insufficient. And it seemed obvious to Jim that this was mainly because the group received insufficient support—not enough treatment for the problems they brought with them, too little in the way of lessons on how to live in an apartment, and no community.

The Street Team all agreed with Jill, who said: "I still believe that everybody should get the chance to live independently in an apartment, and if they can't manage that, we have to try to find another housing option that's a better fit. Because there were people who just looked like a mess outside, and then they did really well when they got housed, and you don't know who those people are until you give them a chance."

There had been many modest successes, in which evictions were avoided thanks to periodic professional cleaning of the patients' apartments. And there had been some astonishing victories. For instance, a man in his early fifties, the dreadful age when rough sleepers often died. This patient had slept in a church doorway on Commonwealth Avenue. Jill had known him for years and had never seen him sober: "He even used to drink shampoo!" (Mouthwash was a common beverage, but shampoo, which also contains alcohol, was a first for Jill.) Around the time when the housing experiment began, the man was offered one of the vouchers. He had just come out of detox programs and he was placed in an apartment near Brookline, a wealthy "high-opportunity" suburb, and the location, it would seem, made all the difference. He started taking courses at the library and community center, courses in computers and cooking—and presumably one in zoology, because he kept several aquariums full of tree frogs, and a bucket of crickets in the shower. Otherwise, the apartment looked like a tidy, well-appointed grad student's place, with houseplants by the windows, books lying around on a desk, and a functioning computer. This man became a member of the Program's board, a paradigm of the salvation that housing could bring. He continued to flourish for a decade, and died of cancer in his sixties, old age for a rough sleeper.

4

~~~~~~~~~~~

Eulogies for Barbara

Barbara McInnis died in 2003. A minor car accident while visiting friends in Maine left her with a crack in her femur, which led to a stay at a hospital, where she suffered a rare but lethal interaction of anesthesia and the drug she took for diabetes.

She died on a Sunday. Jim was in Newport for the weekend. She had called him at one in the morning, something she never did except in emergencies. She had trouble speaking. She gasped that she couldn't breathe. Thinking she might have an embolism, Jim called her floor at the hospital. There was no doctor around. Jim talked to the charge nurse, who said they had just checked on Barbara—she was fine. The nurse was wrong, and Jim sensed it. "I should have gotten in the car and just gone right up there to Maine." Even if he had driven a hundred miles an hour, Barbara would have been dead when he arrived. But regret has its own logic.

Memories of Barbara lingered. Larry Adams, a formerly homeless member of the board, recalled that he first met Barbara in the subway station in Chinatown, when he was about to commit suicide: "I was getting ready to jump onto the tracks, and this woman I never seen before, she comes up and puts her arm around my shoulder. 'Young man, are you getting ready to do something?' I said, 'No.' She said, 'Come walk and talk with me,' and we walked over to Pine Street."

She had already been celebrated in song. Years before her death, back when he'd just begun to receive her tutoring, Jim was driving down to Newport for the weekend, and a song with the lilt of an Irish ballad came over the radio, a man's voice singing:

> *I was lying alone like a ship that had sunk,*
> *Shivering and sick from the booze I had drunk,*
> *The highway was roarin' right over my head,*
> *The city of Boston had left me for dead,*
> *When along comes a woman as big as a bear*
> *In an old overcoat with a scarf in her hair,*
> *A kind voice but tough like she'd paid her dues,*
> *My name is Barbara, would ya like some hot soup?*
> *Barbara McInnis, a friend of the poor,*
> *Standing there with us through hard times and more,*
> *Barbara McInnis, the salt of the earth*
> *May the world someday remember her worth . . .*

Jim pulled off the road and sat for a while, until the surprise wore off. The lyrics came from "A Song for Barbara," by a folksinger named Ben Tousley. He had volunteered with Barbara at the Stone Soup Mobile Food Service, which brought soup and bread and pastries to poor and homeless people in the South End. Ben remembered her bear hug, as did Larry Adams, as did Jim: "She'd just envelop you, and nobody could say no after that."

Jim knew almost nothing about her former life, but she still inhabited his present. Back when they worked together, he got into the habit of quoting her and, at times, citing her as the source of his own ideas. Now when giving speeches, he was still quoting her and inventing quotes for her. On occasion, he invoked her memory to answer criticism.

People who worked and proselytized on behalf of homeless people formed a loose confederation, with one shared interest and many differing opinions. In recent years Jim had heard that some in the alliance claimed that the Program belonged to "the homelessness industry," which misspent resources that should be used for creating permanent supportive housing. Also that the Program was an insidious part of that status quo: It propped up an unjust system by successfully treating homeless people with diseases like AIDS, weakening one of the housing movement's chief arguments—"housing is health."

Almost always the criticism came indirectly, from friends of friends. This was convenient for a person who hated confrontations. Jim could reply forcefully but indirectly, to a friend of the critic, or sometimes to me in the privacy of his office or car. Often he'd start by invoking Barbara: "The older I get, the more I realize how wise she was. I remember somebody coming into the clinic, and saying to Barbara, who was working like hell, 'What are we going to do to fix this problem of homelessness?' And she looked up and said, 'Are you kidding me? I'm too busy. Don't ask me a question like that.' That was her way of saying, 'Stop torturing me with what society isn't about to do. Let's just do the best we can right now and take care of these folks.'"

Jim paused, then wrapped up his case: "But do I want to hold that up as a gold standard? No. I want to hold it up as, 'This is what we do while we're waiting for the world to change.'"

• • •

Barbara lived on in other ways. In 2008, the Program created its first real headquarters, inside the shell of an old city morgue, situated at

780 Albany Street in the South End. It was four stories tall, with brick walls and large windows, each surrounded by a limestone frame and topped with carved medallions. The upper three floors were made over into a shiny respite hospital with 104 beds, a new "Barbara McInnis House" to replace the previous one. The building was formally named for a donor, but most of the people who worked there called it "Seven-Eighty," and rough sleepers in need of a rest knew the building by the name of the respite inside. "I want to go to Barbara McInnis," they'd say.

On a springtime morning in 2017, I walked with Jim down Albany Street, looking up at Seven-Eighty as we drew nearer. It had been constructed in 1929 in a style known as Egyptian Revival, and it remained a substantial, handsome building. Rain showers in the night had left dark streaks on the window moldings and the frieze below the edge of the roof. As we stood across the street waiting for the light to change, Jim glanced up at Seven-Eighty's rain-blemished façade. On days like this he didn't much like the building's looks, he said. "It looks like it's weeping."

He wasn't commenting on the sights in front of us, but the ambiance was troubling. Seven-Eighty's neighborhood was an urban hospital zone. The air carried the usual anxious sounds of such places—angry car horns, hurry-up sirens of police cars and ambulances, dinosaur roars of truck and bus engines. But these felt like an oddly distant backdrop to the main spectacle, which was Boston's narcotics epidemic on parade.

Crowds filled the sidewalks on Mass Ave and Albany Street, many staggering men and women among them. Lone figures in apparent stupors went wandering into the intersection against the lights, yelling at the cars and trucks, while Boston drivers sped around the stoned jaywalkers. A block down Albany Street, a group of men were shooting up in a doorway, and along the front wall of Seven-Eighty, half a dozen men and women stood stock-still, like marionettes at rest, bent forward at their waists, heads down, arms hanging loosely, knees deeply bent. Jim knew some of those people as patients. Their symptoms were familiar. Unmistakably, they had ingested cocktails of drugs that induce sedation, prescription drugs such as the antiepileptic gabapentin ("johnnies") and the benzodiazepine Klonopin ("pins").

An island in Boston Harbor—Long Island—had served as a sanctuary for a large homeless shelter and various treatment facilities, including one for drug addiction. By 2013, the bridge to the island had grown so dilapidated it had to be shut down. To make up for the losses, the city had added about six hundred new shelter beds in Seven-Eighty's vicinity. And because drug overdoses were rising dramatically in Boston, the authorities had also expanded an existing methadone clinic and created a new one. The two clinics lay about a mile from each other on a stretch of road that the local papers nicknamed Methadone Mile. Seven-Eighty's corner lay roughly in the middle. Methadone was a safe and effective drug that could easily be administered in doctors' offices, but federal policy insisted that the job be done in dedicated clinics. The result locally was a tide of about 1,200 people daily traversing the Methadone Mile. Most of them, Jim figured, were managing their addictions, but some, maybe three hundred, still craved opiates and represented likely customers for drug dealers, who had entered the neighborhood in force. Other people seeking drugs had followed the dealers in turn. Collateral damage included many new cases of HIV, street gangs, sex trafficking, used needles on the sidewalks. Recently, an intern had collected ninety used needles lying within five hundred feet of Seven-Eighty's front doors. The neighborhood, Jim remarked mordantly, had turned into "an enterprise zone."

Across the street, on the sidewalk in front of Seven-Eighty, a young man on a bicycle brushed my shoulder. He was threading through the crowd, saying in a quiet voice, "I got johnnies, I got pins."

Sanctuary for many of the city's thousands of homeless lay just beyond, inside Seven-Eighty's front doors. To Jim's regret, preserving the peace now took a team of security guards and a metal detector. But the lobby was busy in ordered and productive ways. It was like a train station's concourse, flanked by vital services, a sense of the size and diversity of the Program on display. A steady flow of patients passed through the lobby during the day, some on crutches and canes. The vast majority were not the rough sleepers sought out by the Street Team but the city's sheltered homeless. Many headed for the pharmacy window, where around 1,500 prescriptions were filled each day. Others stopped at the dental clinic, which employed three full-time dentists, interns from Boston's dental schools, and technicians who fabricated about 350 sets of dentures a year. Some patients climbed a broad stairway, which led up to the Boston Medical Center Clinic, the largest of the Program's thirty clinics. This one included eighteen exam rooms, special treatment for HIV and hepatitis C, and care tailored to the needs of transgender homeless people. At the back of the lobby a set of three elevators carried disabled patients up to the large BMC Clinic and respite patients farther upstairs to the floors of the Barbara McInnis House.

The drug epidemic had infiltrated Seven-Eighty's lobby. Every day—even many times a day—a siren drowned out all other sound and a robotic voice called out, "Code blue!" During the planning of the building, Jim had imagined that single-use bathrooms would foster dignity, not the risk of a quick death from respiratory failure induced by fentanyl. The staff had adapted. Now if a person went into one of the two public bathrooms and didn't move for a minute and forty seconds, the siren and code blue would sound, and within thirty seconds a team would arrive.

No one here stepped over inert bodies. No one had died from a drug overdose inside the building. But the effort this took was taxing for everyone. In an article in *JAMA*, Jesse Gaeta, the chief medical officer, pleaded for a different approach, unpalatable to many, anathema to politicians, but backed by experience and sympathy:

> . . . I wish I could be with [these people] before they injected, that I had more chances to really know them before I'm hovering over them on the grimy bathroom floor, sliding an oral airway into their throat.

. . . We must be able to create cleaner, safer spaces for
people to consume drugs and be connected to help. Super-
vised consumption sites would not only play an important part
in stemming the tide of opioid overdose deaths for people
downstream in this epidemic, but they would also reduce the
trauma associated with injection drug overdoses—for both
people who use drugs and the people who care about them.

Dr. Gaeta had dreamed up a more limited form of succor, known
as SPOT—Supportive Place for Observation and Treatment. It was a
soundproof room, off the lobby, with eight adjustable cardiac chairs
where people who'd been brought in from the streets slept off whatever they'd ingested, usually drug cocktails. Jim had doubted that the
project would contribute much, but over just a few years it had produced a library of information about the drug epidemic, and it had
offered patients a serenity that no busy ER could provide, while likely
sparing the Boston Medical Center's emergency department several
thousand visits. The recovery room lay behind a wooden door. Passing by one morning that spring, Jim stopped and, staring at the door,
he declared his change of heart. "SPOT!" he exclaimed. "It's the
kindest, gentlest thing going, for the roughest-living people. It's all
these people sleeping in there, being cared for by these wonderful
nurses. It's the foot soak clinic!"

He had said he was going to resist nostalgia. Obviously, he didn't
always succeed.

5

Living Life Backwards

Jim turned sixty-nine in March of 2017. Many of his college friends had retired. Some had grandchildren enrolled at Notre Dame. He still went to work every day, and helped to care for a daughter, three years old. Her name was Gabriella. A surprise for Jim and Jill. Soon after she was born, they had brought her to meet Jim's mother, who was in her late eighties then and in a nursing home. She was delighted, of course, to meet her new granddaughter, but at one point she said, "Why the hell did you wait so long, Jim? You're living your life backwards."

Spending time with Gabriella made him feel like a tourist in his own youth. "I came so close to missing this," he'd say. In his errands around Boston, he would peer out the windshield at playgrounds and note the addresses of ones that looked especially well equipped. On some mornings Jim found it hard to leave Jill and the warm little child who had crept into their bed and was sleeping beside him. But except on the days when he drove Gabriella to school, he still rose early and headed for work, eagerly more often than not.

Home for the three of them was a wood-frame three-bedroom house situated in a quiet, outlying corner of Boston, half a dozen miles from the city's downtown. Jim liked to leave by 6:30, before the roads filled up. At that hour, he could drive to headquarters at Seven-Eighty in about eight minutes and to Mass General in about twelve. Those sites had become the two fixed points on his compass—the renovated Egyptian Revival building encircled by Boston's drug epidemic, and the giant, world-class hospital where he had trained.

He had mostly invented his current job. It was miscellaneous, both office-bound and mobile—Street Team meetings on Mondays at Seven-Eighty, the van on Monday nights, doctoring at the Mass General Street Clinic on Thursdays, street rounds on Fridays, visits to patients in respite and apartments and nursing homes when he had time, and many meetings of the Program's senior management. He also took calls from nurses at Andrew House, the detox facility where he had moonlighted in the early days, and where he still served as medical director. This didn't take much time away from other duties, because the nurses' calls often came when he was driving among the stations of his work. He'd listen, then diagnose and instruct.

"Doreen, *never* let anyone come back from the ER without taking both blood pressure *and* pulse."

"Yes, sir." The nurse sounded chastened.

An unintended effect, quickly softened. "Doreen, you're doing great. Thank you for giving me that history."

He spent about a week every month traveling to give lectures, sometimes in towns and cities nearby, sometimes in places as distant as Los Angeles and Sydney, Australia. The board encouraged his trips. They viewed him as an ambassador for both the Program and the wider cause. They wanted him to do more lecturing, and to spend time writing and thinking about the big issues surrounding

homelessness and medicine. For some time, they'd been gently suggesting that he "step back" from his duties with patients and the
Street Team.

Jim toyed with that idea. Riding the van on a quiet night, in the
dappled semidarkness of the cabin, he said, "I have this vision of like,
the old bus of Ken Kesey, and picking up our people and going on
trips. You know, to the zoo, to the movies, to the beach, just gather
everybody and go, three days a week go and do something."

On another nighttime ride, he offered me a summary of what he
felt the Program had become, which was something like a summary
of his career. What he'd helped to build was now the country's largest
medical system wholly devoted to the care of homeless people, but its
size was, after all, a reflection of an ugly truth about America. What
pleased Jim was the Program's design: "If you're homeless, we have a
great deal for you. You have doctors of your own. You can page them
twenty-four hours a day. We will see you at a clinic at Mass General,
which is a pretty good place to go. And when you're admitted to a
hospital, we'll be involved in your care. And if you need a place to
recover, there's McInnis House. If you're housed, we'll see you at
home. There was none of that when we started. The homeless people
didn't know the name of any doctor."

He paused, then added, "People will say, 'All right, but it's just for
the homeless.' Yes, but as an example of how to approach the problems of medicine in the United States, it's worth looking at."

Jim had begun to call himself "redundant," a now unnecessary
part of the operation. Whether or not he believed this, he wasn't in-
clined to give up his doctoring. Many longtime patients—"the old
classics"—had died. He felt obliged to stand with the ones who remained, in the dark if need be, as Barbara McInnis had said. Dozens
still relied on him. Frankie, for instance, who while homeless had
managed to become an ordained minister. He used to preach con-
vincingly to his compatriots and others, in actual services on the Boston Common, but drinking and pulmonary embolisms had finally left
him incapable of that. He had gotten housed at last but was losing

track of time and would have Jim paged at all hours, sometimes mistaking night for day. Jim would call him back, and Frankie wouldn't answer because he was growing deaf and couldn't hear his phone ring.

There was Susie, a former pop singer who had belonged to a band that once opened for B. B. King. She was a college graduate and suffered from the same problem with alcohol as Frankie, as did most of the old classics. "I like my beverages, Jim. You know that." She refused to be counseled about her drinking or to admit it was the cause of her many ailments. She often called Jim, but usually at times when he was in his office and could put her on speaker, then catch up with his email, while listening: "Holy socks, Jim! I haven't seen you since Moby Dick was a minnow."

And there was BJ, a patient for more than twenty years, the ultimate survivor among them, with one leg lost to infections from frostbite. Jim couldn't desert him now, and the new guy, Tony, was becoming more interesting by the day.

It seemed obvious: Jim would keep on growing old with his patients for some time to come.

V

Searching for Meaning

1

A History of Tony

Some patients never revealed the slightest details of their pasts. The man who had called himself a judge, for instance. Jim used to find him lying drunk on a sidewalk, and the Judge would awaken and adopt his dignified persona, lifting his head from the pavement and saying with the roundest of Os, "Oh, *good* evening, Dr. O'Connell." He had never been a judge—a friend who really was a judge had determined this for Jim—but he never abandoned the role, not even on his deathbed, when Jim sat beside him, holding his hand, wanting to ask him who he really was.

Jim had gone with Barbara McInnis to the funerals of several patients whose histories they didn't know. One time she'd remarked that this was probably for the best, "because we don't want the past to cast any aspersions on the person that we're celebrating." The

warning applied with equal force to the living. When he helped patients apply for Social Security Disability, Jim had to assemble sketches
of their lives. In all cases, he made it a practice to restrain his curiosity
and not push for details. But some patients eagerly volunteered their
stories. Tony Columbo was one of those, and Jim was happy to
listen.

· · ·

Tony had been born on the Charlestown Bridge, in the back seat of
his father's car. "You were a troublemaker from the start," his mother
liked to say. He grew up in Boston's North End, known to outsiders for
its Italian restaurants and American heirlooms—the Old North
Church, Paul Revere's house. "The healthiest place in the city," Jane
Jacobs called the neighborhood, in *The Death and Life of Great American
Cities*. The streets, she wrote, had an "atmosphere of buoyancy, friend-
liness and good health."

The North End of Tony's childhood was a harsher place. Outsiders used to say that a single woman could walk its streets in perfect
safety, but this was true, Tony said, only if the woman was white. His
neighborhood was far from universally healthy: "There was an old
saying that, back in the North End, the Italians lived by: That your
wife stays home, barefooted, black-eyed, and pregnant." He said he
witnessed his first murder when he was six or seven. He was walking
down Hanover Street with a bag of groceries when he heard a *pop, pop,
pop*, and, turning the corner to Prado park, he saw the older brother
of a schoolboy friend shooting another teenager, the kid standing with
his back to a wall, his body jerking with each pop of the pistol, then
slumping to the ground—whereupon the gunman turned to Tony
and said of his victim, "He looks like a sacka patatahs." Tony dropped
his bag and ran home to a scolding from his mother, which ceased
when he told her what he'd seen.

Tony insisted that his parents had done the best they could, but his
father, he believed, was doomed by genetics: "Come to find out, a lot
of my father's brothers and sisters, they're psycho. The reason is my

grandmother married her first cousin, which was legal in Italy. She got married at fifteen. So my mother married a guy that was mentally incested." His mother wasn't faint of heart, he said. She would cook liver for dinner knowing that Tony's father hated it. He'd come home and throw the liver on the floor, and in no time the fighting would begin, Tony's father hitting his mother, Tony's four brothers and sisters trying to intervene and getting hit themselves. In the aftermath, there would be blood on the walls, chairs and tables overturned, and, one time, the TV screen smashed.

Clumps of his mother's hair would be lying on the floor, and Tony, the baby of the family, would pick them up and take them to her in her bedroom, where she lay sobbing. He remembered a fight when one of his siblings called the police, and a local cop came up to the apartment but merely sat at the kitchen table, smoking a cigar and drinking a glass of some liquor or other, and saying to Tony's father that it was time for him to calm down now. Calling the police was futile, and also dangerous, because after the cop left, his father ripped the phone cord out of the wall and beat up Tony's brothers. But Tony was his favorite. His father never beat him up. Would it have been better if he had? Sometimes Tony thought so.

When the fights started, the children would usually run and find a neighbor—Blackie Pete or Big Sam. Or they'd go to one of their "uncles," members of the Anguillo family, the Mafia royalty of the North End. Tony's father worked part-time for them as a bookie. He also drove a truck. The Mafia bosses would warn him not to beat up his wife again, or else. But soon enough his mother or siblings would commit another offense—leaving an ice cream container on the table, for instance—and another melee would follow, and his father would have to keep the news from their uncles. "It was war for days," Tony told me. "We weren't even allowed out of the house. We'd stay five days, no school, no nuttin', because he beat everybody up so bad, wouldn't let us out, so our 'uncles' wouldn't find out what was going on."

Sometimes after a brawl, he and his siblings managed to retreat to their grandmother's house. They also went there for Sunday dinners, which were all Tony knew of consistent family harmony. When Tony was sixteen, that sanctuary disappeared. His grandmother was murdered, by Tony's namesake, his uncle Anthony, who stabbed his own mother to death because she wouldn't give him $100 for heroin.

Physically, Tony took after the men on his mother's side. At ten he was taller than his barrel-chested father. Tony told me: "Me and my brother, we made an invention. We took a board and we glued a knife to it and we were gonna put it under my father's mattress, so when he laid down he would lie on it. We tried to poison him. We put Drano and stuff in his coffee. He went to the hospital, he never knew. We used to dream about him dying, wanted to kill him, yet at the same time I loved him, he was like the closest to me."

When Tony started tenth grade, the family moved to Revere, a working-class suburb adjacent to Boston. He hated it. He had done well in his North End elementary school. The nuns had him skip third grade. But in Revere, he often cut classes and boarded the trains for the old neighborhood. He quit school altogether at sixteen—"I was too busy making the money." By then he'd found various occupations. He and a couple of friends broke into a high school biology lab one night and emptied the formaldehyde from the jars holding specimens of reptiles and amphibians. They used the formaldehyde to manufacture ersatz angel dust, which they sold. What else did he do? "Some fireworks. Burning restaurants down that wanted insurance. If you parked in my friend's parking spot, I cut your tires, put mothballs in your trunk, blow your car up." He described, in alarming detail, how he made incendiary devices.

He had never played organized sports, but he learned to fight on the streets of the neighborhood and spent some afternoons at a little storefront school for martial arts. He also spent time in juvenile detention and at least two long stretches at the Lindemann Mental Health Center, the longer stretch after he tried to shoot himself, at fifteen. One of his sisters saw him take a pistol out from under his mattress, and when he left the house, she called the police, who caught up with him in a Walgreens parking lot in Revere. He tried to run, found himself surrounded, put the pistol to his right temple, and pulled the trigger. Somehow he missed, the bullet merely grazing the back of his head. He would have tried again, he said, but the police were on him too quickly.

By then he had already collected an array of diagnoses at the Lindemann Center—attention deficit disorder, possible schizophrenia, bipolar disorder. The doctors had treated him with psychoactive drugs. Tony told Jim the names of the medications and the dosages prescribed. The list was credible, its implications troubling, Jim thought: "They tried him on everything. That points out to me that he must have been really difficult to control, that they were struggling to calm him down."

. . .

That was the account of his childhood that Tony gave to Jim and me, in the early months of our acquaintance. Documents verified its broad outlines—his grandmother's murder, his stays at the Lindemann. Other claims were demonstrably true, such as his skill at martial arts. And details he offered lent some of his stories credibility—for instance, that it was raining the day he tried to shoot himself and that, as they took him away, he heard the policemen saying to each other, "Fuckin' kid. Now we gotta clean our guns."

His stories were also sprinkled with inconsistencies, especially with dates, and he left some matters vague. He said he was introduced to sex by a sixteen-year-old girl, a relative, on the floor in the corner behind the stove in the family's tenement. He was twelve. A year of initiation followed. He volunteered this story, and said it had this long-lasting effect: "Because of that, I never loved anybody. Never fell in love. I've had two girlfriends and I never—like sex is dead to me. Even to this day, it doesn't—like I'm dead in my mind to a lot of things. It's crazy." He also said he was kidnapped and raped by a neighbor. This happened, he thought, when he was twelve or maybe fourteen. There was in fact a well-publicized case in which a neighbor of Tony's supplied boys to a group of male pedophiles, some of them prominent citizens. But Tony was only eight at the time.

The events, if real, lay in the distant past. Maybe he misremembered his age, or the psychological wounds had distorted his memory. Whatever the case, Tony spoke of that experience with puzzling nonchalance. Perhaps he feigned indifference in the fear that Jim and I would think the crime had left him prone to sexually abusing others—a disputed assumption about the victims of sexual abuse, but still widely believed. Or maybe Tony claimed to be a victim of a notorious crime in lieu of something a former Catholic altar boy might have thought more shameful. As in the rest of Boston, some boys of the North End had suffered sexual abuse by priests. On at least two occasions, Tony vehemently insisted that had never happened to him.

According to official records, the crime for which Tony went to state prison was sexual. When he was twenty-six, he was sentenced to twelve to eighteen years for "assault with intent to commit rape." Four other related charges were tacked on, including "assault and battery with a dangerous weapon." The victim was a seventeen-year-old male.

According to Tony, his actual crime had nothing to do with sex, but with forcible robbery of drug dealers, a business that he and two friends had conducted with the tacit permission of Tony's "uncles." To question him for details seemed like a violation of Street Team policy. As for public records, only the outlines of his case were still available: His arraignment, a plea of not guilty, then a plea of not guilty by reason of "mental disease or defect," followed by a stay of about a month at a mental hospital for evaluation, which found him "criminally responsible." Then Tony pled guilty. After the judge sentenced him, he tried to withdraw the plea, but the judge denied the motion.

He served the full term, eighteen years. But in cases like his, cases in which one is convicted of a violent sexual crime, a sentence doesn't ever really end. Tony left prison branded as a "level-three sex offender," the highest level of classification, which carries a lifetime of punishment.

• • •

Tony's stories about his years in state prison came with a touch of nostalgia. When he went in, he imagined that he would commit suicide, he said. But then routine took over. "Days go by, weeks go by, months go by, it flies by," he said. And then one day he realized that prison had become his world. "Some people wake up ten years later and find out they're in prison. It took me about five years. One day I woke up, and I see the wall, and I'm like, 'There's no more to life. This is it.' Horrible things I saw by then, but I said, 'This life here is actually better than it was when I was outside.' And what I meant by that, I was sitting there thinking, 'Today when my cell door opens I gotta go meet this guy, that guy, it'll be showtime, I'll have a nice tea, then I'm gonna go work out, then I gotta write somebody a letter, then I gotta go do this and do that and play cards.'"

He also spent time in the library, and, he said, he put some energy into making sure that he committed enough offenses to keep himself in maximum security for most of his last eleven years at the state prison in Shirley, Massachusetts. At Shirley Max he had his own cell. Its door was steel and plexiglass. Sometimes when he heard it slide shut at night—it didn't shut with a clang, just a little thud—he would open his eyes and look at the door and in his mind he would be lying awake, gazing at the door to the bedroom he had shared with his brothers, fearfully waiting for it to open and for his father to appear, on his way to hurt their mother in the adjoining bedroom. Tony would awaken from this memory of sleeplessness with relief.

Of all the prisons he saw, he liked Shirley Max best, because after a few years, he knew everyone there. He was known as Big Tony and Big Man, he said. He was all of that back then—not just six foot four but also, once he started lifting weights in earnest, nearly three hundred pounds. He used his size and strength to create an informal

profession, a purpose for himself, which was administering rough justice, jumping into the middle of fights in the yard, and protecting the
weak inmates. He claimed that the guards and wardens loved him
because of his knack for breaking up and preventing fights, though by
his own account he also joined some that turned into riots: "A lot of
my situations were because I helped a kid out or looked out for them,
when a gang rival come on to them and stuff. If they're out in the yard
and they get jumped by five people, I wouldn't let it happen. And if I
jumped in, a lot of other people jumped in." And he also became an
informal counselor to young convicts, especially young Black men just
entering prison. A couple of them actually named their own children
Tony, after him. Or so he said.

"I took kids out of gang lives, I changed people from wantin' to
kill themselves. I was involved in a lot of stuff. My happiness, my high,
my biggest drug, was never money. There was nothing bigger to me
than some of the young dudes' stories, how they grew up. How they
would get up in the morning and have to push the roaches and cigarette butts off the table to eat the pizza for breakfast, while, you know,
Momma was smoking crack. And some of them, their Mom sold
them. They'd be sleepin' and wake up and two guys would be molest-
ing 'em in the bed while Momma was home. I mean horrible stories,
and when I'd get close to them, a lot of these dudes—young men
then, grown men now—I'd talk to them in the cell and I would share
a little bit about myself, and they would be like, 'Yo, I want to talk to
you.' And for some reason, everybody like confessed and opened up
to *me*. There was a kid that came into prison for a drive-by. He's got
four bodies under his belt and he's hard-core, don't give a *fuck* about
anything, and he's sitting in his cell crying, telling me about how he
woke up being molested, and how he seen his sister being sold, and
how it was on the streets, and now he's doing a life bid. And he'd be
looking at me like I have some wisdom for him."

During the first months after meeting Tony, I thought that those
accounts were too self-serving to credit. But as time went on, a witness
surfaced, a friend of Tony's. A middle-aged Black man, Isaac, who

had served time with Tony at Shirley Max. He spoke with a soft, melodious southern accent: "I know a few people, you know what I'm sayin'? Tony had befriended them in prison, and became close with them? Well, I could tell you about Tony. From my perspective he's always been a good guy. He always overextended hisself. He's always been that person that always overextended hisself, put hisself last all the time."

I asked if he remembered Tony fighting at Shirley Max. Isaac said, "You bein' in prison, people always gonna test you, when they think you're soft. People's always gonna test you, that's just proven. Tony was tested a few times. He always fought. Did a little hole time, come back out, still was a humble dude. Very generous. Always, always gave hisself. Even if he didn't have, he'd try to find and give it to you. That's been him."

• • •

Tony recalled vividly the day he was released—at the end of May 2013, when he stood at the front door of the Suffolk County Courthouse, facing freedom. It was the kind of moment we say we'll never forget—and usually don't. The glass doors opened before him, and after eighteen years he was looking out at the city where he was born and raised. He started walking, downhill from Pemberton Square toward Washington Street, looking for old landmarks. The Woolworth Building was there, but the store was gone. Jordan Marsh seemed to have turned into Macy's. He spoke to a passerby. "Excuse me. Where's there a phone booth?" People drew back from him and walked away. Finally, a woman stopped. "What are you looking for?"

"A pay phone."

"Hon," she said, "where have you been the last fifteen years?"

He went to get a coffee at a fast-food chain store and was peering around under the sinks of the bathroom looking for a way to turn on the water when a fellow patron demonstrated how sensors controlled the faucets. "Wow!" Tony exclaimed. He added, replying to the man's puzzled look: "Dude, it's a long story."

He headed toward the North End. When he got to Cross Street, he stopped and stared. He'd been a young man when he last saw this place. He was forty-four now, and he felt, as he would later put it, that he had been removed from time. The high trestles of the Southeast Expressway were gone, and so were most of the things that used to lie in their shadows: Martignetti's liquor store where his mother had worked, the fruit market, the pushcarts, and the big parking lot that they used to call the Underpass, where people went to find a prostitute or drugs and where, as a boy, he'd watched the professionals strip stolen cars—taking their time, because if a police cruiser drove by, it would only be the local cop who befriended Tony's father. He would wave to the car thieves and drive on.

Tony's memories of his first six months of freedom were murky. He thought he'd been promised a room, but he didn't claim it right away and when he tried, it was no longer available. He borrowed the couch of a friend for a while and also slept on pavement. Someone at the Pine Street Inn helped him obtain Social Security Disability payments, and he earned some money working, part-time and briefly, as a bill collector for a Boston drug dealer who went by the nickname Deuce.

After nearly a year on the streets, Tony was arrested and sent back to jail for most of the next. He said it was for shoplifting, but in fact the main charge was failing to register as a sex offender, as he was required to do every month.

When the state released him this time, life on the street was his only real option. Homeless shelters felt like prison. Sometimes he walked the city all night. On the coldest days he took refuge in the underground MBTA Orange Line station on State Street. He would sit there on a bench with fellow homeless people and watch the trains arrive, calculating how, someday soon, he'd time his leap so that the train would still be moving fast enough to kill him painlessly.

He told me more than once, "I was a big man in prison. When I got out, I was a nobody." Old injuries to his back and left knee dogged him as he walked the winter streets, and to curb that kind of pain he would buy doses of Suboxone. Tony had used it in prison—it was often smuggled in. Reducing the craving for opiates was its main effect and purpose, but when taken occasionally, it had a euphoric effect. It also had mildly analgesic effects. If Tony took it every day, it relieved some of his aches and pains. For forgetting where he was, he favored cocaine and the so-called synthetic marijuana known as K2, or spice. He used street opiates like heroin only occasionally and avoided the drug cocktails that many street people assembled from prescription drugs. These usually included benzodiazepines, which had the paradoxical effect of making him anxious and jittery, whereas the cocaine he bought calmed him down.

As the weather warmed, he began sleeping outside, among friends he'd made. A group of them had a spot on the waterfront and invited him to join them. On a Thursday afternoon in 2016, he was languishing with his crew on the shore of Boston Harbor, broke and feeling ill from Suboxone withdrawal and aching in the knees and back. One of his friends—Billy, known as Billy Goat because of his gray beard—said, "Tony, why don't you go to the Mass General. There's a clinic there Thursdays. There's this Dr. Jim guy."

Tony remembered telling Billy he was tired of hearing that name. He said he'd heard about this Dr. Jim in prison, but he didn't believe a doctor was going to help a penniless ex-con. Tony had additional thoughts, which he paraphrased this way: "I've run into doctors everywhere and they're very very very abrupt and very in a cold way. Just want to give you treatment and get you out of there and they're not looking to give you that extra concern or compassionate time, they're not showing any sign of really caring, they're just trying to get the issue moving on to the next person. They look at you like you made your problems, you're an alcoholic, you're a drug addict, you deserve what your burden is."

But Billy Goat insisted: "Tony, I go to Dr. Jim. I think the guy will really help ya. Come on. Just give it a shot."

2

~~~~~~~~~~~~

Inventing a Purpose

I t was a Thursday morning in early spring 2017, six months since Tony had taken Billy Goat's advice. Tony was sitting in the cramped exam room beside Jim's desk, wearing a grin so wide it nearly pulled his eyes shut.

"You heard about next week, right?" Tony said. "Next Tuesday I go to look at a studio apartment in Allston."

"What do you think of that area? You okay with it?" asked Jim.

"*Perfect!* Doc, you can put me anywhere. I know everybody." Tony went on in rising cadence: "My friend at the VA? He says, 'I got a CD player for you, I got silverware.' My place is gonna be fully furnished by people that have places, that really care."

Tony was forty-eight and like a child possessed by Christmas Eve mania. He had never lived in a place of his own.

Jim smiled. "Finally, good things are coming."

But Jim was wrong. Early the next morning, Beckie, the Street Team's manager and housing expert, called to say that Tony wasn't getting an apartment after all. She had found a state-financed housing voucher for him, one that didn't exclude a level-three sex offender. She had hunted down a decent place with a rent that the voucher would cover. But last night a representative of the landlord, a quasi-public agency, had told her that Tony wasn't eligible, because their organization didn't accept level-threes. Beckie was sorry and frustrated, she told Jim. "We came so close."

Jim said he'd let Tony know. The next day was a Friday, Jim's day for street rounds—for patrolling the city between Mass General and South Station. First stop, Mousey Park. Jim headed there.

The March gales were gone. The air felt gentle. You could smell the river, even a faint perfume of spring from the Esplanade. Some patients came to the park on Fridays just to see Jim—for a medical consult or a chat. Some came expecting a pack of cigarettes or a Dunkin' Donuts card from Jim's knapsack or a folded "dead president" from his pocket. Several petitioners were there today, along with the usual crew, for whom the park was a family room and barroom. The old fisherman Karl, in a wheelchair. And BJ, the lone survivor of that Mousey Park photo of the living dead, one-legged now and seated in a red motorized chair. There were also several women, two of them eyeing each other angrily. Tony, still dressed in his five coats, his cold weather garb, stood among them.

Jim drew him away from the others. This was unremarkable, a private consult with Dr. Jim. Tony lowered his head and turned an ear toward Jim, as Jim spoke. In a moment, you could see the bad news had been passed. Tony straightened up and said—as Jim later told me—"I know why."

Tony didn't yell or storm off. On the contrary, he seemed unperturbed. When I went up to him, he told me that he wasn't getting the apartment after all, and this, he said, was because you couldn't use a state housing voucher if you had an outstanding arrest warrant, and he had a charge from two years ago, for shoplifting seventy-nine bucks' worth of clothes. He thought the judge had thrown out that case. No big deal, he said.

Of course, this wasn't true. His disappointment about the apartment must be keen, I thought, a new wound, and as he spoke, I searched his face for signs of this, but there was nothing, just a natural-looking shrug.

Jim had turned from Tony to the others, who were waiting for their consults and gifts. After another fifteen minutes or so, Jim shouldered his street doctor's bag and led a small entourage down Cambridge Street. Once out of earshot of the patients, he said: "Level-three sex offenders aren't eligible for most housing. They're ashamed of their record of course, and no one will hire them, and they'll end up being on the streets. It's as if Tony's been condemned to homelessness."

That was it, then?

"Not necessarily," Jim said. "There may be other, more complicated ways to get him a place."

Tony's situation looked dire to me. He yearned for an apartment, privately: "If I had a place to live, I know I'd keep myself safe, I know I would sleep, I'd set up things nice, I would be proud, I would put ego and pride in it." But a place of his own looked out of reach. Indeed, because of his classification, which was publicly available, almost all avenues to a normal life were closed to him.

· · ·

Clearly, Tony didn't want other rough sleepers to know that an alleged sexual assault on a man was the real reason he wasn't getting housed, and he might not have survived eighteen years in prison if he hadn't become skilled at hiding the fact of that charge. He was also good at hiding his feelings when it suited him. In private, though, he could come unfastened, even floridly emotional.

A few weeks after his hopes for housing were dashed, Tony had a long talk-therapy session with Dr. Bonnar, the Street Team's elderly, white-mustached psychiatrist. Afterward, at the preclinic team meeting,

Bonnar gave this report: "Tony *says* he has no feelings, and yet he shows them all over the place. He's weeping, he's angry. He said he learned the skill of shutting off his feelings in order to survive. I told him this is a survival tactic, this is not something that's sick about you, this is what you had to do. So we started talking about trauma and recovery. He said, 'I'm this way and it's not going to change.' I told him, 'No, this is where you're starting from.'"

Bonnar's account reminded me of talks I'd had with Tony. He would say he had no feelings, and no hope for anything, but it was as though he were asking to be proven wrong. Often he'd declare despair, and the next thing he'd say was that meeting Dr. Jim and the Street Team had inspired the opposite in him. "When I went on the streets after prison, I didn't believe in nuttin' or nobody, but then you meet somebody like Jim who has a buncha people under him that are like him, showing that they really do care." In one of our first conversations, he said, "Jim changed me." And he was going to do for Jim what he himself had done for other inmates in prison. "Here I'm looking at a guy that, thirty years a doctor, and I imagine how many times he's helped out a person. In my mind, he's like that person to me, I'm gonna be that person to him."

The first thing he could do for Jim, he felt, was to clean up his own act. He'd made a start on that, he said. "I stopped a lot of things. I threw away all the pills, the opiates and all, I didn't want to do that no more. Just smoke and drank, stood on the regimen, Suboxone, stood out of trouble, didn't think about robbin' banks or anything anymore. Held my temper in order. Stayed clean myself pretty much. So when I went in on a Thursday I looked a little cleaner, I was a little healthier, and I was more positive."

He seemed to be devising a new start, regardless of his situation. He told me, "I don't have a family anymore. So it's kind of like *this* is my family." He meant the Street Team and its community of patients. In one odd sense, Jim later learned, Tony was making this claim literally, telling fellow rough sleepers that Jim was his great-uncle. Just why Tony did this wasn't clear at the time, but other aims were obvious. He had told Mike, the team's recovery coach, that he'd like to do some of what Mike did and serve as something like a peer counselor to other patients: "I want to go out and talk to people and share my experience as a peer and just encourage them." He'd also told both me and Dr. Bonnar that he'd like to go out with Jim on Friday street rounds, to take Jim to places and people Jim might not know.

Tony was looking for a purpose like the one he'd had in jail, a reason not to throw himself in front of the Orange Line train. And it was obvious that he'd begun to imagine a role for himself with the Street Team, as Jim's assistant on the front lines—an unsanctioned, not yet fully formed idea of a place for himself in the world, which had the urgent quality of a thing conceived in desperation.

3

The Social Director

For Jim, 2017 was a year of worries. First of all, "Trump"—shorthand for the president's attempts to eradicate Obamacare. If successful, it would bring deep cuts in funding for poor people's medicine and, Jim feared, maybe kill the Program.

A troubling philosophical issue also loomed. He served on a panel that was compiling a study of studies for the National Academies of Sciences. The aim was to show that housing for homeless people improved their health and saved the public money, and yet no studies fully supported those widely held claims, none at least that met the standards of the academics on the committee. Some of Jim's old allies refused to give up the cost-savings argument. He wrote me privately: "Housing homeless people is mandatory. A human right. But I have long been skeptical of the drive to show that it saves money, because that leaves housing dependent on whether it saves money. Ridiculous. Who would ever say that Mass General exists to save money?"

. . .

There is a subspecies of doctor for whom visiting patients is therapeutic. Often, when Jim felt discouraged by large problems, he would visit McInnis House, where there were always some Street Team patients. To spend a little time with them restored his spirits, he said.

The Program's latest incarnation of the respite occupied most of Seven-Eighty's second, third, and fourth floors. Most visitors and patients rode up from the lobby on one of the elevators. Jim preferred to climb the back stairs. Once you had made it through the addled crowds on the streets outside and the busy lobby with its uniformed security guards, the floors of the respite felt emphatically serene. It was sanctuary defined by its surroundings, like an oasis by its desert.

The respite's first floor contained a kitchen and dining room, a recreation room, various offices, conference and exam rooms, and a high-ceilinged atrium with a piano and rocking chairs. Outside was the Serenity Deck, where patients could smoke at appointed hours—a source of continuing disagreement. Cancers had for years ranked as the leading cause of death among the Program's patients. How could a medical facility allow smoking? And how could it not, given that the vast majority of homeless people were addicted to tobacco? Jim knew that if the respite didn't let its patients smoke, many wouldn't stick around for medical treatment. Most probably wouldn't come in at all. So if you banned smoking, Jim and others argued, you wouldn't have a chance to help patients in any way, including helping them to quit smoking.

The second and third floors were hospital-like—nursing stations on well-lit hallways, flanked by bedrooms with doors. Only a few rooms were private. The formerly homeless members of the board had vetoed Jim's original plan for single rooms, reminding him that homelessness was a terribly lonesome state, insisting that most people who came to McInnis House would want company. This was certainly true of Tony, who was increasingly in residence, and who seemed on his way to becoming the protagonist of the place.

Jim would be walking toward the dining room on the second floor, looking for familiar patients, and he'd see a long torso bent over the dining room's trash barrel, like a scavenging bear in a park. Tony would emerge with silverware and unused packages of butter and mayonnaise that his fellow patients had discarded. Evidently, "Trump" had inspired this. "They throw good stuff away, Jim. I tell 'em, 'McInnis is in danjah. If we don't save money, this won't be here for us. We need to work together. Little things can save us, like don't steal the sheets.'"

Tony seemed to have invented his position piecemeal, adding new roles from one stay to another. By the end of summer, he'd assumed the role of triage nurse, taking Jim to meet residents in need of special help. For instance, a man Jim already knew slightly—he had a disconcerting habit of removing his glass eyeball to get one's attention—who was being discharged the next day and wanted to be allowed to stay a little longer. Or an old boxer who wanted to be reunited with his wife, who was lodged in a nursing home.

One afternoon Jim came upstairs and got held up for a while by a series of old classics for reunions and consults, and finally made his way to Tony, who was standing in wait, off to one side of the corridor just beyond the nurses' station. He wore the freshly laundered sweatpants and T-shirt that Julie, Jim's assistant, had saved for him—Julie now made it a policy to go through the piles of donated clothing and reserve the extra-large sizes for Tony. When he had come in from the streets a week before, he'd been filthy and unkempt. Now even under the bright ceiling lights, he would have withstood a drill sergeant's inspection—clean fingernails, a fresh shave, a recent haircut that had cleaned up his balding crown. He could have passed for an aging sports star. He greeted Jim and at once began a report on fellow patients:

"Sally's sayin' she's gonna leave. I'm tryin' to talk her out of it. Timmy wants to leave, too. Timmy, he looked like me when I came in. Drunk."

Jim nodded. "He needs a break."

"I told him that, too," said Tony. He went on: Andy had planned to leave this morning, but Mike Jellison, the recovery coach, had talked him out of it, and by the way, Nick was about to lose his housing *again*. And even though Jackie looked clean, he was undernourished—"He don't eat much at all, Jim."

BJ almost always figured in Tony's reports, and the news was rarely good. BJ had refused to come into McInnis, or he had left McInnis AMA, because he got a check in the mail and missed the bank run, so he took off to cash the check and find some crack cocaine. "BJ's big time wit' crack now, Jim. That's all he talks about. How do you go from alcohol to that? Big jump. I don't know how he got on it, but I know the last check he got, he had four hundred seventy dollars, and he blew it all on crack, and he lied, he said someone ripped him off."

As Tony briefed Jim, like a resident reporting to the senior attending physician, a steady stream of nurses and aides and housekeepers passed by. Most said hello to Jim. All greeted Tony.

"Who's the nurse that just went by?" Jim asked.

"Carol," said Tony. "She's being trained."

This kept happening, Jim asking about one or another of the respite staff who walked by, Tony telling Jim their names and sometimes rating them—this one was new but she'd be fine, that one was having family troubles—and finally summing up: "Everybody has a flaw, but when you put them all together, they're awesome."

• • •

Tony the social director. It seemed like a good development to Jim, both for Tony and McInnis House. "He pays attention, and he's here day and night. So he's a great resource." Omar Marrero, the respite's manager, agreed. Tony had cooked up a plan to ease traffic in the dining room, which Omar had partly adopted. Tony had also become a detective, or, as Jim put it, a secret agent. He had cased every corner of the respite, it seemed. He showed Jim and Omar the various spots that the security cameras didn't cover, the sites for illicit activity. He led Jim out to the smoking deck, which was shrouded from the street and other buildings by fencing covered with black cloth. "See this, Jim?" In a corner, hidden behind the cloth, a thin cord was tied to the fencing. Certain people, whom Tony wasn't going to name, would tie a pillowcase to the cord, put something heavy in it, and drop it down to the sidewalk, where other unnamed people would wait until the security guard wasn't looking, then fill the pillowcase with a bottle of vodka or K2 packets or a baggie of heroin. And did Jim know about cutting a tennis ball in two? You put some pills or whatever inside, then glued the ball back together and tossed it up over the fence onto the deck. Or, he explained on another occasion, certain people would carry a cane when they went out to get their methadone at one of the neighborhood clinics. On their way back, they'd buy some drugs on the street, take the tip off their cane, put the pills or the baggie of powder inside, put the tip back on, and limp across Seven-Eighty's lobby, past the security guards, through the metal detector, and onto the elevator up to McInnis House.

Tony said it was partly on behalf of the nurses that he passed this kind of information to Omar and Jim. Some patients high on alcohol and drugs got into fights, which could get out of hand—"I'm worried about the nurses. They're sweethearts, they're gonna get hurt." He had intervened already in a couple of brawls between patients outside the third-floor nurses' station. He also said he worried that someone would overdose inside the respite and die, and Jim's reputation would be destroyed, and maybe McInnis House would get closed down. He had told other patients what he was doing. "Don't use booze and drugs in here. You can do it outside. *I* do it outside, but don't do it in here."

His favorite McInnis House nurse, Heather, told me that Tony didn't always follow his own rule. Once in a while he lapsed, she said, maybe when he was offered a drink from a contraband bottle of vodka or a hit of K2 out on the smoking deck. But he didn't bring in alcohol or drugs himself, and he didn't sell them inside. Heather felt she would have known if he did.

One time, Mike Jellison, who had very experienced eyes, saw Tony handing a five-dollar bill to a woman patient named Jane, who was in the midst of a difficult detox from heroin. Mike reported back to the Street Team that Tony seemed to be dealing inside McInnis House. But when Jim made inquiries, Jane told him that she had been threatening to go back to the streets and heroin, and that Tony was counseling her to stay and finish her treatment. Tony gave her the five dollars, she said, to buy candy from the vending machine in the atrium, in the hope that candy would dampen her cravings. Later, Jane told Mike that once in a while Tony did in fact play the middleman in a few drug transactions inside. And this was also believable.

Jim's informal titles for Tony expanded to include not only secret agent but also "counselor" and "social director." Twenty years ago, when the first McInnis House had opened, the Program had invented a formal position that encompassed those roles—milieu director. Jim and the staff had thought the respite needed someone to manage its social life and keep out drugs and alcohol, especially at night. A security guard had seemed too threatening, too nearly penal. Instead, they'd hired a formerly homeless man who had gotten sober and was savvy about substance abuse and widely respected by the staff and patients. He'd served well but then relapsed. Occasionally during the past year and a half, Jim had let himself imagine Tony reviving the position.

However, there was a stark difference between Tony inside and Tony after two or three weeks of rough sleeping. Further evidence came one night in a telephonic drama, which began with Jim's receiving a page from Tony asking that Jim call him. When he was living on pavement, Tony couldn't keep a phone for more than a week or two.

Still, he managed to page Jim frequently, usually from a friend's phone. Sometimes Jim couldn't answer right away, and when he did, the friend with the phone wouldn't know where Tony had gone, and the message to call Tony would hang around in a corner of Jim's mind like an unfinished chord. So on that night, Jim called him back as soon as he got the page.

Tony delivered a long monologue, complaining about the unfairness of the world—by then a familiar theme. Perhaps an hour later, he paged again. Jim called back, and Tony said he had been about to bed down in Pi Alley, but Elizabeth, a fellow Street Team patient, had just shown up. She was slurring her words. "She's drunk, Jim," Tony said. "So I guess I gotta take care of her."

Having such a job for the night had cheered Tony up completely. Jim could tell from his voice. But then, several hours later, when Jim was at home, he got this message, in the form of a text from the page operator, quoting Tony: "I'm being arrested. I don't know what's going on."

Minutes later, another text: "Please tell Dr. O'Connell thanks for everything."

There was no callback number. Jim lay awake for a while that night, waiting for bad news that didn't come. In the morning he saw on the manifest that Tony had gone into the Mass General ER in the night but had soon departed AMA. The following evening, Tony appeared in the lobby of Seven-Eighty looking too discouraged and disheveled for questioning. It was after five, the downstairs parts of the building closed. Julie talked the security guards into letting Tony use the clinic bathroom to take a shower. Her cache of extra-large clothes was over at Mass General, but Mike Jellison managed to scrounge up a clean outfit for Tony, and Jim secured a bed for him upstairs in McInnis House. After all of that, however, Tony wouldn't agree to come inside. He said he knew that an enemy of his was staying in the respite, and he didn't want trouble. Tony walked out onto Albany Street, vanishing into the dark.

Jim's memory of the incident contained a touch of parental anxiety. The child is leaving for the world; the parent can no longer prevent the worst but still feels responsible. Jim told me, "My fear is the call that says he's dead. It's so fragile out there. There's no place for him to turn."

4

~~~~~~~~~~~~~~

Autumn Street Rounds

S ome rough sleepers get good at hiding, even a big man like Tony, who could use light and shadows to make himself disappear in a doorway. John Cotrone had a manner that could make him disappear in plain sight. On Friday mornings, at a little before nine, he would be seated at a table, inconspicuous amid the rush hour clamor of Finagle a Bagel, a coffeehouse near Mousey Park. He was in his early sixties, of average size, with clean hands and clothes, a neatly trimmed gray-and-brown beard. A mustache hid the gaps among his few remaining teeth. Nothing suggested that until recently he'd spent his nights behind a dumpster at Brigham and Women's Hospital—lying there only half-asleep, he would say, and with one eye open. In the coffee shop, he was the picture of a person minding his own business, his eyes seemingly trained on no one and nothing. In fact, they were on duty.

"Here comes the cause of all my trouble," John announces as Jim walks toward the table, smiling, his street doctor's bag slung over his shoulder. John laughs, lowering his head toward the tabletop, his beard muffling the sound. He has already bought two cups of coffee, one small for himself, the other a regular with cream and sugar for Jim—coffee just the way he likes it on Friday morning. John has made this one of the things Jim can count on. John is also Jim's advance scout for Friday rounds. Like Tony, John invented jobs for himself. He would walk the early morning streets, gathering news and rumors and noting the whereabouts of other patients, and end up here around nine o'clock to give Jim his briefing.

Once in a while on Friday, Tony would burst into the coffee shop looking for Jim, and John would slip away and out the door. He had nothing against Tony, but he seemed to feel that someone that large and vigorous was worth avoiding just in case.

John said that he used to fall down drunk, and that he'd been pushed out a window once or twice, but his nose was straight and unscarred. Even back in his days of drugs and hustling he must have been good at staying out of the way. He grew up without a father and in a tough neighborhood, on Mission Hill in Roxbury. His mother let him walk to school alone. He was six when he first decided to walk past his school and spend the day at the Franklin Park Zoo. This became a habit. He was kept back in first, third, and fifth grades, and he quit school for good in sixth, already a teenager. "I was drinkin' at ten, twelve," he said. "I didn't do dope until I was eighteen." After he discovered heroin, he sniffed it for a while and then injected it—for decades. When his superficial veins collapsed, he injected it subcutaneously, into the skin of his legs, sometimes into the backs of his hands, and, most painfully, into his palms.

He'd never had a job. He'd done some small, nonviolent thieving to get money for heroin, but mainly he stemmed, using a wheelchair for a prop. He collected several of those from sidewalks outside the hospitals and kept them chained together in an alley. His most profitable area was outside Fenway Park, where he went for years without ever seeing a baseball game. He would sit in his wheelchair at a spot where arriving players would notice him—the Black players were the most generous, he said. Near the ends of games he'd move his wheelchair over to the special exit for wealthy patrons. "Oh, I miss those days," he told me. "Oh, I killed 'em." By way of illustration, he told this story: "I was sittin' in my chair, and these two old women came up. They said, 'We've been saving up for you all winter. We want you to have this.' And they handed me fourteen hundred dollars in cash." He shook his head. "I guess they were pretty disappointed."

I asked him why. The women couldn't have known he was faking, that he didn't need a wheelchair.

He said, "They knew when I got up and ran."

Why did he run?

To find his dealer, "the dope man."

John had remained unhoused until several years ago, when the Program had found him a room. The change brought him a new and dangerous privacy. "When they gave me that room, I don't know why I didn't die. Go in and shoot up." One morning, he woke with a hypodermic needle in his eye.

It was Jill, then the physician assistant on the Street Team, who helped him change his life. He agreed to let her send him to a detox. He stayed clean briefly afterward, then relapsed. But he agreed to go back, and this time, after merely ten days of clearing his system and with nothing more than Jill's encouragement, he quit all of it, both drugs and alcohol. He had managed to stay sober on methadone.

Once John quit heroin, he felt compelled to go straight—to his own mild disappointment, it seemed. "When I stopped doin' dope, I couldn't do that wheelchair or break the law. I don't know why. Maybe I was afraid of goin' to jail." He also realized that he hated his lodging house, both the communal bathroom and the fact that the place was "full of drunks," one of whom would stand outside and yell at night. He went back to sleeping outside, under the dumpster.

Beckie, the team's master of all trades, had put his name on several waiting lists for housing, as she did for all the patients, and just recently John had been transplanted into a studio apartment, owned by an organization called Hearth, devoted to providing housing for the homeless elderly. His place had its own bath and tiny kitchen, and maybe most important, a front desk and security—features that in Jim's experience greatly reduced evictions by discouraging parties among the newly housed. Beckie got John a flat-screen TV. When it arrived, John complained that it was too small, but then called several times to tell her how grateful he was. "What I love about him, he's so grouchy," Beckie said. "One time I bought him a medium-size coffee and he said, 'Don't you know I like small?'"

He had refused many offers to have his teeth fixed at Seven-Eighty's dental clinic. He had an array of other medical problems. Jim sent him to see specialists, but those visits only rarely came off, because John would walk out if the doctor kept him waiting more than fifteen minutes. And yet he would wait all day to see Jim. He kept track of Jim's schedule and coached Julie. "Don't forget to remind him it's Jill's birthday tomorrow," he'd say. Or: "Jim won't be here tomorrow. You know why? He's goin' to Denver." And Julie, who knew where Jim was going because she had arranged the trip, would thank John for reminding her.

Not long ago, Jim packed a suitcase full of clothes he no longer wore and took it to Mass General to donate. He was rolling the bag through the hospital's central corridor when John approached, asked what was in the bag, and hearing the answer, said, "I'll take those." Several protégés ranked Jim as utterly hopeless on preserving boundaries between patients and providers. One explained, "The same people calling seventeen times all night long. Why does Jim allow this? Is he encouraging the patients to think this is okay?" But in fact Jim was startled and discomfited when he saw his own old clothes on John. "It gave me a freaky feeling." Patients morphing into secret sharers—maybe this was a line for Jim, which John had discovered by crossing it.

Still, John had special standing. He represented a species of achievement that had been rare over the years. His wasn't the story of a life interrupted by homelessness and then resumed. It was an escape from addiction and the streets, achieved without the foundation of a former, richer life. And for that reason, it was also only a partial success. "Once people like John get housed, they realize they have nothing in their lives," Jim said. "How to fill their lives with something meaningful?" At sixty, John was still adjusting to indoor living, and most of what he had to keep him purposefully busy was the help he rendered Jim.

. . .

Friday street rounds always began at Mousey Park. Jim called it "the center of our universe." It had become another of Tony's theaters of action. The other day Jim had found him standing there, earnestly counseling a fellow rough sleeper who had been grieving for weeks over the death of a former girlfriend. As he approached, Jim overheard Tony telling the man, "You have to stop feeling guilty about her." And then Tony turned and said to Jim, "Can I talk to you later, Doc?" Then Tony went back to his counseling, and Jim walked away, thinking, "This is pretty cool." For Jim, the park's atmosphere had improved since Tony's arrival a year ago. When he wasn't around, the place felt diminished.

It was a Friday morning in October. When Jim said goodbye to John and walked out of Finagle a Bagel, heading for the park, the weather was like a memorial to summer, sunny and warm, and the scene in the park was much as usual—a smattering of men and women sitting on the concrete ledges and the benches, some slumped forward over their knees, rough sleepers' gear lying here and there in garbage bags and knapsacks. The place felt grimmer than usual.

Tony was missing today, and, more significant, so was the park's main fixture—BJ, the one-legged man with the red motorized wheelchair. His remaining leg had become incurably infected, and yesterday surgeons had amputated it. Right now BJ was lying in bed close by, but far away, in one of the hundreds of rooms behind the shiny windows in the towers of Mass General, which loomed over the neighborhood.

Karl, the former fisherman, had already heard the news. He was one of BJ's longtime drinking companions. When they drank heavily—as much as a gallon of vodka a day, Karl told me—both men would suffer a neuropathy that left them unable to walk, "legless" in street lingo. Karl had another odd affliction. Years of prodigious drinking had altered his speech to something like the opposite of Tony's. Each raspy word seemed laboriously hauled up out of the well of his chest, so that Karl sounded drunk even when he was sober. Strangers routinely treated him as if he were drunk, including staff in emergency rooms, so he tended to avoid the ERs, even when he needed help because of the maladies brought on by heavy drinking.

Karl sat hunch-shouldered in his wheelchair now, talking about BJ. "It's going to be . . . a challenge," he said in his halting cadence. He added, "I believe . . . his life will begin to suck . . . right *now*."

As always during this first stop, Jim looked around for people who were ill, while receiving petitioners angling for money or a bed at McInnis House. Jim's professional companions today were one of the Street Team's veteran psychiatrists, Eileen Reilly, and a young woman psychiatrist in residence at Mass General. After about half an hour, Jim and his entourage said their goodbyes to the patients in the park and headed off. They walked side by side up Cambridge Street, past various sleeping places that patients favored: A patch of pavement under a roof and behind a pair of large concrete planters that Tony called the Flower Pots; a small, roofed alcove beside the Wyndham hotel that Tony also favored but hadn't named; the grounds of the Old West Church, where, according to the signs, everyone was welcome. Homeless people were included, Jim explained, so long as they didn't drink there or urinate on the grass. Every place on rounds held memories. Jim remembered a morning years before, when he and others searched that churchyard after a blizzard, looking for a patient who usually slept there, and the man suddenly emerging from a snowdrift, shaking the snow off and laughing, then bragging about his hardiness for weeks.

Jim and Eileen paused every fifty yards or so to chat with rough sleepers who were stemming on the sidewalk. Some were equipped with advertisements, hand-lettered on cardboard, such as these, assembled from many Fridays:

HOMELESS AND DISABLED SEEKING HUMAN KINDNESS

IT'S MY 40TH BIRTHDAY PLEASE KILL ME

I NEED A DRINK

EVERYTHING HELPS

NOTHING HELPS

Up ahead, just past the wrought-iron gate to the churchyard, a cardboard sign—HOMELESS THANK YOU—was propped against a blanketed form. A new Street Team patient, a schizophrenic woman, lay beneath the blanket. Eileen lifted a corner and peered in, just to make sure the woman was breathing. And as the small group walked on, Eileen explained that there wasn't much else she could do at the moment. At some point, she might try to get the woman placed under the control of a court-appointed "guardian," usually a long and difficult legal process. More immediately, she could "section-12" or "pink-paper" her—that is, file a formal request that the woman be involuntarily committed for evaluation, in the hope that she'd be hospitalized and treated.

Eileen had worked among Boston's homeless and mentally ill people for decades. Hospital care and therapy really could improve the lives of patients, she said. She'd seen it happen. But the system was broken. There weren't enough places to send people in distress, not in timely fashion, and very few facilities provided adequate treatment. As for pink-papering, patients couldn't be hospitalized against their will, unless they were found to be dangerous to themselves or to others. And this was a hard case to make if a mentally ill person had managed to survive on the streets for years. As a result, the attempt to get a person hospitalized usually failed, and failed attempts amounted to arresting already confused people, then holding them for seventy-two hours, and finally letting them go. In Eileen's experience, patients tended to remember those impositions bitterly. Many refused to speak to her afterward, which meant she lost all chance of helping them.

On Summer Street, as if to prove the point, they paused beside a woman lying in a doorway. It was always the same doorway. She'd been pink-papered a few years back. Jim greeted her by name and with his customary, "How are *you*?" She looked up at him, grimacing, and said, as if holding up a sign: "No inquiries. No homeless outreach."

At Street Team meetings, conversations about mental illness sometimes broadened. What could the team do, what should they do, about rough sleepers who refused all help but were confused and couldn't take care of themselves, or were in danger of dying from what—in the respectful, nonstigmatizing lingo of the age—had come to be called substance use disorders, or SUDs? Did involuntary commitments for treatment violate patients' right to self-determination and their right to take "reasonable risks"?

Some favored treatment. Mike, the old navy man, disagreed: "Our folks have the right to make their own decision, even in the face of death."

Jim managed a synthesis, what he seemed to consider the great lesson of his years—that sooner or later every rule got contravened by another. In his experience, pink-papering often didn't work and could be worse than doing nothing. And yet he remembered occasions when he wished he had filed the form. He told the team this story: "I once knew a lady, really psychotic. I used to see her every week on the van, for something like ten years. She lived on a stoop by South Station, surrounded by all sorts of junk. She refused to come in. She refused all help, and everyone on the van thought it would be a bad idea to try to get her committed. So we just kept on offering help, which she refused, and we didn't pink-paper her, and then one day she had a psychotic break and the police arrested her, and she was sent to a mental hospital. Years later, I was in another town at a meeting, and she was there. Well-dressed, well-groomed. I went up to her and I said, 'You look great! It's so good to see you.' And she looked back at me and said, '*Fuck you*. You left me out there for ten years and did *nothing*.'"

· · ·

Some of the misery encountered on street rounds was easily leavened—by examining the wound, the dermatitis, the not-exactly-benign-looking lump on the forehead, and then inviting the patient to go to Mass General, where at least one of the Street Team's providers was on duty every weekday but Friday. Sometimes the remedy was simple—a rough sleeper saying he needed a pair of size 11 heavy-duty boots, which Jim would promise to bring him. Sometimes, though, the crew came up against something unspeakable. On this warm October Friday, the victim was an old favorite, a woman Jim remembered as once having been pretty and mischievous, now with no teeth and confined to a wheelchair, but still alert and sassy—she had a cackling laugh. In emergency room notes from the night before, Jim had read that she'd been drinking, had met a man who threw her in the trunk of his car and later raped her and punched her several times. The ER had treated her physical injuries. When the team on rounds ran into her, she'd just been released and was heading for Mousey Park. Jim asked if she would go to McInnis House. As usual, he added, "Or no?"

"I'm not ready. You know what I mean, Jim."

As the crew moved on, the young psychiatrist in training asked Jim, "She was raped last night? Can one bounce back that fast?"

"I can't figure out trauma on the streets," Jim told her. "Our people get drunk, and they kind of blame themselves. She wasn't outraged by it."

Later, toward the end of rounds, the young psychiatrist said to me, "I'm trying to figure out why one feels uplifted by this work." She added, "The word 'saint' comes to mind." She was referring to Jim.

· · ·

He had never forgotten Barbara's advice to beware of zealots and would-be secular saints. It irked him to be called a saint partly for that reason, and also because he knew it wasn't true. One night, on my way to join the van, I saw Jim coming from the opposite direction. This was in the parking area outside the Pine Street Inn, and the artificial lighting and geometry left me in shadows while Jim was entirely visible. He was looking down at the pavement with his jaw set, his mouth severe, as if he was glaring inwardly at a recent or future annoyance, maybe at the prospect of a van ride with me and my questions. When he saw me, his smile blossomed, and he said his "How are *you*?" But from then on I realized, with some relief, that he wasn't always what he usually seemed to be.

He, too, got annoyed, angry, tired of it all. He had moods and had learned a face for hiding them, which he wore with uncommon consistency. Maybe this wasn't surprising, given the terrible restraint in his childhood home, where the children and the father never argued for fear of causing the mother to leave again. If you learn to wear a happy or a placid face early in your life, maybe it becomes a reflex.

His job was difficult and often discouraging, but he enjoyed it most of the time, especially its clinical and social work sides. Medicine fascinated him. He felt the satisfaction all craftsmen feel in practicing their trades well. He liked doctoring people who desperately needed his help and usually thanked him for giving it, and he enjoyed, even admired, many of his downtrodden patients. Far from saintly, he simply felt that he was a fortunate man.

Rounds progressed down Summer Street. Then South Station came into view—a grand old neoclassical building with a huge clock that rose over its rounded granite façade. It was the last stop on Friday rounds. As Jim and his small crew approached the building, Eileen spotted one of her special patients sitting on a ledge outside the station's northwest entrance. Eileen and the psychiatric resident sat down with her, and Jim and I walked on toward the train station. I was still thinking about the young psychiatrist's remark. I wondered if Jim felt that the Street Team's work was "uplifting."

He said, "Long-term, if you step back, it's really depressing, but there's some kind of joy I feel from day to day, and it worries me. I realize when I go to work, I love it, the people I work with and for. It's satisfying and fulfilling. It makes *me* feel good, but sometimes I wonder if we make our patients' lives better." He'd been thinking all day about BJ's case. He said he'd felt glad when he got word that the amputation had been successful. BJ's life had been saved, but at the cost of his one remaining leg—a cause for relief, but nothing more. "I thought, How can I be *glad*?"

Standing near the station entrance, Jim said he'd also been thinking about the Street Team. He felt as though he was seeing his own past through them, watching them realize, as he had, that they could do a lot for patients from day to day but not much to fix the real causes of their misery. When he had felt near despair, both exhausted and awake to how ineffective his efforts were on the grand scale, he'd had Barbara McInnis to counsel him, to tell him, "Who are you? God? Your job is to take care of that broken foot." It was his turn to play a role like Barbara's with the newer members of his team, to help them find defenses against spiritual exhaustion. If he could.

· · ·

Jim couldn't find any patients inside the station. He and I walked back to Mass General, where he led the way through long hallways and into the proper elevator and finally to the door of BJ's room.

Jim entered loudly. "BJ! We were outside and couldn't resist comin' in to see ya."

BJ's twin stumps lay in outline under the sheet, one longer than the other. A trapeze bar, something like a pull-up bar, a piece of a jungle gym, hung over him. "Have you tried moving yourself up on that?" Jim asked.

"I'm waitin'," BJ said. "For a monkey that didn't get in yet." His nose was gnarled into something like a fist, and he had a roughened yet quiet voice to match. He looked as if he'd lived a life that couldn't be numbered, but he was only fifty, and he still had—astonishing to Jim—a healthy liver.

Although they differed in details, most of the autobiographies that Jim had heard fell into general categories. BJ's was of the white-middle-class-kid variety: Parents who drank a great deal, then quit and became anti-alcohol evangelists, but did so when BJ was already a teenager, already fond of drink and rebellious, with vodka as his weapon and eventually his way of life. What Jim admired in BJ could perhaps be summed up in the man's nose. It was a badge of endurance. "He's a gentle guy, but his nose has been moved around many times. He's the one person who has the respect of just about all the street people. And they all keep trying to take care of him."

They chatted for a while, Jim hovering beside the bed.

BJ said, of the latest amputation, "I didn't want to do it. I had no choice."

"Well, everybody's asking for you," said Jim. "Just so you know that."

BJ ignored this. He said that the surgeon had taken his leg above the knee. "I wish they had gone lower. But they couldn't."

"Because that infection was just so socked into the knee, BJ." Was he in pain now?

BJ said he was, in spite of many painkillers. But he said so only once. His main complaint was different. "It's like I've been kidnapped, Jim."

"You're being held hostage."

"Yeah!" BJ went on, "I gotta learn to walk. I may not be able to . . ."

"So you want to walk again. You want to get up and walk."

"I want to try. I have to stay sober." He made a small, wry sound in his throat. " 'Course, I been saying that for fifty years."

5

Success

Caution was one of Jim's themes in these later days of his career. He wanted to temper expectations among the relatively new members of the Street Team. He also felt freshly plagued by the looming changes in health care finance, which might, he feared once again, support only the kind of success that could be numbered in years of life saved or illnesses cured. He had come up with a defense for that eventuality and had been repeating it. He'd say that most of the Street Team's patients suffered from chronic, incurable illnesses and that most of the medical help the Street Team provided was "good palliative care"—care that focused less on trying to cure those illnesses than on providing relief from their symptoms.

But if you belonged to the team, you knew that recovery from the cycles of chronic homelessness was possible. Evidence of this appeared nearly every Thursday, when a middle-aged man with a small service dog on a leash came to Street Clinic to pay a social call on Jim. A decade ago, this man, Joe Meuse, had set a city record for being carted into emergency rooms dead drunk—216 visits on a gurney in the space of eighteen months. Now he had an apartment, a driver's license, a car, and a job, which involved driving several professional women to work and taking care of their dogs.

You could also cite the four members of the Program's board who had once been homeless. There was Larry Adams, whose rescue had begun decades back, when Barbara McInnis stopped him from committing suicide in the Chinatown subway station.

There was Sara Reid, who was born a boy but knew she was female from the age of five—"And I knew I wouldn't make it to six if I told my dad." After long travails, which included homelessness, she had found a harbor at the Program.

There was Sara's colleague Derek Winbush. He'd grown up in a Black neighborhood in Boston, but had been sent to a suburban school because his mother wanted him to get a good education, and had been razzed in his neighborhood for not being Black enough. Trying to prove that he was tough, and listening, as he put it, to the "false wisdom of the streets," he ended up in state prison at eighteen. The driver who took him to Walpole, in a bus with bars on its windows, had tried to comfort him, saying, "Don't worry, kid. Just act as bad as you did on the street," while Derek sat weeping in fear. For years after prison he took and dealt drugs and lived in other people's apartments and abandoned buildings. But he was clean and sober when some members of the Program discovered him and asked if he would join their board.

• • •

The fourth once-homeless board member was Joanne Guarino. She had a reputation for lively public speaking at various events. For seven years in a row, she had told her life story to the new students at Harvard Medical School. I went there to hear her perform for the eighth time, on an August afternoon, in the Bornstein Family Amphitheater.

She looked very small, seated in a chair in the well of that spacious auditorium—165 new medical students in starchy white coats rising before her. She had arrived at the theater in a wheelchair pushed by Jim's assistant, Julie, who was Joanne's friend, confidante, and, today, her hairstylist. (Earlier, back at Street Team headquarters, Joanne had said to her, "I have a brush with me. I was hoping you could fix my hair like yours, in a ponytail.")

Looking up toward the students, Joanne cocked her head to one side. The effect was coquettish, but she did this only to improve her view of them. One of her eyes was glass. She had lost the real one years ago, on the streets. Joanne had many stories. Julie's favorite dated back to the latter part of Joanne's younger days, when she was trying to pick up a guy at a pub, and the fake eye fell out and rolled down the bar.

Jim stood at the lectern beside her chair. He said to the students, "Hey! So listen, it's a treat to be here!" He addressed brief remarks to the white coats: When he was a student here, he never realized that homelessness and premature mortality lay in the very shadows of Boston's great hospitals, but he hoped they'd take that fact to heart. Then he turned to Joanne. "I am incredibly honored to introduce you to the students once again."

A young colleague had told Jim that she felt very nervous listening to Joanne give a speech. "Because I never know what she's going to say."

Jim had replied, "Neither does Joanne." Now he retreated to the doorway, leaning against the jamb with his arms crossed, smiling and on guard.

Head still cocked and looking upward, she began—in an accent like Tony's, one of Boston's working-class accents: "Anyway, I'm gonna tell you a little story about myself. I was homeless off and on for about thirty years. When I was young, my mother left six kids behind, and I didn't have a mother growing up, and because of that I was sexually abused as a child, and that went on for years and years."

It was a family friend who abused her, while her father was at work—her father would have killed the guy if he'd known. The abuse ended when Joanne was twelve, but devolution followed: Early pregnancy, abortion, a biker boyfriend who died of an overdose, drug and alcohol addiction, a good marriage that merely interrupted her descent.

She told the students: "I was a victim of all this stuff and it was my mother's fault, and I just ran with that for years and years and years, and then finally it stopped working. I had like this hole in my body, I just needed somebody to fill it. But it was an *inside* job. I thought it was an outside job. God and me was the only ones that could fill it. But I didn't know that at the time. Even though I went to Catholic school. And that's another story."

There was a stirring in the crowd, a hint of laughter. Joanne ignored it, but then one of the students' phones started playing a ring tone.

"Shut that off!" said Joanne.

"Sorry," said the student.

"It's okay, honey," Joanne called to her. "You all right? I have to be silly sometimes, because sometimes my story's a little difficult."

Then she went on with it, until finally Jim called to her from the wings, "You should talk a little bit about your experiences with doctors. That would be . . ."

"Yes, that's my plan now," Joanne said, but for a time she continued the story of her homelessness: Being raped, contracting HIV, losing an eye to a stab wound, and finally suffering an accident while riding on the back of a motorcycle. She ended up at McInnis House, where her life began to change.

"What they told me at McInnis was that you matter in life, and Jim tells me this still all the time. I was at McInnis for like four months, I think. I probably wasn't supposed to be there four months, right?

But I was there because they kept thinkin', She's gonna get it, she's gonna get it, and I didn't think I was gonna get it, but somebody believed in me more than I did and that was why I did get it, because somebody believed that I could. But then the problem was that I got sick. I got sick with hepatitis C, and I had HIV, which turned into AIDS. I now have rheumatoid arthritis, and"—she turned toward Jim—"what's the new one I got?"

"Pulmonary hypertension."

"Oh yeah. Which I just received recently. And that's because, I think it's because of the hep C, the rheumatoid, and somethin' else, and now I don't breathe good anymore."

Still, she had been free of alcohol and narcotics for many years. She had also earned a place in her daughter's life, managing to win her forgiveness—only, she thought, by forgiving her own mother. "Which took a while," she said. Her path to recovery wasn't easy to trace. It had many sources, she believed. Even drugs, which kept her from suicide—"I was so high most of the time I couldn't think about being depressed." For many years she had seen Jim out on the streets ministering to other homeless people, but she had hidden from him—out of shame, she would say—until she'd had the motorcycle accident that took her to McInnis House, where she couldn't avoid Jim or the ministrations of the other doctors.

Getting housed had also happened gradually. She'd lucked into her first place, but she was still drinking and drugging then and invited friends to join her. She got evicted and lost her housing voucher, but with help from Jim and others, she enrolled in a program that consisted of a year in a halfway house, receiving instruction on how to survive indoors. By then, she couldn't even remember how to write a check: "My brain was like mush." But she stuck it out, was placed in a beautiful apartment in a town outside Boston, got evicted from there because the landlord wanted a higher rent than her voucher paid, and finally was quickly rehoused in a newly renovated apartment in her old hometown of Everett, a short drive from Boston.

The place was fine, her health less so. The bones of her hands were so twisted that she sometimes couldn't open any of her many pill bottles—one time not long ago, fumbling with the lid, she'd ended up dropping all of one medicine into the toilet. Her rent was paid, but she had only $700 a month for everything else, and it was never enough for her to get ahead on her bills. But she was grateful and proud.

She wasn't just housed. She had a position and unpaid work to do for the board. She gave lectures, such as this one, and she spoke her mind at board meetings, and the members in suits and dresses listened and more than once had followed her advice. The latest of her contributions was a pamphlet, in English and Spanish, published by the Program and distributed to patients newly housed. It was titled "Housing Guide: Tips and Tools for a Successful Housing Experience." Joanne had created it with the help of an intern, partly in memory of her own struggles and those of friends—such as her fellow board member Larry Adams, who had fallen into a deep depression the moment he got inside, or the man who had pitched a tent in his new apartment. She remembered that at the start of her second try at indoor life, she found herself asking the refrigerator what she was supposed to do. Her housing guide provided the answers that she'd spent a long time finding. It had sections labeled "How to Settle In," "How to Stay Safe," "How to Buy Groceries and Do Laundry." The section called "How to Keep Rooms Clean" offered advice such as, "Put things away when you're finished," and "Wash dishes after you use them."

When she finally got launched on the theme Jim had requested, she said, "I think one of the things I would share with you as new doctors is to have compassion. Because you're gonna see—as you look at me today, you see me in this cute little ponytail and my hair green, white, and whatever, 'cause I'm adorable . . ."

The students erupted, first laughter, then applause. It was as if they had been listening in suspense, wondering how Joanne's story would turn out—or whether she would survive the telling of it—and now she had finally released them. Earlier that day, in private, she had told me about the rich boyfriend who owned a Rolls-Royce and an airplane and had given her a large diamond ring, which she had ended up hurling into the waves off a beach in Florida. "I tried to love him, but I just couldn't. I was very young and very cute, and I broke a lot of hearts." And at that moment in the amphitheater, I realized that in spite of her missing eye, her hands mangled by the unchecked joint-eroding inflammation of rheumatoid arthritis, she still had the power of attraction. And, of course, that attraction now had everything to do with her manner, her frankness, her humor, and her pluck, and the fact that those traits had survived in spite of great misfortune.

"But at one time I didn't look so adorable," she said to the faces ranged above her. "So when I went into the hospitals when I was sick, some doctors were real nice, some weren't. When you're homeless, you look like crap, like I probably did. No, I *did*. I didn't have this belly, I was like a hundred pounds, if that. Now I'm fat. A little bit. Right? And if I could say anything to you guys about what's important, we do know our bodies. If I tell you I have a pain in my heart, chances are I have a pain in my heart. You gotta listen, that's the key. You have to have compassion. That's the other key. You have to just not be afraid to touch anybody, not be afraid to feel and care and to allow people to tell you what's going on with their lives."

They should put themselves in the position of their patients, she said, especially the ones who looked as she had when living on the streets. Occasionally, she had chances to do that herself, in the course of her work. "I run around like a crazy woman. I'm on the board of directors. I'm on numerous consumer boards. I just got a call today to be an ambassador for another coalition over in Jersey—New Jersey— that I'm considering doing. So I'm very busy doing all kinds of things for Health Care for the Homeless. I travel all over the place.

"But I am not getting better. I'm still sick and I will always be sick, and I will die being sick, but it's the care that I get that keeps me com-passionate, and keeps me saying, Screw it, I'm gonna get up anyway.

And there are days when I just want to throw the towel in, and then I think of someone like Jim and I go, Oh no, Jim needs me. I'm up. And I go. Even when I'm crawlin' I'm still goin'.

"But this is how I believe in you guys. I believe in every single one of youse, and I want to invite youse to come to Barbara McInnis House, so I can give you a tour. And Julie over there, that beautiful girl standing up in the corner, she will give you some cards if you want to go." She turned toward the doorway. "Is that what you wanted me to say, Jim?"

"Yes."

More laughter, more applause. The dean came to the lectern and asked the students for questions. A young fellow piped up: "I want to thank you first of all so much for coming in and talking."

"You're welcome, honey," said Joanne.

The young man wanted her advice: How to be sensitive to the feelings of a patient who has been abused and homeless? Should a doctor withhold certain information, for instance?

"Jim's listening," she replied. "Listening, sometimes mirroring my conversation, 'cause I'm Italian and I talk too fast sometimes, as you can tell. I love to hear people say the truth. I need to hear the truth when I'm sick. I need the doctor to tell me I'm sick. And I don't want to hear that I'm doin' good when I know that I'm not doin' good. And I think that's another thing you're gonna . . ."

She paused. "I never cried this way, why am I crying? I apologize. But the thing is to tell the truth, and they've been always honest with me, even when I didn't want to hear it. But it's good when a doctor's bein' honest with me. They're there for you, like lovingly. You know what I mean? Just not bein' *shithead* doctors, you know?"

The room erupted again—laughter, resounding applause, and the dean's amplified voice declaring: "You heard it here. Another question?"

VI

A System of Friends

1

~~~~~~~~~~~~

Winter Comes

On a chilly Monday night in December, Jim was heading for the vans parked outside the Pine Street Inn men's shelter, when up ahead in the gloomy half-light, the hulking figure of Tony appeared. He was dressed in sweatpants and a hoodie. He had come for a "loan," but first he wanted to describe his odyssey last night. His knees had been aching, no bed was available at McInnis House, so he went to the Mass General emergency room, where they wrapped his knees in elastic bandages—he pulled up the legs of his sweatpants to show Jim; the wrappings were now bunched around his ankles. Then the ER doctor sent him back to the street, at two in the morning.

"It was a good thing, though, Jim," Tony said. "Because BJ had got thrown outa the garage at North Station. BJ says to me, 'Tony, I'm freezin'. Get me a blanket, please.'"

After a little more chat, Jim handed a folded bill to Tony and they parted, Tony disappearing into the night.

On board the van, the lights of the city flashing by, Jim told me about a recent dinner where a group of doctor friends had discussed the current state of their profession. One had said, "What's happened? The joy's gone out of medicine."

I wondered how Jim felt about that. He had said he found joy in his work. Could he say more?

"It's a system of friends," he said. "And that's where the joy comes from, I think. In med school there were a lot of professional boundaries you were told to keep. 'Be friendly but not a friend.' But if we tried to keep that boundary the way we were taught, we would get nowhere with this population."

The van was passing St. Monica's church in Southie. Jim looked out the window and noted several people sleeping in its doorway. He wasn't sure he knew them. If not, I thought, he would soon enough.

• • •

The news at Monday's Street Team meeting featured John Cotrone, Jim's shy and wary advance scout for Friday rounds. John had stepped off a sidewalk and a hip bone had snapped. He was only sixty-three, but his body was older. He had called Jim from the ER.

"I went to visit him," Jim told the team. "I haven't been doing it much anymore, since Gabriella was born. But I realized how important it is to visit people in the hospital. John was alone in the dark. I asked him why he wasn't watching the TV. He said, 'I don't know how to work it.' He was just lying there, nothing to read, no one to talk to." Jim added, "He's in the Connors Building. Seventh floor, room twelve."

In a few days, John was sent home to the studio apartment that Beckie had found for him. It was in a well-maintained building situated in a gentrified part of the South End—a very quiet place. Jim took me along to visit. This was the season of truncated daylight, already dark outside by the time we arrived. John lay in his bed with the lights out, images from the TV playing over his blanketed form. Jim turned on a light. The rooms looked tidy, indeed almost unused—nothing on the walls, no chairs for visitors. It seemed in principle like a perfect place for a rough sleeper to have fetched up at last, but when I said as much on the way out, Jim replied, "It's a step up from under a dumpster. It's lonely, though. All he has is that TV. It would be a good thing to do in old age, wouldn't it, pick ten people to visit every day?"

. . .

BJ, now legless, had been transported from Mass General to a nursing facility, but in the late fall he had argued his way out and back to the city—in effect, to Mousey Park. He didn't have an apartment or even a room. Because he was disabled and carried no criminal record and cost a lot in the way of emergency services, he'd been given priority for housing over the years. He'd had five different places, but he'd lost each one—mostly because he needed help getting around and had invited various rowdy friends inside. Now he was likely to be stuck outdoors for a long time, because he had fallen off the increasingly exclusive priority list, the "chronic list," for housing. "We have entered the theater of the absurd," Jim declared. "The city no longer considers BJ chronically homeless."

BJ was out in Mousey Park again, shivering in his electric wheelchair by day, sleeping on pavement during the cold and soon to be snowy nights, and offering a mixed blessing to Tony, who, without having been asked, was trying to help BJ with the labors of survival. It seemed as though every time Jim came out to the park, he'd find Tony hovering over BJ. Then Tony would take Jim aside and complain about the job.

Over the years, many rough sleepers had tried to take care of BJ, but none, Jim thought, as conscientiously as Tony. In the evenings as winter loomed, the pair would make their way down Cambridge Street, tall dark Tony striding along beside BJ in his motorized wheelchair, heading for one of the outdoor sleeping spots with an overhanging roof. Tony would lift BJ off his chair and lay him down in one of the sleeping bags he'd scrounged from some charity or Good Samaritan. Or he'd spread some of the ubiquitous government-surplus gray blankets on the pavement and deposit BJ on them.

I have a photograph of the two of them in the alcove by the Wyndham hotel, bedded down side by side and fast asleep under blankets, with their hats and coats and gloves on, like a pair of grizzled Boy Scouts. In the mornings, Tony would wrap up BJ's soiled blankets, collect the empty bottles and the mess of food wrappers strewn around the campsite, dump them in a trash can, then go to Dunkin' Donuts to get breakfast for both of them.

BJ was often drunk by afternoon. He'd drive his chair into Mass General, in the area of the Street Clinic waiting room, and if he was drunk enough he'd run into people. "If he had legs, people would beat him up," Tony said. "They see he has no legs, they give him a break. He hits me with the chair. He doesn't mean to, but he's drunk." BJ would apologize, saying in his garbly, after-vodka voice, "Sorry, Tony. I didn't see you."

"BJ," Tony said, "I'm the size of Texas, I'm as big as Godzilla. You didn't *see* me?"

Riding his electric chair outside, BJ would sometimes tip over onto the sidewalk, and Tony would set his chair upright and put him back in it. Tony kept an Allen wrench in one of his many pockets for making small repairs when the little red vehicle broke down. He cleaned BJ up when he soiled himself. After the first snowstorm, Tony told him that they both had to go into McInnis House and rest up until after Christmas. BJ agreed, but after Tony went in, BJ didn't follow him. In the hallway just beyond the third-floor nurses' station, adorned with a few Christmas decorations, Tony gave Jim his report: "Just to let you know, heads-up, BJ's throwing up. He's throwin' up a lot."

"He does that sometimes," said Jim.

"But he's strictly straight alcohol now," Tony continued. "No water, no food, a gallon of vodka. I mean I'm drinking wit' him, but *nobody* can keep up wit' him, and it's just strictly no food, no water.

And then he's mad at me because I keep falling asleep. I'm passin' out. He wants me to stay awake, running back and forth through the snow, get him this and that. I said, 'Dude, I can't do it anymore.' So we made a deal. Monday I stood with him, and he swore to God he'd come in wit' me till it warms up. He lied."

Jim said, "I don't think he intends to lie, Tony, but then at the last moment he goes, 'I can't do it,' and he feels badly. I've been down that road with him many times."

But, said Tony, BJ had confessed to vomiting blood. "And I warned him, 'You puke one time blood, I see blood, I'm calling an ambulance.' Now if I call an ambulance on him, he has to go. Right, Jim?"

"No," said Jim. "Everyone has the right to refuse an ambulance, anytime. As long as the EMTs don't think you're crazy."

Tony's face went dark, sudden shadows in the doorway. His voice was vehement: "He's only got two arms left! They're gonna fall off pretty soon, too! I told him, What are you gonna do, wait till you lose your arms?"

• • •

On the last Street Clinic Thursday before Christmas, John Cotrone shuffled into Mass General on a walker and reclaimed his long-established place as Jim's first patient of the day—a concession that Jim made to John's age and impatience. John got some subway and meal tickets from Jim, and a Dunkin' Donuts card, and while Jim checked his vitals, John offered him advice.

"Hey, Jim, where are you takin' Jill for Christmas? Switzerland? Hawaii?"

"Home," said Jim. "What am I *giving* her is the question."

"You should be takin' her on a nice two-week vacation."

Jim replied with his stethoscope. "Deep breath and hold it, okay?"

• • •

When Tony had been sleeping outside for a while and came to Thursday clinic, he invariably brought some of the street's chaos with him in the form of complaints about fellow rough sleepers. Each week there were different culprits—people he befriended and tried to help, and who ended up rifling his pockets and knapsack while he slept in exhaustion or in a stoned and drunken stupor. It seemed to Jim that Tony was always looking for a trustworthy friend, and was usually disappointed.

He did have one faithful friend who, he swore, had never betrayed him—Rocky, an older man. He'd entered McInnis House for good a few months ago with terminal cirrhosis.

There was a bustle in the room the December evening before Rocky died, nurses and aides coming and going, fellow patients slipping in for a last look at their compatriot. When Jim stopped by, Rocky had fallen into a coma. Jim watched from across the room. Tony was standing beside the bed, towering over his friend's inert form. Only half an hour ago, Rocky had asked for a bottle of orange soda, but he had gone comatose by the time Tony returned with it. Now Tony held the bottle in one hand, and in the other a damp sponge attached to a stick. He was swabbing Rocky's lips with it, just as the nurses had taught him, and he was sniffling.

After Rocky died, Tony left McInnis House AMA. Jim arranged for him to return a few days later, and Tony said he would stay this time until he got his knee fixed. But just before New Year's he departed again, carrying a garbage bag of gear, striding out into the midst of Boston's fiercest cold snap in a century.

· · ·

On the way to his exam room on Thursday morning, Jim was pleased to see John Cotrone sitting outside the Walk-In Clinic. John had ditched his walker and now had only a cane. He was chatting with Angie, who needed company more than ever these days. She was a short, stout, silver-haired woman with tawny skin and high cheekbones. Both she and John made a habit of refusing to go downstairs and mingle with the others in the Street Clinic's waiting room. "I should talk, but they could at least clean themselves," Angie explained. "It smells so bad down there. I got a weak stomach, I guess." She was also one of the old classics who insisted on being doctored only by Jim. She liked the other providers but refused their services. "I'm used to Jim."

I sat with John and Angie sometimes on those early winter Thursday mornings. They were like an elderly couple who liked to share complaints about the world and reminisce about their good old days—in their case, about the big scores they'd once made from begging. Angie, too, had given up that trade. "He doesn't want me stemmin' anymore," she said, speaking of her current boyfriend.

They talked about doings in their community. Angie had seen BJ drinking in the park this morning, in his wheelchair, out in the cold. "I told him, 'You're a fucking asshole. You got no legs!'"

A tall man in a velvet-collared chesterfield coat, a prominent citizen, was passing by just then. He paused in front of John and Angie, bent down, and, smiling, put a finger to his lips. "Shhhhh. Shhhh."

"Oh, sorry," said Angie. As the man moved on, she lowered her voice and said to John, still referring to BJ, "I love him like a friend, but he's a fucking asshole. Out there in the winter. Now I hear he's stuck in the Public Gardens. His chair ran out of power."

Angie's father was part Cherokee. "I loved my dad. But he had a drinking problem like me." She said her mother beat her routinely with kitchen implements. Angie's route to homelessness had begun after one hateful year of high school, followed by an early pregnancy, lots of drinking, and a boyfriend with whom she joined the carnival. She had lived outdoors in Boston for twenty years, with two different boyfriends. Both routinely beat her. She'd spent a long outdoor stretch with the last of them, mostly sleeping on benches on the Esplanade beside the Charles River. She remembered the nights as "beautiful sometimes, cold sometimes." They'd wake up with snow on their blankets. Jim had met her there on the van, almost twenty years ago. For a while he'd found her hard to like—"Until I began to see the lovable little person inside." At one point, he arranged for her to stay at McInnis House for two months, to keep her safe from that last boyfriend.

A decade ago, she'd managed to find a room—a small single room with a bathroom down the hall—and she'd stayed there ever since, paying the rent with her Supplemental Security Income. Five years ago, after her latest boyfriend had died of cirrhosis, she decided to get sober. "Me and my old man used to go through like two and a half gallons in a day. And then when he passed away, that was it for me. I quit the day he died. I had a hard time when he passed away. Some days I'd be so fucking down in the dumps, I'd walk up the street, all the liquor stores right there, I'd walk by and do I want to or don't I?" She had held on, with help from the Street Team. Lately, she'd tried to reconnect with her daughter, but had failed so far. And now her landlord was selling the building where she lived. The place was going to be gutted and turned into condominium apartments. And she was on the verge of losing her tiny home.

On the bench beside John, she poured out the story. "I been goin' through a bad fuckin' time. I'm being evicted. Some people came to measure my place. I had to let them in. I said, 'Go tell the landlord he's a fucking asshole.' What the hell are they doin' putting people out in the winter? I went to court. I went to Chelsea Housing. I can't be out on the streets. Not at my age. That's fucking crazy. Don't throw me out on the street."

John listened, eyes focused on something far away.

. . .

Inside Mass General, squeezed into the exam room for the Thursday preclinic meeting, the team exchanged news on Tony: "He has type 3GA hepatitis C, with a whopping viral load of seventeen million," said Jim. Tony would need treatment, but the new drug, though expensive, would likely cure him.

Tony also had a legal problem. "He's in violation of registration," said Beckie. That is, Tony had failed again to register as a sex offender. "So he could be arrested anytime."

"Yeah, he's lying low," said Jim. "As low as he can."

A flurry of laughter rippled through the team, all packed together in the room. Jim went on, thanking the nurse practitioner, Katy, for getting the results of Tony's latest blood tests. These showed that one of his medications had fallen far below therapeutic level. "He's probably not taking it," Jim said.

Katy smiled. "I did increase it, the med he's not taking."

Jim smiled back. "If they're not taking it, double it."

• • •

Out in Mousey Park, a woman patient of many years stood before Jim, her face wreathed in a hood, tears freezing on her cheeks, as Jim explained that every bed and emergency cot in McInnis House was full. He knew she hated shelters, but there was no alternative right now.

Only one case of frostbite had appeared at Thursday Street Clinic so far, and the patient lost only some fingertips. Meanwhile, Tony had disappeared.

2

~~~~~~~~~~~~~~~~

Tony's World

Ona very cold Saturday early in the new year, Jim stopped at South Station with Jill and Gabriella for a quick lunch. They were sharing a pizza when Tony appeared—the tall, dark man of many coats. It wasn't clear where he'd come from. Had he known that Jim would be there with his family? Not possible. And yet on arriving, he reached into one of the pockets of his outermost coat and produced a gift-wrapped package, a brand-new Cabbage Patch doll for Gabriella. Later, Tony told Jim, "A lot of people steal for their kids. I'm like, Come on, stop smoking your crack for a day and buy the kid something legit, don't give the kid stolen stuff." This by way of assuring Jim that the doll wasn't stolen. Tony added that he had wrapped it himself. Probably he'd been carrying it around for a few days.

Jim took a picture of Tony with Jill and Gabriella and the doll—in it Tony wears a catlike grin. Then they parted ways, and Tony disappeared from the Street Team's view. This was normal. He tended to make quick departures. Two weeks later, on a Friday morning before street rounds, he made one of his unexpected entrances—storming into Finagle a Bagel with a dramatic story, delivered in a nearly incoherent torrent of words, in a voice going hoarse: He had warned the drug dealer Deuce not to sell meth near Seven-Eighty, and now Deuce was attacking him, but Tony was going to go on trying to keep meth out of Boston. "It's my people, my city, I'll stop it if I can!"

After a while, he jumped up and went out the door. He strode right past Mousey Park and down Cambridge Street. Jim and I and the day's psychiatric resident followed. I asked Jim if he was alarmed by Tony's state. He said, "I'm *completely* alarmed." Jim caught up with Tony, and as he grew calmer, street rounds became something like a sightseeing trip in Tony's Boston.

It began with a descent into the State Street T station and a passage through its complicated pedestrian tunnels, Tony showing us the way he got to the train platforms when he had no pass or money— moving swiftly up to the entrance gate for wheelchairs and handicapped people, moving with a light-footed grace surprising in such a large man with a bad knee, then reaching a long arm around the side of the gate post, waving his hat in front of the sensor, and stepping through the opening.

Tony said that if he found himself downtown in the late morning, and it was cold outside and he was still tired, he would come to this subway platform and sit on the farthest bench, the place where he had once sat imagining suicide. If he lay down on it, the Transit cops would throw him out, but if he remained upright, they left him alone. He had to struggle to stay awake sometimes. To me, this was another fact of homelessness that was hard to imagine, a weariness so great that Tony had to fight to keep from dozing off on a busy subway platform, amid the loud, repetitive squawkings from the PA system and the screeches of braking trains—like cries of tormented souls, I would have thought, to a mind on the perimeter of sleep.

After he got out of prison, Tony said, he used to come down here late at night and hide from the Transit cops and workers until the system shut down, at one o'clock. Then he'd explore the tunnels. During his first few winters, he had found some abandoned stations that he'd heard about from old-timers, stations reachable only by walking the tracks—walking with an ear cocked because, after hours, trains would be moving at high speed to and from service depots. Down in the tunnels, he'd also found several empty storage rooms suitable for sleeping and partying. To get to one of the best, you crossed these tracks in the Orange Line tunnel to the door on the other side. So far as Jim could tell—and he'd been looking for the signs—Tony had no romantic attachments, with men or women. But he was very gregarious, and he'd lost access to that room because he'd invited friends there, and they had exposed the secret by coming out of that door in the daytime. "Shoulda never shown it to those idiots. Shouldn'ta never did it. They fucked it up. Transit was like, How long have you guys been going in there?"

One time, Tony said, he'd been sitting by the platform and witnessed a lovers' quarrel. It ended with the young woman pulling a gold ring off her finger and hurling it over the edge of the platform onto the tracks. Some hours later, when the coast was clear, he climbed down to the tracks and retrieved the ring from the vicinity of the electrified third rail.

Often he carried a knapsack full of tools for moments like that. He was carrying it now, and he showed it to the young psychiatrist and Jim. He pulled out bungee cords, flashlights, half of a pair of scissors for picking locks, an extender, and a heavy glove with a rubberized palm. "That's for the third rail. You gotta carry a flashlight. And use the glove and the extender. It's fun, though."

• • •

Some of the accounts Tony had given Jim and me made his Boston seem like a survival course, where just waking up in the morning wasn't a given, and where a person was obliged to practice what Tony called "hustle." Early last winter he'd stayed for a time at a friend's apartment, but the man had invited in all sorts of other people, and twice Tony got robbed when he fell asleep. Losing stuff by one means or another was the normal plight of rough sleepers, Jim would say, but no other patient seemed as vulnerable to losses as Tony, especially to thefts. He did take some precautions. For instance, he had persuaded one of the Street Team—a member Tony wouldn't name—to hold some of his prescription drugs. But he kept getting robbed, often by the same friends. The problem, Jim had begun to sense, was that Tony had some inborn need to trust people, and to forgive them when they betrayed him so that he could trust them again.

For warmth, Tony picked up blankets here and there. From time to time, he carried sleeping bags, but bedding was even harder to hang on to than cellphones. In Tony's opinion, the heavy cardboard used for boxing up and shipping stoves and refrigerators made for the best mattresses—he knew the stores that put that cardboard out on the sidewalks for trash pickup. Whether he bedded down indoors or outside, he rarely got a full night's sleep. When he managed to doze off in Pi Alley, the rats would wake him. One time, a patron of a nearby bar must have stopped and dropped some money on his blanketed form. Later, he'd been awakened by other night owls trying to steal it. He called this "People trying to do you a favor and causing you trouble." If he passed out from exhaustion or from smoking K2 or crack cocaine or drinking a lot of vodka, he didn't rouse easily, but those were the times when the alleged friends camping with him were likely to empty his pockets—none would dare try when he was awake. He tended to favor women as nighttime companions. Not for sex, but because he liked the feeling of protecting someone vulnerable, and because he didn't like to be alone and women companions tended to rob him less often than men.

He had said that on many nights he didn't sleep at all. "Sleeping's overrated," he told me once. In the warm seasons, he would walk the nighttime city, and sometimes stop at Mousey Park or another lighted public space and pick up the litter. After he finished one cleaning job

of that sort, a cop in a squad car called him over—to say he'd been
watching Tony work and wanted to thank him. Why did he do this
volunteer maintenance? "I like it. It calms me down." As a bonus, he
always found useful stuff among the litter, mostly snipes—cigarette
butts with a few drags left. Taxes meant to discourage smoking had
made cigarettes extraordinarily expensive. K2, the dangerously unpredictable synthetic marijuana, cost much less, and some of the
team's patients had started using it in lieu of tobacco. In any form,
including snipes, cigarettes were precious items, and among fellow
rough sleepers Tony was a notorious mark. When he had a pack, he
ended up giving most of it away, and would then find, to his fury, that
others did not reciprocate.

On an average morning, he was on the move by six or seven at the
latest. He'd look for a bathroom. Public ones were scarce in Boston.
Sometimes he had to settle for the corner of an alley, but if he was
downtown and made it to midmorning, he'd just walk into the rest-
room at Chipotle or even better the one at Marshalls, always clean in
his experience. He'd walk in confidently—"as if I own the place"—
which was how he would enter the staff shower room up on the eleventh floor at Mass General. If need be, he could get a shower at the
Kingston House shelter near Seven-Eighty. He liked to be clean, especially before Street Clinic.

Since prison, he'd lost about sixty pounds. Food was an after-
thought. When a Good Samaritan or street friend handed him a sandwich or a slice of pizza, he'd realize, "Oh, I was hungry." If he did go
looking for food, dumpsters behind police stations could be productive.
And half-full garbage bags in the alleys behind pizza shops often had
unsold, unsullied slices in them. Sometimes he found what he needed
lying right on the pavement—sandwiches still wrapped up, and even
packs of cigarettes and unscratched scratch tickets. "God makes it happen." He didn't stem, he said. "And I don't boost stuff." That is, he
didn't steal, except for that time when, a month or two out of prison,
he got caught shoplifting some winter clothes. Or on those occasions
when, for no other possible reason besides divine intervention, a

good-looking prize appeared right in front of him—for instance, a couple of years ago, a pawnshop with no one at the counter and easy access to a box full of rings that turned out to be worth a lot less than their tagged prices.

. . .

On the way out of his underground world of tunnels and trains, Tony led us past a little alcove behind an escalator. This was a good place to hang out on a rainy day, he said, especially if he had an outstanding arrest warrant, because the cops had to ride up the escalator to nab him. Before they got there, he could jump up and hit that red button and the escalator would halt: "Hey, I'm sitting on the cardboard, they're comin' up, they're three or four feet up, I open my eyes and I said, 'Assholes,' and I hit the button and I beam right up the stairs, hit the cawnah, hit Cheeseboy Alley, go into the alley, and they see me. I go down Cheeseboy Alley. My knees were still good, I jump up and grabbed the fire escape. I had cops walk under me so many times. We used to sleep sometimes on the fire escapes. I could tell you a story, but I used to be able to jump up and pull myself up and the cops would be walking underneath and they'd never look up."

We emerged from Tony's underworld into a part of Boston's Freedom Trail. There were pre–Revolutionary War monuments all around us: the Old South Meeting House, the Old State House, the Granary Burying Ground, the site of the Boston Massacre. Tony's special sites included the Irish Famine Memorial, which he called the Circle. He had sold that gold ring he retrieved from the subway tracks—for far too little, he said—and had hosted a party of street friends near the memorial. It was a favorite hunting spot. "People sitting on the benches there, they lie down, fall asleep, wallets fall. I find stuff all the time. Insane the stuff I found." Recently, for instance, a gold chain of obvious value—"14 k" was inscribed on it. The other homeless people at the Circle had told him to sell it. But he'd told Jim that he was going to wear it for a while, on the off chance that it had sentimental value for the owner, who would see it on him and give him a small reward—"twenty dollars or something"—which was far less than the chain was worth, but would leave everyone happy. No doubt he would sell it when he lost his cards and his Social Security got stopped again, but good intentions also counted, at least to Jim.

Tony took us over to Spring Lane and told us to look up. "The sculptures and stuff up there on the original buildings cost hundreds of thousands of dollars! Boston's one of the most art cities, and nobody ever looks up! And these are the oldest buildings in the world! These buildings are *ancient*."

Tony proceeded to rattle off information from the plaque in the wall beside us. He did this without looking at the plaque. Evidently, he had memorized its contents. "This is Spring Lane. Know why it's Spring Lane? Back in the seventeen hundreds this was a spring. This was a spring where people used to come down, wash their clothes and get their water. This was a rivah. That's the name." I was struck by the performance. Clearly, he had sobered up from the drug he'd ingested that morning, whatever it was.

Tony had told me, "I notice everything, and I don't forget anything."

Jim believed this, with a caveat: "Tony's very perceptive. He sees into things. But he can't manage himself."

Part of the reason had to be alcohol and drugs. Mike Jellison was the team member who knew that territory best. He knew firsthand where the illness had begun for many of the patients he was trying to help: "What's the best antidote to homelessness? Drugs and alcohol are your best friends, and then because they work, you get addicted, and that's a whole other thing. How can you live on the streets without self-medicating? *I* never could."

3

The Beauty of Human Connection

The psychiatrist Eileen Reilly had been with the Street Team for decades, and to her it seemed as though their work existed outside of time. "You go away on a sabbatical, and when you come back, nothing's changed." Jim often recited those words, and would add, "There's both a comfort and a terror in that."

For me, after spending time in the team's company, a certain coffee shop was no longer just a place to get a good muffin, but also the shop across the street from where Harmony and Jake liked to camp, with their caravan of shopping carts and roller bags and witchcraft equipment. Certain sights had acquired meaning—walking up Bromfield Street around dawn, I saw a man in a janitor's uniform sloshing a bucket of water across the pavement of a doorway, and I wondered if I knew the person who had spent last night on that patch of concrete. Predictions of winter storms and plunging temperatures could still make me imagine boats tossed in heavy seas beyond Boston Light, but now they also summoned faces: In Mousey Park, in McInnis House, in the Street Clinic waiting room, on snow-lined streets in the headlights of the outreach van. And Seven-Eighty had come to feel like refuge. I had been given a key card, which let me move freely through the building.

Julie had given me my first tour of Seven-Eighty. Some months later, mildly puzzled, I told her that I hadn't heard any members of the staff speaking angrily to anyone there. She said, "It's gentler than other places that I know. People don't yell at each other, at least in my presence. Sometimes patients do, of course, but not very often. It's almost like the waters get calmer. Everything's done by dialogue, in open conversation. It's like a cult that isn't one."

She was in her midthirties. She'd been Jim's assistant for about three years. In her previous job, she had risen to executive director of two schools for language-impaired children and adolescents. She was looking for a new challenge when she happened to visit Seven-Eighty with a group from her church. She returned and spent several Saturdays with patients in the recreation room of McInnis House. The patients' frank gratitude affected her strongly: "Thank you for spending your Saturday afternoon with me." "Thank you for coming here." "Thank you for helping me with this art." "Thank you for listening to me."

The experience made her curious about the disheveled men and women she saw in the city, begging at a corner or sitting on a bus or slumped against a wall. Outside, some invisible barrier seemed to block all pathways between them and her. Inside McInnis House, though, homeless people acquired identities. She also got a glimpse of how happy most patients seemed in the nurses' company. She tried to explain her feelings in a note: "What I know for sure is that there seems to be something about being *with* someone (and I mean really with them, not distracted by cellphones or computers or with an intention to fill a medication or fill out paperwork) that dignifies his/her existence. What's interesting is that I, too, in these moments, feel that same deep sense of gratitude. Maybe I have holes in my life that patients fill? Or maybe there is something to be said for the beauty of human connection that reminds us how complete we already are?"

Not long after her stint as a volunteer, Julie gave up her job and title and a large chunk of salary, and went to work handling Jim's professional life—she was the first assistant he'd ever had. She told me: "It just felt like I was *called* to do it? I never know what that phrase means, but it was like someone whispering in my ear, 'Just take the leap of faith and do it.'"

Twice as many women as men staffed the senior management. Women nurses were everywhere you turned. I wondered if this explained the general atmosphere. Julie said she thought it might. She was distinctly feminine herself, in what seemed like an old-fashioned way—always carefully and practically dressed, no high heels but stylish flats like dancing slippers. Beckie—the cheerful, overworked, multicompetent case manager—once called Julie "the most reasonable person in the world." To me, she had charisma in the original sense, a gift of grace—poised to listen and to say the right thing at the right time. She said that the organization's best qualities reminded her of her grandmother. "She always cared about how I was. She was open, she was loving, she was grounded."

Julie was overqualified to serve as Jim's assistant. Still, the job had its complexities. "Jim says yes to everything. I'm the one who has to say no."

She also took on the arrangements for team activities, bought the presents for teammates' birthdays, helped to manage the chaos on Thursdays down in the rowdy Street Clinic waiting room. She visited patients with Jim in nursing homes and apartments and upstairs in McInnis House. By now she knew all the patients. She had a knack for calming the drunk, the stoned, the angry. Tony seemed to view her as a sister and therapist. He called her often just to talk, from the street on a friend's phone, and very often from upstairs in McInnis House, when he was managing its milieu. Mostly she listened in on what she called "Tony's argument with God." She thought of him, not without fondness, as "just a very big kid."

· · ·

The Street Team's headquarters lay deep inside Seven-Eighty—across the lobby, up a stairway, through two doorways that required electronic ID cards, down another stairway into what had been the morgue's lobby, where some of its Egyptian trappings were preserved— carved replicas of sphinxes serving as newel posts for another set of stairs, which led down to the basement, once the building's underworld, where the bodies had been kept.

Half a dozen steps down a hallway from the old lobby, the walls were covered by framed photographs of men and women, most with weathered faces, smiling for the camera. These were photos Jim had taken of patients over the years. They marked the Street Team's territory, a back office with the team's desks and computers scattered here and there. Jim had the only private office. Beside it was a simple room with bookcases, a sofa and chairs, a small fridge and coffeemaker, and a sign on the wall that read THE LIBRARY. At its far side, just beyond a pair of sliding doors, usually open, was Julie's desk. As the first members of the team arrived for Monday meeting, she'd turn from her computer to say, her voice rising at the end: "Hi, *Jim*! Hi, *Mike*!" She greeted everyone in this voice, as if she were singing their names.

The midday Monday meeting in the library was long and leisurely compared to Thursday's preclinic meeting at Mass General. Kevin, the younger doctor, had suggested that it be more "regimented," but Jim had demurred. He wanted the meeting to remain informal and its time frame elastic. "Flexibility is going to be the name of the game. Because this is a high-stress job." And so Monday meeting remained a time to regroup, maybe even relax. Everyone had an actual seat. Most brought lunch. And there was ample time to talk about patients and problems and odd events in their world.

One day, as the members trooped in, some just returning from street rounds and shedding winter coats, Jim pointed to a small, neatly sealed box on the coffee table in front of the couch. "We have a mystery here. We don't know whose ashes these are." They were the remains of a patient, but which patient? "I'm telling you guys, we need a detective."

Mostly, they discussed the problems of new patients and the recurring problems of rough sleepers who had been in their care so long as to seem like aging relatives. After a while, Beckie would say, "Okay. Who are we worried about?"

This question was one of Monday's routines. The first times I heard Beckie ask it, I was puzzled. What had they been doing for the past hour if not worrying about patients? But eventually I realized it was a matter of degree, that Beckie was really asking: "Who are we *very worried* about?"

· · ·

On one of those Thursday winter mornings at Mass General, John Cotrone came into the exam room without a cane, sat down beside Jim's gray metal desk, and in his beard-muffled voice, declared, "I'm getting three to four hours of good sleep."

Jim turned to him, beaming. "John, this is such good news! I can't tell you!"

"And my weight just went up five pounds."

John's friend Angie wasn't doing as well. The sheriff's office had delivered her no-fault eviction, Beckie still hadn't found her a new place, and John wasn't going to linger and gossip with her anymore, not at least until this was over. "Ahhh, they'll get her a place. I don't want to listen to her moanin' about it."

"The beauty of human connection." Julie's phrase seemed like an idea to hang on to, like a bright thread that wove through the trials of winter.

But of course connections sometimes broke down. Angie now sat alone outside the Walk-In Clinic, a white-haired orphan, on a chair in the bright hospital hallway. Julie was passing by, on her way to the cupboard where she kept donated clothes for patients. She stopped. "Hi, *Angie!*"

Angie looked up at her, and said in a quavering voice, "I'm scared!" Then she burst into tears. Julie, her own face suddenly flushed, sat with her for a while, and then Jim came out to the hall. He stood in front of Angie, listening to her describe the futile search she'd made for a new place—not for anything special, just a room she could afford. "I'm driving myself crazy, I'm smoking almost two packs a day. My old man said, 'Angie, you got COPD, I think you better slow down.' That makes me want to smoke more."

Jim nodded. "I know what you mean. So we've been trying to find you a place. We're not going to give up. You wouldn't consider coming to McInnis House, even for a couple of weeks?"

"No. No way."

"What *would* you do?"

"Go outside. I'd start my own shit again. I can't go outside and not drink. And it's five years since I quit." She began to sob.

Jim gazed away for a moment, as if looking for something coming down the hall. Then he smiled. "Hey, can I show you a picture that'll make you laugh? Do you know where we were last weekend?"

"Florida," Angie said, sniffling. "Disneyworld." She wiped her eyes.

"So look at this." He took his cellphone out of its holster, fingered the screen, then handed it to her—a snapshot of Gabriella with a Disney Cinderella. "Is that perfectly her?"

"Awwww. Beauty-*ful.*"

"She was like, she was a princess."

"You don't got one with you and Mickey Mouse?"

"Noooh, I don't. I don't have any of me and Mickey Mouse. Sorry. Isn't that kind of cute, though? She's like a little human being now. I'm refusing to acknowledge that. I keep thinking she's a baby."

At the moment, cheering Angie up for a while was all Jim could do for her. Later that day, Beckie told him that Angie's name had risen to the top of the housing list in Chelsea, but then, at the last minute, the authorities there had denied her application on the grounds that she had criminal convictions. One dated back nine years, the other twenty-five. They had sent Angie a letter giving her until the sixth of the month to appeal. Angie had received the letter on the seventh. "In their denial they made it sound like she lied," Beckie said.

She sounded angry, as did Jim: "The *last* thing she needs is to have someone else make her feel like a piece of shit. She's been a *model* tenant. She has done *nothing* wrong since she stopped drinking nearly five years ago, and her partner died and she was a mess, but she didn't relapse."

"She calls every day in tears," said Beckie. "I have gone down every road I can think of. She says, 'I know you'll solve this. I have faith in you.' I want to say, '*I* don't.'"

· · ·

The previous summer, Mike had predicted that BJ wouldn't be alive come spring. Kevin had agreed, and so had Tony. While most of the city's homeless people remained in winter quarters, BJ sat shivering, day after day, in his little red chariot out in the park. Tony often attended him, passing the bottle of vodka, but he wasn't nearly as worried as he'd been. He reported, "BJ's the king of the idiots, Jim. He's gonna outlive all of us."

In February, the temperature hit seventy for two days, a record. Then arctic cold returned. Outside, it felt as though the wind was being piped down the streets. Jim altered Friday rounds. For several weeks, while the freeze continued, he and Eileen skipped the walk and took the subway directly to South Station. There, one day at noontime, they found a man named Arnold. He was sitting at a table in the mezzanine, above the food court. He was dressed in sweatpants, his large midsection hanging down in a loose T-shirt, as if inside a sack. The mezzanine was crowded, but there were empty chairs and tables all around Arnold. Jim had never heard his life story, but he knew his present well. The man was seventy and disabled. What Jim found easiest to like in him was his defiance of the world's authorities, the way Arnold cussed out police and judges to their faces, in effect saying, "I've lost everything, but I still have this power, and you can't take it away." But when he was inside nursing homes or shelters, he could be feisty, foulmouthed, and lewd. At the moment, he was banned from every place of shelter in the city, including McInnis House.

Jim and Eileen and the day's students—two young women psychiatrists in residence—sat down at Arnold's table. Jim asked him how he was doing.

"Well, so-so," Arnold said. "I have a stench right now, because I'm incontinent. What can I do about that? I fix one thing and another pops up. I can't win. I can't win for nothing. It was six months I've been walking around. I was soiling *everything*. I even got a violation at Barbara McInnis for exposing myself, because the diaper fell. It don't stay. You know how diapers are. Fell down. My pants fell down. I got kicked out of there. Indecent exposure. I can't do anything. I'm in the nude."

"So where are you staying?" Jim asked.

"Out on the streets. *Now.* If I go back to the shelter, they would have to find me another set of clothes, clean me up. Would they do me that favor? Emergency rooms don't have showers, so I'm screwed. I don't know where I can take a shower now and clean up. St. Francis House, they barred me."

Jim turned to the young psychiatrists. "Arnold has been challenged everywhere." He turned back to Arnold. "And there is literally no place for you to go now?"

"They're gonna throw me out of *here*." He meant out of the train station. "I've been thrown out of every place. A miracle would have to happen for me to be able to be fixed up. A miracle. This is my thirtieth year homeless. Thirty years homeless. I can't do it anymore. I'm not a young man. If I was younger, I could. When I was younger, I relocated twice. I may have to relocate to the middle of the woods where there's nobody, and if I die out there, that's the way it's gonna be."

In a moment, without warning, Arnold began to rage about Irish security guards and police—"Mick cops" who rousted him from places like this and from Mass General's waiting room. How good it would feel to empty a revolver's six bullets into them. As he spoke, expelling fury, tears collected in his eyes and meandered down his cheeks. He wiped them away with his wrist and turned to the young women at the table. "I'm cynical. Homelessness makes you that way. It makes you hate the badges."

Eileen—seasoned, judicious—stared past Arnold, evidently deep in thought. Jim turned to her. "What do you think we should do?"

She looked at Jim, lips pursed. She didn't speak.

This wasn't a new predicament. A few weeks before, McInnis House had banished Arnold, passing him on to the Boston Medical Center, which passed him on to the Pine Street Inn, which sent him to Mass General's emergency department, which sent him back to the lobby of Seven-Eighty. The young doctor Kevin had found himself confronted with Arnold, sitting in a wheelchair and dressed in a hospital johnny with his ingrown Foley catheter hanging out of his penis. Kevin had spent hours getting Arnold admitted to a shelter.

Now, at the table in the train station, Jim asked Arnold where he wanted to go. A nursing home, said Arnold. To get into one, he'd have to go to an ER first, Jim explained, and Arnold agreed to that. The next hour was a labor of phone calls, which ended with EMTs wheeling Arnold out of the station to an ambulance.

We walked toward the subway. "I never saw Arnold cry before," Jim said to Eileen and the students. "It makes you realize. All that anger is from a broken soul."

• • •

Arnold's hope for a nursing home failed. A few weeks later, he was back on the streets. Tony ran into him near the waterfront. Arnold wanted to go to Mass General. Tony wheeled him all the way there. When they arrived, Arnold asked him for a cigarette. Arnold didn't drink or do drugs or even smoke, but he said he needed money and he thought he could sell the cigarette to someone. Tony gave him several and went looking for Jim.

4

~~~~~~~~~~

Sisyphus

A Sunday evening in the dead of winter, and in the atrium at McInnis House, the windows were black mirrors reflecting images of a dozen men in a circle of rocking chairs. It was an old habit of Jim's to visit the respite on Sunday nights. Nowadays Tony took it upon himself to make it a gathering, extending invitations, moving the chairs into place. The group had just gotten settled when Tony said, "Wait a minute. Ronnie's not here." He jumped up and went off to Ronnie's room and brought him back to the atrium, mussing up Ronnie's hair as he led him to a seat. Jim watched all this with amusement. It reminded him of summer camp, with Tony as a counselor.

Tony kept handing out cigarettes from the pack that Jim had given him, and when other patients wandered in, he invited them to grab a chair. When Nick said, "They don't know how to do eggplant parm here," Tony at once defended the respite's cook: "What are you talkin' about? Everyone says the food is great." He looked around the circle. "What do you guys say?"

They shrugged, some nodded. One of them smiled and said, "I'm staying out of this."

Jim suggested that young people were taking over the turf these veterans had held for so long, down on Cambridge Street and in Mousey Park. Billy Bianchino, a small, muscular man, corrected him: "Comin' in, not *takin' over.*"

Jim smiled. These new people were "infiltrating," he said. "You guys are the tough Mousey Park crew."

"Yeah," said Tony. "And look at us." He swept a hand around the circle.

One of the men had shuffled in on a walker, another had an IV hookup hanging from his arm, two sat in wheelchairs, one with a fresh bandage on a recently amputated leg. They all looked older than they were. And yet for all of that, each was sober and shaved and dressed in laundered clothes. They cleaned up well, especially Tony and the man with the walker to whom Jim had said, "You look like a prep-school kid!"

Seated among them, Jim let himself imagine that this was just a group of old friends, just regular Americans getting together. But the spell lasted only while he kept himself from enlarging the context to the world beyond the atrium's night-darkened windows, where people like these slept on cardboard and concrete. He told me later he was thinking that most of the men in those rocking chairs wouldn't ever get a job. They had no skills, or they were too sick or too old. "So it really is respite, before they go back into the darkness."

· · ·

The next day, I found Jim in his office and we ended up chatting about Tony. "He's fine again now, in great shape, social director of McInnis House," Jim said. "But that means that one day sooner or later he'll leave without much warning, if not AMA." Sure enough, a few days later Tony announced that he had to get out of the respite. Everyone there was asking him for help, he told Jim, and he no longer had any to lend. "I've just given up."

Jim's response was also predictable, in keeping with a longstanding, informal rule for the respite: "Make sure people feel welcome when they come to McInnis House, and don't make them feel bad when they leave." Jim gave Tony some money and cigarettes, and asked him to please take his hep C meds on schedule while outside. Promising that he would, Tony picked up the cane that one of the nurses had brought him—he had cut his toe, his knee ached—and stumped out onto Albany Street. Afterward, Jim commented on this latest desertion: "Things change like mad from day to day, but not much in the long haul. Sisyphus again. Tony's the quintessential example for me."

Every patient had patterns, even if they were erratic. Tony's was cyclical, and McInnis House a principal way station. Under the rules, patients could leave McInnis at will, but they couldn't simply walk back in. Getting admitted, or readmitted, was a formal process, involving a medical exam. And there had to be a bed available. Rough sleepers were only a small percentage of homeless people in need of medical respite. But the Street Team had an informal claim on about 12 of the 104 beds at McInnis House, and Jim could usually find one for Tony, within a day or two at most. Jim made the effort mainly because after a few weeks outside, Tony was the picture of medical neediness—pressured speech, racing pulse, exhaustion, delusions, and always the swollen, painful knee. Moreover, McInnis as a prescription for Tony had the kind of transformative effect that any doctor would relish. And once restored in body and mind, Tony became a useful presence—to Omar the manager, to the nurses, to Jim.

On average, patients stayed at McInnis House for two to three weeks. Omar sometimes asked Jim to keep Tony there longer, but Tony usually left before Omar or Jim would have liked. Tony would get tired of his self-appointed roles, especially when it came to mediating arguments among other patients, who, he felt, didn't appreciate his efforts. Lack of proper cigarette etiquette—so many failed to return his generosity—stood for a variety of offenses. Or vexing problems with his medical insurance and Social Security would crop up, and he'd stalk out of the respite, heading for a state or federal office to try to fix the issue. Or check day would be approaching, the day when Social Security payments came and he could afford to buy a few things, including alcohol and drugs. Or he simply couldn't resist the pull of what he called *outside*. Behind every departure loomed his two decades of prison. Once in a while his tongue would slip and he'd refer to a floor in McInnis House as a "tier," and then exclaim: "Did I just say that? I'm not in prison. I don't *think* I am." Often he spent a few days deciding to leave AMA. One time, he found himself near Seven-Eighty's front door and simply eloped.

He'd gone downstairs for a dentist appointment. The door to that clinic was at the front of the lobby, to his left. To his right, tall windows opened onto Albany Street and sunlight. The wide front doorway lay straight ahead. The weather was warming. He kept walking and was gone for nearly three weeks.

When Tony left the respite, he would live outside for varying periods, ranging from a week to one or two months. Sooner or later, he'd appear out of the dark at a van stop or he'd come to Street Clinic in extremis—dirty, exhausted, depressed, and talking maniacally fast. Once inside McInnis House, he'd sleep for a day, sometimes a day and a half, then revive and resume his roles as unlicensed milieu director. Usually, the cadence of his speech slowed day by day to something like fast normal. The atmosphere inside seemed to restore him. Undoubtedly, prescription medications also helped. Suspecting that Tony suffered from both bipolar disorder and attention deficit hyperactivity disorder, Dr. Bonnar had put him on a regimen of two drugs: Ritalin for the ADHD, which Tony had used before and liked, and lithium, an old and sometimes very effective treatment for bipolar disorder, especially its hypomanic phases.

But Tony didn't take those drugs when he went back to the streets.

Bonnar couldn't let him have the Ritalin, because routine tests showed that Tony always used cocaine when he was outside, and the two drugs make for a dangerous combination. As for the lithium, Tony felt it robbed him of the edgy vigilance he needed on the streets.

Sometimes his returns to McInnis House came quickly, as when he found Jim at a van stop on a Monday night and said, in a panic, that he was covered with bugs and fungi. He showed Jim a bagful of the evidence—just pieces of lint. Tony declared that the things turned into plants, which turned into something like flowers. "Nobody believes me, Jim. This ain't fair!" Jim brought him in, and with some misgivings, he had the staff put Tony through the decontamination process as if his delusion were real. A few days later, Dr. Bonnar reported, "When I saw Tony today, he said the bugs were gone. In my experience, the delusion usually comes with drug withdrawal. It's called formication."

More often, Tony returned to McInnis House gradually and without drama. He often left the respite abruptly, AMA. For a while afterward, when he visited Jim at Thursday clinic, you could tell that Tony was still taking pains with his hygiene. Eventually, though, Tony would visit the office and afterward Jim would get out his can of air freshener and spray the room. This was one usual sign that Tony would soon need to get off the streets. By then his mood would be corroded with complaints of cosmic proportions, devolving into self-pity. To wit: "I do ten good things, twenty bad things happen. I've stood there when it's freezing cold, and I say, What's next, God? Are you gonna freeze all my fingers, you gonna start *snappin'* them off?" Small human betrayals also added up. He bitterly recalled all the things he'd done for BJ, saying, "And so many times he's laughed at me and turned his back." Others did him wrong, too, such as the crazy woman he'd saved from being robbed, who turned around and robbed him a night later.

Of all betrayals, deaths of friends were the most grievous to Tony. There had been dozens in the five years since he'd left prison. The latest had come in the midst of an impromptu carouse of Street Team regulars on Congress Street—an argument over $20 fueled by vodka and crack, between two childhood friends, one stabbing the other. Tony arrived moments later, yelled at the clerk in the convenience store to call an ambulance, then took charge of the half-dozen Street Team patients standing there, drunk and stoned, herding them into a nearby parking garage and bedding them down on stairwell platforms. He arrived at Street Clinic the next day, alternately weeping and raging to Jim and Julie, his voice comprehensible only in snatches: "I haven't slept for days . . . When I was kid, I seen people murdered. It didn't bother me. Now a fuckin' bird dies and I can't stop crying . . ." (He had tried to nurse a sparrow back to health some nights before, and had failed.) "I seen so many dead people . . ."

In the aftermath, Tony came down with pneumonia. The window in his room at Mass General looked out on the Charles River and the Esplanade, a lovely view, but when I came in to visit, he was lying in gloomy light with the curtain closed, and he wouldn't let anyone open it, for fear that something would go wrong and he'd be punished. I had the impression he'd been lying there marinating in long, bad thoughts. In a hoarse half whisper, he said street friends had been telling him that he was going to kill someone soon, just like that Street Team patient who had knifed his old friend the other night. "They say, 'You're next, Tony. I see it in your eyes.'" I think that before I arrived, he'd had a dream in which he killed someone, and I think the dream still hadn't left him—because in a low, incoherent mutter, he seemed to be reviewing events in his mind. Then he declared, "No, I didn't!"

He went on, fully awake now: "It's so crazy. I feel like I'm living in this world wit' this person that wants to try so hard to do some good, but he doesn't have the power and the resources, and when he does something, he lets down the ones that help him." *This person*. He meant a version of himself. "Now it's come to a point where—I hit Timmy in the head wit' a brick, all right? I caught him stealing from my friend's pocketbook, he told me he was gonna boot me in the face. I hit him wit' a brick, but I made sure he wasn't bleeding after, and he seemed okay before I left."

Tony sometimes boasted about being an enforcer on the streets. But what I heard now was the voice of a worried mind.

"Jim's got the heart of an angel," he went on. "When I hurt people, I feel I hurt Jim. Like I'm the guy— People he's trying to help and cure? I'm the guy that makes them sick again." Tony paused. "It's easier to hurt people than it's hard to help people."

• • •

In the circuit of Tony's current life, things always fell apart, but between the breakdowns there were weeks-long periods of sanity and order, and moments of grace.

One afternoon on his way to Mass General, Jim was passing by Mousey Park and witnessed what looked like the start of a catastrophe. Two men standing face to face at the center of the park. Rabbit, despised and derided, whose invariable pattern was to provoke the person most likely to beat him up. And Leon, street tough, among the most dangerous of the team's patients. "It has nothing to do with strength," Jim once explained. "It's what he will do to you before you realize he's doing it."

Rabbit was in full voice: "Your mother is a Black motherfucker. She's a whore."

Leon snarled back. "Don't you *dare* talk about my mother like that."

"Oh yeah, she'd suck my cock."

Just then—before Jim could act—Tony jumped up from the bench at the rear of the park, strode up, and stepped between the two men. "Rabbit, that's an awful thing to say! Stop it!" He turned to Leon. "Leon, you know he's just trying to piss you off. Don't take the bait. Let's just walk away, 'cause you would kill him if you hit him, so let's walk away."

Tony put an arm around Leon's shoulder, and walked him out of the park. From a little distance, Jim could see Tony bending down, talking to Leon. But the danger wasn't over. Rabbit wouldn't quit. "Your mother must be very ashamed of you!" he yelled, and Leon turned and headed toward him fast. Tony blocked the way. "I'll get him outa here, Leon. Let me take him outa here." Then Tony laid an anaconda of an arm over and around Rabbit's thin shoulders and walked him quick-time up Cambridge Street. Jim followed them for a few blocks, and from a distance witnessed the peaceful end of the affair—Tony and Rabbit sitting on the steps of the West End library, in earnest-looking conversation.

Jim was impressed. "It was so deftly done and so patiently done."

Surprising Jim was part of Tony's pattern. He had grown up in the North End when it was a bastion of virulent bigotry. One might have expected him to share the racist views that came spewing out of the mouths of many older white patients when they came to Street Clinic drunk. But this was the dissertation Tony offered on prejudice during a session in Jim's exam room: "Some of these guys use the N-word connotative and denotative. My belief's in this. Be very open, don't judge a person by race, religion, sexual preference, political beliefs, or other aspects. When you start judging a person by their weight, their color, their disablements—there's different forms of prejudices. And one of the things that we do when we do those things is we close our minds. Sometimes we do it in an ignorance way."

To hear Tony talk, you realized that during his years in prison he had joined a long tradition of self-educated inmates, reading widely and eclectically, and with an enthusiasm unspoiled by intellectual snobbery. Tony liked suspenseful action and adventure novels, and also Freud and Jung. Abraham Maslow was a special favorite. "I related to him a lot. Reading the Bible about the Romans and stuff. Maslow would relate the verses in the Bible, he would break them down, how certain phrases in the Bible is a form of psychology that we practice today."

Then he asked me, "Ever read the psychologist Watson?"

I confessed that I'd never heard of him.

"He's my favorite medical writer," said Tony.

He also told me, "I love art! Ever hear of the artist Martisse? He's my favorite!"

Tony said he'd discovered Matisse in his teens, during his stays at the Lindemann Mental Health Center, where several reproductions of the artist's prints had hung in a psychiatrist's office. "And the doctor explained who Martisse was, and I bought prints, and I had them in a room where I was staying. I don't know what happened to them."

· · ·

Tony had never been to Boston's Museum of Fine Arts, or even visited its neighborhood. I went there with him one morning, along with my wife, Fran, an artist and art teacher. Tony had been out on the streets with no respite for the better part of a month. Boston's weather having turned into an approximation of spring, he was wearing only two coats. The outermost had ragged, soiled cuffs. His hands looked sooty, his fingernails like black half-moons. When I met him in Mousey Park earlier in the morning, he smelled of liquor. Now he smelled of hangover, of a good time turned sour, moist, overripe. When we walked into the museum, I felt embarrassed in his conspicuous company and embarrassed for feeling embarrassed, but then I told myself that he could easily pass for a starving artist. He didn't do anything untoward, didn't knock anything over or get too close to paintings and sculptures or use profanity once he realized there were elderly women around.

Fran took him to a large abstract canvas by Helen Frankenthaler. "Frankenstein!" Tony exclaimed, reading the caption on the wall. Then he glanced at the painting. "That kind of looks like the face of a dude I beat up."

Fran ignored this. She said, "I don't see any creature of any kind," and Tony made a nervous chuckle and stared at the Frankenthaler as Fran offered ideas about what else he might find in the painting, perhaps the creation of the Earth. Fran added, "She didn't put anything on the canvas to begin with. So the paint is soaking in, making stains."

"I see the stains," said Tony.

"I'm interested in that kind of thing and the way the paint—"

Tony interrupted. "Those are autumn colors."

Fran: "Yeah. And desert."

Tony: "Why does she do dark down here?"

Fran: "It's just to orient it in space. It's like creating landmarks, to create the feeling of space."

Tony: "You look at this and I know a few people go, 'What is that, kindergarten art?' People don't see what you just said, though. The creation of Earth."

Fran: "I'm not saying that's right . . ."

Tony: "No, but I see what you're saying. But I seen something else. I was fooling around, I says, 'I see the eye, dude I beat up, his face looked like that,' but then I seen—"

Fran: "You're right. It looks like a bloodshot eye."

Tony: "She uses yellow and green but there's two blues there and nowhere else."

Fran: "I just noticed that."

They went on for a while, trading observations, until Tony asked, "How much is that worth? What if I cut it out and roll it up right now? How much would I get for it?"

Fran laughed, then excused herself for a moment, and while she was gone, Tony said to me, "I seen it in my mind. She opened it up by speaking."

He was full of questions for her, about the varieties of paint and their properties, the techniques of printing, how metal sculptures are made. They moved on to other paintings. He seemed to like all of them. He exclaimed over a Vlaminck: "It's awesome. I like the colors. Look at the trees. Notice how the leaves are all crinkled up like they're burning?"

Eventually, he wearied. His damaged knee ached, he said. But then Jim arrived, fresh from Street Clinic, and Tony agreed to make one last stop, at a show of works on paper by the artist Egon Schiele, mostly figures, some drawn without hands or feet.

When Fran read from a caption that Schiele had spent three weeks in jail, Tony said, "Three weeks? I spent more time on the toilet." At one point, he remarked that a woman in one drawing looked like his mother after his father had beaten her. Then he chastened himself:

"My mind goes too many places. Yeah, sometimes it does. So I'll shut up."

With that, he seemed to sweep all distractions away. He became intent on the drawings, moving from one to another, saying, "That's beautiful. That's awesome. I wonder how he does it. He uses a lot of orange. Every picture. The lips." He said to Fran apropos of Schiele's palette: "I don't want to sound stupid, but in school, kids will often use pretty colors and things like that. You see them and you think, Wow, I couldn't do that now."

After a while, he came to a drawing that made him stop and stare in silence. It was a nude, a woman seen from behind. She stands in the classical pose called contrapposto, in which the body is relaxed with one hip slightly cocked. Tony murmured, as if to himself, "Kinda looks like, that looks like the, the statue of, uh, David."

Fran turned to him, with wide eyes and a smile, a gratified teacher. "I was just thinking that!" she said.

I said he must have taken an art course back in his school days.

"No. I just—it's me." Tony laughed. "Did *I* study art? I looked at people. They were in prison."

"But you must have studied Michelangelo," said Fran.

Tony said, "Frannie, I'm *Italian*. I read, but the statue of David, the Colosseum, Michelangelo, whatevah. I'm *Italian*."

Growing up in the North End, he would have seen many souvenirs of Italy's treasures, in postcards pinned on walls and figurines on tabletops. I could picture him as a boy picking up a little metal statue of David and his dark brown eyes studying it with the same intensity he applied to Schiele's drawing. The connection he'd made between the modernist drawing and the Renaissance statue was the kind of insight you'd expect from an art historian. I shouldn't have been surprised.

Tony told us he had a place to sleep that night. We put him and his damaged knee in a cab, and as we watched it pull away, Jim said, "I just can't help thinking what he could have been."

5

Boundaries and Limits

The memorial service of 2018 was held on a warm sunny morning in May. In Mousey Park, thirty sunflowers surrounded the linden tree, the name of a departed rough sleeper attached to each stem. Tony had wanted to come, but Jim hadn't told him the date, knowing that if he did, Tony would insist on attending and leave McInnis House AMA.

Listening to Reverend Tina read the most recent list of the dead, each of the names a trunk full of memories, Jim had moody thoughts. These dead had been part of his extended family for years, but he didn't know most of the people who were replacing them. Getting to really know a new generation of rough sleepers would take more years than he had left. He said that he told himself, "This is a natural evolution. I have to get used to it."

A few weeks later, the team held a retreat in a borrowed conference room, high above the streets in a Boston skyscraper. Jim had prepared a history lesson, with some startling old photos of elderly patients when they were young, which evoked double takes and exclamations—"That was Frankie?" "That can't be BJ!" He'd also retrieved a mission statement dating back to the time of the Street Team's creation. The Program itself, he explained, had been created to serve only as a catalyst, as an attempt to inspire the city's health care system into adopting homeless people as full-fledged patients and not mere charity cases. The Program, large as it had become, was just a part of a much bigger system and the Street Team just a small part of that part. What role should the team play now?

The question had urgency because of all the new faces appearing on the streets. Who among those newcomers should the team take on as patients and follow all the way, from the streets and, with luck, into housing? "Who is ours?" Jim asked. "The issue for me is, who gets into that group? We can't take on four thousand patients." Then he turned the question around. "How do we not burn out?"

Beckie said she already felt like a doorkeeper at Thursday clinic, always obliged to turn some people away. "It doesn't feel good," she said.

Mike said, "I feel overwhelmed sometimes with the substance use. How to help our folks a little more? Because all our folks have substance use disorder. I feel spread a little thin."

Dr. Bonnar was just a few weeks from retirement. "The only contact our patients have with the rest of humanity is us," he said. "One thing I'm hearing is that we all want to be everything to everybody, and one thing we need to do is, *not* to try to be that."

"It's hard to have anything left at the end of the day," said another team member. "We have to be careful to set boundaries and limits."

Jim, known for having none or very few of those, agreed in principle, recalling a time long ago when everything had seemed simpler, when no one on the team yet had children, and when, as he put it, "the days could be endless."

The tone of their voices wasn't proud or whiny. No one talked about quitting. It sounded as if they were just naming insoluble dilemmas of the job, airing them out like laundry in the backyard. At one point, Jim said, "I think one of the burnout issues is, most people get to the streets for complicated reasons. The process of trying to fix those can be lifelong. And Sisyphean. How do you get your joy and fulfillment out of that process?"

6

‧‧‧‧‧‧‧‧‧‧

The Gala

When Jim spoke to groups about the plight of homeless people, he usually showed photos and told stories. The world he described was harsh, but his tone was always agreeable. I once listened to him speak to a smattering of employees at a big engineering firm, a high-tech branch of General Electric. The setting was a suburban office complex, where streets had names such as Results Way and Value Way. During question-and-answer time, a company employee who looked to be about thirty raised his hand and said, "So I live in the city and I have desensitized myself to these homeless people." Suddenly, his voice breaking, he said that he had learned first to step over people sleeping in doorways, and now he'd mastered the art of not seeing them at all. "And they're not even *evil*."

I was struck by the emotion in the man's response. Most people who came to Jim's talks already knew the abstract truths about American homelessness—that it is the direst form of poverty, that it consigns people to appalling miseries and kills them well before their time. The mild tone of Jim's slide-show stories let a listener take in that reality through the experiences of actual people. The effect, for some at least, was to make a harsh part of the American world new again, and visible.

One of the important talks Jim gave each year was at the Program's main fundraising event, its Medicine That Matters Gala. It was a rite of Boston's charitable springtime—a vast hotel ballroom, dresses and suits, photographers, speeches, and pledges at the end. At the 2018 version, the crowd filled every table, a throng of the dutiful and dedicated from the medical establishment and the wealthy donor class, also the wives of Boston sports stars and clergy and politicians, including Mayor Marty Walsh and Governor Charlie Baker, and many less illustrious citizens who simply wanted to attend and contribute what they could.

There were many speakers. Jim mounted the stage near the end, to applause mixed with a few whistles and cheers. He told the crowd he was nervous. "All that we do every day is really dependent on your support." This was audience flattery but true enough, given that private donations paid for shortfalls in the general budget and for some of the costs of the dental clinic. Moreover, the person in charge of Medicaid in Massachusetts, the governor, was there.

Huge photographs of half a dozen patients hung above the crowd like billboards. From the podium, Jim ordered up another giant picture on a mega-TV screen: A small, thin Black man wearing a furry hat with earflaps, seated like a trophy on top of his head. "This is a person many people here know. He used to hang in and around Boston Common. This is one of his winter hats."

Jim had met the man, Michael Henry, on a cold winter night thirty-two years before. He'd found Michael sheltering in the kiosk of the parking garage on Boston Common. His life story had a Dickensian flavor: Childhood in South Carolina, a violent father, not much schooling, flight to Boston with his mother when he was a teenager. He couldn't read or write, but he had made friends all over the affluent area between Charles Street and the State House. Many gave him money faithfully. "But he was very furtive in the night. He disappeared in the night. He didn't want people to know where he was." He would sleep on a friend's back porch in the neighboring town of Chelsea, or near his stemming spots. Lately, Jim had often found him camped in a small, half-subterranean alcove in a defunct church soon to be turned into condos on the back side of Beacon Hill. Michael had lived in various outdoor places for thirty years, and for most of that time he'd been a patient of the Street Team. Not long ago, he was diagnosed with advanced metastatic cancer. He was being treated now at Boston Medical Center. "By a wonderful team of specialists," Jim told the crowd. "Then he came to our McInnis House, where he would take his medicine, and he's doing really well now. And thanks to Beckie, our team manager, he's finally going into housing."

The story of getting Michael housed was more complicated than Jim let on. Beckie had vowed to find Michael a place but right away had discovered that he wasn't on the city's "chronic list." This meant he had no chance of getting a place in the foreseeable future. He'd been homeless and living mostly outside in Boston for three decades, but those years didn't count. To qualify as chronically homeless, you had to be seen by the outreach van and have your name recorded at least once every month for the past three years. But the outreach van had rarely encountered Michael because of his habit of nighttime furtiveness, which had helped him to stay alive on the streets.

One didn't have to be a cynic to realize these absurdities arose from the city's desperate need to limit the size of the chronic list. The mayor had promised to end the chronic form of homelessness in Boston. Over the past two years, in a nearly impossible rental market, his people had managed to find housing for almost a thousand. And yet during that time, the numbers of homeless people in the city had grown.

Beckie had persevered. She found something called the Homeless

Set-Aside Policy, created because of the restrictive nature of the chronic list. It actually set aside only a handful of apartments, but when Beckie went through Michael's records for the previous three years, she found that while his nights of homelessness hadn't occurred in a pattern that fit the formula for "chronicity," they added up to eight hundred nights, the largest number for any candidate. He had risen to the top of that special list and now was guaranteed a place.

In the interest of brevity and diplomacy, Jim spared the ballroom audience this tale of Beckie's victory over administrative obfuscation. He brought another photo up onto the huge screen: Michael in a hospital bed, smiling up at the camera. "This is him early this morning, at McInnis House, where he's still recovering, but about to go into housing."

Jim paused for a moment, then said, "So that's the good side of things."

He summoned another giant photo: A woman, no longer alive, smiled out at the crowd of faces in the ballroom. Her short sandy hair looked professionally cut and combed. She wore jeans, a T-shirt, and a stylish-looking black jacket. Her smile opened on an even row of white teeth. "This is Rebecca, but Rebecca's story is not quite as nice in the end. She was one of our very favorite women on the streets. We met her in 1992 when she was living on Long Wharf on the harbor. It's probably the nicest outdoor place to sleep—during the summer. During the winter, it's probably the coldest."

She had lived with her boyfriend and a group of other homeless couples on the waterfront, where they drank and took cocaine together, alternately helping and fighting one another. Jim had treated her for broken facial bones, an epidural hematoma, two subdural hematomas, and most significant later on, a shoulder separation.

Jim knew her to be tough: "She did not back down from *any-thing*." But she also had a gift for charming people and could make herself look presentable in spite of heavy drinking and doping and sleeping in a park. Her life began to change when death dissolved the old Long Wharf crew. She went voluntarily to detox and then to a small respite for women. In her street days, Rebecca had contracted hepatitis C, curable for some back then but only after a long and difficult regimen, so wrenching that a conscientious doctor would put the patient on suicide watch. Rebecca stuck it out, and she also managed to quit alcohol and drugs for good.

During that period, she'd also had time to plan a new life. "Rebecca was able to go quite smoothly from living by the ocean to living in an apartment. And she decided to do it on her own. She found a place in Dorchester and got a job working in a laundromat." She emptied the machines and ironed clothes. She loved to iron, she said. She never applied for rental assistance. For nine years, she paid her own way. Another photo appeared on the screen: Rebecca and her boyfriend standing in the foreground of her apartment. "This is her home. She made it into a real home."

For tidiness, Rebecca's several rooms would have met the standards of a Dutch housewife. And she had decorated the apartment, with framed mirrors, photos, reproductions of paintings, lacy curtains, end tables, lamps, two comfortable sofas, many chairs. Candlesticks stood on a glass-topped dining table, where she sat Street Team visitors down and fed them sugar cookies just out of her oven.

Jim described some of her accomplishments. She'd been the first Street Team patient to acquire a valid driver's license. Then she'd scraped up the money to buy an old car. And instead of casting her boyfriend aside, she'd housed and fed him, and she also took in and helped care for a child her boyfriend had sired.

"The problem was, one day she came to our clinic with shoulder pain . . ." This pain turned out to be the symptom of non–small cell lung cancer, in a late stage. The Street Team had missed it for a time, because the sore shoulder was the same that had been dislocated. Eventually, she was admitted to Mass General's cancer center. "She had surgery, she had radiation, and she had chemotherapy, and then she moved into immunotherapy. And despite having stage four lung cancer, she was alive four years after her diagnosis."

During her last stay at Mass General, Rebecca had her boyfriend wheel her out to Mousey Park, where she met up with a bunch of old compatriots, still homeless. "And this picture, this is the last picture I have." Up on the screen, Rebecca sat in a wheelchair in the park, smiling toward the camera and holding up the two-fingered victory sign. She was plucky and determined, given to saying, "Heaven don't want me, and Hell's afraid I'll take over." In fact, she was dying when Jim took the photo, and as he now explained to the silent crowd, she was also in the process of being evicted from the apartment she had rented, her home for nine years.

Gentrification was spreading all over Boston. Real estate developers had bought the building in the working-class neighborhood where Rebecca lived. They planned to turn the place into condos. They'd offered to sell her the apartment, for $245,000. She'd actually tried to find a way to raise the money. Beckie had managed to stave off the inevitable for a while, but a week after Jim took that last photo, Rebecca received her official eviction notice. She paged Jim. When he called her back, she was crying so hard she couldn't speak. Her boyfriend had to give Jim the news. At that moment, Jim had realized that her apartment stood for everything she'd accomplished in her life. And now it was being taken away. "She was devastated, because she had spent nine and a half years in that apartment, had paid her own rent, never had a single complaint on her record."

If Rebecca had been housed with public assistance instead of paying her rent by herself, she would have kept her housing voucher, and the city would have prevented the landlord from kicking her out until she'd found another apartment. "She made the mistake of doing everything right," Jim said.

The photo of Rebecca in her wheelchair, holding up the victory sign, remained on the giant screen. Jim said to the crowd, "The sad part of her story is that after all these years she ended up dying of her cancer one week before she was going to be evicted from her house. In the end she died *frantic* that she was going to lose housing."

The story seemed unusually painful and damning for Jim to have told on a night for diplomacy. Maybe for that reason, he closed with praise for the donors in the audience. "I think if you would ask any-body in our program, they'd tell you it's such a privilege to take care of people, to have an opportunity to know them over time and learn their stories and the courage that they live with. So I would just end this by saying thank you for letting us do this."

He paused for a moment, as if he wasn't sure he'd finished. Then with a nervous-sounding laugh, he said, "Okay," and walked off the stage.

7

_{~~~~~~~~~}

The Prism

The obvious remedy for people without a place to call home is to provide them with a home. From a distance, the problem and its solution could still be framed that simply. It was in this spirit that Jim had written, more than a decade ago, his faux prescription for a studio apartment to cure all the ailments of Boston's rough sleepers. But his views had changed in the years since Housing First arrived. Now he observed ironically, "Housing turns out to be more complicated than medicine. I wish we had a cocktail of drugs that would cure people of being homeless."

At the gala, before he made his exit, Jim told the audience, "I like to think of this problem of homelessness as a prism held up to society, and what we see refracted are the weaknesses in our health care system, our public health system, our housing system, but especially in

our welfare system, our educational system, and our legal system—
and our corrections system. If we're going to fix this problem, we have
to address the weaknesses of all those sectors." It was a bleak assessment, implying that the only cure for homelessness would be an end
to many of the country's deep, abiding flaws.

When Jim spoke at the gala in 2018, 38 million Americans were
living in what the federal government defined as poverty. For an individual, this meant a yearly income of $12,140 or less. In Boston, a
person making that little couldn't have afforded to rent much more
than a storage locker. For a family of six, the poverty line was $33,740,
about half the cost of a one-bedroom apartment in most inexpensive
Boston neighborhoods. Poverty and homelessness were clearly related.
They were not uniformly shared. Black Americans represented only
13 percent of the population, but, by one estimate, 40 percent of all
homeless people. It was easier for some groups to become homeless
than others, and for everyone trapped in it, the state of homelessness
was poverty in its most visible, savage, and lethal form.

Homelessness was fed by racism, income inequality, and a cascade
of other related forces. These included insufficient investments in public housing, as well as tax and zoning codes that had spurred wide-
spread gentrification and driven up rents. Many poor and moderately
poor Americans lived with the fear of losing housing, which can itself
harm bodies and minds as well as social relations in families. One recent study had found that "unstable housing" was accompanied by a
twofold increase in diabetic emergencies. Illnesses such as diabetes,
and all sorts of accidents and injuries, could lead to homelessness,
which itself bred other illnesses, such as PTSD—redefined by one
practitioner of street medicine as "*persistent* traumatic stress disorder."

Jim believed that housing was a right and a necessity, but only a
partial solution. For most of the Street Team's patients, and for
many rough sleepers in other locales, housing without adequate social support often led to eviction and worse. Most people who briefly
fell into homelessness could probably manage apartment life well
enough on their own. But for everyone, a dilapidated and poorly

situated place could be a poverty trap and a way back to homelessness, or the site of an early death.

A study in Boston had shown that average life expectancies varied dramatically between the city's rich and poor neighborhoods, by thirty years in one pairing. Environment could be destiny in neighborhoods where violence was common and residents lacked access to anything except fast food and convenience stores. One recently housed Street Team patient had been receiving a great deal of social support from a caseworker, and yet she was spending most of her nights and days on the streets again because she had been placed in an apartment building where someone routinely stole her electricity and Social Security checks—and because one day a neighbor had broken through the screen in her ground-floor window and stabbed her with a butter knife, leaving her with a collapsed lung. Standing outside that building one day, watching rats scurry around the garbage pails, Jim remarked, "This is where the city is placing people and claiming victory."

He had seen much better examples of housing projects. In Denver, for instance, the Colorado Coalition for the Homeless had used a time of recession to buy distressed properties and had created about 2,000 housing units, virtually ending homelessness in the city—for a while. San Francisco's public health department had done something similar, converting empty public buildings into about 1,800 apartments. Both examples had made Jim wish the Program had bought its own collection of abandoned buildings in Boston, back when they were numerous and cheap.

But just as in Boston, the cost of housing in Denver and San Francisco had risen outlandishly, while the pool of homeless candidates for housing kept growing. "They've now got a problem that's worse than when they started," Jim told me. "And this was done by brilliant people who worked really hard and solved the problem. But they had no way to stop it from getting worse over time."

On a recent trip to Southern California, Jim had been given a tour of the fifty-square-block section of Los Angeles known as Skid Row, where about two thousand people were living on pavement in terrible squalor. Tens of thousands more were living under freeways and beside riverbeds in the greater Los Angeles area. When he returned, Jim told the Street Team: "L.A. makes me feel like we're playing in a bathtub here in Boston. The dimension of the problem is beyond all imagination. Tents and encampments all over the place. L.A. would have to create housing for at least sixty-six thousand."

In 2016, the city of Los Angeles had conceived an ambitious new project—to develop or acquire, in the course of ten years, 10,000 units of housing for homeless people. To pay for this, they had floated a $1.2 billion bond, which would be used to leverage about $2.8 billion more from private and other public sources. In 2022, the city controller reported "mixed results." Housing was being created, but the cost for each unit was rising "to staggering heights"—on average, to more than $600,000 per unit.

Jim was sometimes asked what single thing he'd do to end homelessness. On one of those occasions, he cited large population studies about the tight connection between health and educational status. If he had the power, he said, he'd pay public school teachers $200,000 a year and maybe thirty years later homelessness would become a rarity. Maybe what he called "the faucet" would be turned off. More often, he spoke of a more general solution—"What we need is a new war on poverty."

In Los Angeles and many other locales, the chasm was widening between those who could afford the necessities of life and those left in poverty. But the problem of homelessness had become too large, too visible, too offensive to be ignored. And it was clear that public support for remedies could be marshaled. Seventy percent of voters in Los Angeles had approved that $1.2 billion bond, and the voters of Los Angeles County had also approved an increase in their sales tax, to finance support services for the newly housed. Other promising projects were underway in Los Angeles and in many other regions and cities, and more were being planned: The conversion of hotels, motels, and vacant apartment buildings into decent low-income housing, as well as programs providing rental assistance and job training and a large menu of other support services. In 2021, California's governor had signed a bill to spend $12 billion to combat homelessness throughout the state.

Jim especially admired the work of an old friend named Rosanne Haggerty. In New York City, back in the early 1990s, she had led a successful effort to transform a run-down hotel in Times Square into apartments for poor and homeless residents of the neighborhood—a building with nicely renovated rooms and also a gallery of offices where residents could get haircuts and help in arranging doctors' appointments and applying for Social Security. Jim told me that when he first visited the place, he thought he might like to live there himself.

Since then, Rosanne had founded an organization called Community Solutions to work on a much grander scale. In 2010, it had launched the 100,000 Homes Campaign, with a staff of about a dozen who worked to help about 190 different communities find housing for chronically and extremely vulnerable homeless people. The organization didn't contribute money, only expertise. An assessment by the Urban Institute confirmed that the project had helped to get 105,580 people housed. Since then, Community Solutions had set out to help willing cities and counties achieve "functional zero"—defined as "a future where homelessness is rare overall, and brief when it occurs."

For Rosanne, much of the overall problem lay with fragmentation among social service agencies, both public and private. Her favorite slide displayed in sequence the forty-two different steps that six agencies and a landlord had to complete to get one homeless veteran housed in Long Beach, California. Part of the cure, Rosanne believed, lay in creating systems dedicated to solving each community's issues. All the relevant agencies in a city or region would be represented in a single command center. The coalition would share responsibility for each homeless individual within its jurisdiction, making sure that each person was known by name, with the causes of their homelessness diagnosed and solutions tailored to each. The system would constantly improve itself through an "iterative cycle"—tackling a problem, studying the results, then doing the job better.

Rosanne described the strategy as "a public health approach—science-based, data-driven, collaborative, prevention-oriented." By 2018 the organization was assisting dozens of cities and counties, with measurable success. In 2021, the MacArthur Foundation gave the group $100 million, to accelerate its work.

Jim emphatically agreed with Rosanne when she said that the term "homelessness" failed to capture the complexity of the problem. Her strategy reminded him of the early days of Boston's AIDS epidemic, when the disparate branches of medicine finally began to work together and each sick patient was given a case manager with the power to negotiate all the systems of care. He agreed with what seemed like her fundamental goal: "Each person we see in the shelters and out on the streets, somebody has to own responsibility for knowing that person and getting them housed." He imagined that was possible now in many American communities. But he had his doubts when it came to the most burdened places, such as New York and Los Angeles.

Rosanne thought that Boston's problem was not so large that it couldn't be solved, and rather quickly, if only the local government would get its act together. Jim wished he believed that. "You could change all the zoning laws in Boston right now, and create a more coherent system, and because of the costs it would still take us years and years and years to build enough affordable housing for everyone who needs it." Just to house the current chronically homeless population, the city would have to find 1,000 units right away, he figured, and it would need to come up with another 400 to 500 units per year just to keep up with the growth of homelessness, which at the moment seemed inexorable.

Jim remembered Barbara McInnis telling him, "We're way down on the solution scale." He found that if he thought hard for too long about the dimensions of homelessness and all the forces ranged against great progress, he grew hungry for the clinic, his colleagues, his patients. "I don't get despairing," he told me. "But it's much easier to just go take care of people." For all its limitations, that work felt full and rich and edifying, and real.

Rosanne Haggerty told me, "Jim is doing exactly what he should." Medicine alone couldn't begin to solve homelessness, she said. "This is really about accountability, system design, performance. Until that's fixed, Jim is basically standing at the bottom of a cliff, trying to save people."

VII

The Night Watchman

1

~~~~~~~~~~~

The Worry List

Jim went to Australia for two weeks of November 2018. He lectured for the cause, toured some of the country's homeless facilities, and saw old friends. He got back in time for Monday meeting in the library. When Beckie asked her weekly question—"Who are we worried about?"—Kevin said without a pause, "I'm worried about Tony Columbo."

"What's going on with him?" Jim asked.

"One day he's appropriate, and another he's wildly hyped up," Mike said. He'd been trying to work with Tony, telling him to stop worrying about everyone else and start taking care of himself—Mike's gentle way of saying that Tony had to deal with his own drug problem. So far the coaching hadn't taken. "He was hyper all last Thursday and into the night," Mike went on. "K2 don't do that. It's more like cocaine or meth. He was all by himself, rolling around in a wheel-chair upstairs, self-dialoguing by the front desk."

"That's unusual," said Jim. "He usually has someone with him."

Kevin added, speaking to Jim: "The other piece was, he had a real hard time interacting with anyone else on the team while you were gone."

Some months ago Tony had exclaimed to Jim—with an under-tone of complaint—"You don't stay in Massachusetts for more than a week!" Several of Tony's other abrupt declines had begun when Jim went off on a trip. But the issue at the moment was what to do for Tony. Kevin suggested a psychiatric ward. Jim wanted him to detox at McInnis House. Jim's opinion amounted to a final decision, framed as a suggestion, in the style of language known to some as "Jim." And then the team went on, adding names to the week's special worry list.

• • •

Six months had passed since the internecine squabble that led to one patient killing another and Tony's wild grief. Since then, his pattern had held—lengthy sojourns at McInnis House, followed by quick exits, by disappearances, and finally by resurfacings. He would come out of the dark world of alleys into the lights of the van or into the waiting room of Mass General or the lobby of Seven-Eighty, with the filth of the city under his fingernails and on his clothes and with what Jim called a "cocaine-depleted" look on his face, as if he were trudg-ing back to McInnis House from a battle zone. Then he would quickly revive.

But the intervals between the stages of this pattern were growing shorter—the same pattern but more tightly woven. Jim remarked on the change: "He's becoming a full-time job, you know?"

Tony's next several weeks began with an ungovernable fear that he was being pursued by the drug dealer Deuce and his henchmen, which drove him to the Mass General ER, and from there to one of the small, for-profit mental hospitals that specialized in Medicaid patients—Tony called the place "Planet Zerk." A return to McInnis

House followed, where the usual sequence got squeezed into less than a week: Twenty-four hours of sleep, followed by the resumption of his self-appointed duties—"Jim, they're stealin' Band-Aids and bacitracin from the exam rooms. I'm gonna put a stop to it"—then a sudden AMA departure in the night, because he believed that Deuce had people inside plotting against him. Two days later, Jim found him on the upswing, preventing an incipient knife fight between two other patients in Mousey Park, and the next day Tony came to Street Clinic and for the first time in weeks surrendered a urine sample, which was clean of all of his favorite narcotics. And then two nights later, he lay inside Mass General's Acute Psychiatry Service, strapped to a gurney, in florid, thrashing paranoia. He was about to be sent back to Planet Zerk when Jim intervened.

It was a Sunday, the day when McInnis House was short-staffed and patients weren't usually admitted. Over the phone a weary-sounding nurse told Jim that they couldn't admit Tony today.

"Yes, we're going to take him," Jim said, violating his near-sacred rule against overtly pulling rank, then softening his tone—saying he'd be glad to do the admissions exam if she was too busy.

Tony spent a month in the respite, but the death of yet another friend had inspired a new, dark fantasy—that people who got close to him were bound to die. He felt he had to leave the respite for fear of having the same fatal effect on others, especially on Jim. He said he was going to camp in some tunnels in another town, where he'd be safe.

A week later, Tony was lying on a gurney in a room at the Mass General emergency department. Jim stood looking down at him under fluorescent light. They made a contrast of colors—Jim's ruddy face, silver hair, cheerful necktie, set against the big dark figure under white sheets. The gurney was just big enough to accommodate Tony. He looked like a cyborg, the human part bristling with tubes and wires, the machine part all beeping, blinking animation. "How you feelin'?" asked Jim.

Tony's voice came from somewhere deep and far away. "Hurts."

"Yeah. You got some broken ribs here." Actually there were three, one displaced, which usually signifies a powerful blow. Probably a baseball bat, Jim had said on the way over. "I'm not even gonna ask you what happened," he said to Tony.

"The streets, the wonderful streets," Tony murmured.

He had been found on Blossom Street near the Wyndham hotel, a short ambulance ride from the hospital. He had been lying in a pool of blood, with a deep knife wound in his right thigh. The wound had required surgery. Jim lifted the sheet and examined the result. "This looks like they did a great job. It's all sewn up." And then, after saying that McInnis House would be ready for him when the hospital let him go, Jim said, "Tony, we're going to let you rest. I'm going to peek in on you tomorrow, to be sure you're okay. Is there anything you need right now?"

"Get me a life. Or a gun." Tony laughed a little, then winced.

Jim made his uncertain, hostess-like chuckle. "Let's try the life."

2

~~~~~~~~~~~~~

Button-Down-Shirt Moments

One way to avoid despair in street medicine is to redefine success, as the recovery coach, Mike, would do. Trying to help patients free themselves from the relapsing illnesses of addiction—his job seemed designed for despair. But he had buoyancy. "I measure sobriety in hours," he'd say. The former fisherman Karl had failed to stay housed many times, but when he was about to be given another chance, Mike declared, practically shouting by the end, "I think he might make it this time. You know why? He asked me for button-down shirts. He might not stay sober, but he might learn to manage and not be on the streets living in his own shit and piss. Button-down shirts! No one ever asked me for that! It's a first! It's a frickin' sign! For now I have a saying: I'm havin' a button-down-shirt moment!"

• • •

In early summer, Beckie found a place for Angie, the white-haired patient who, like Rebecca, had been terrified at the prospect of going back to the streets. Her new place was a subsidized apartment in a town north of Boston. The building looked like a worn motel, made of flaking concrete and weathered aluminum, but there was a T station nearby, and sea air and cries of gulls outside Angie's windows, and unlike the virtual janitor's closet from which she'd been evicted, this apartment had its own bathroom, bedroom, living room, even a real kitchen where her boyfriend could produce the Puerto Rican cuisine that she loved. On top of that, she had acquired a family.

She told Jim the story: "I was in the grocery, shopping, and the phone rang and I'm like, 'Yeah? Who's this?' And this voice said, 'Are you my mother?'" Angie paused to wipe her eyes. "It was my daughter! She thought I was dead." Angie said she'd visited her daughter and met her grandson. "It was beauty-ful. He's doing great! And my daughter's doing excellent. She's gotten married. So I got a son-in-law!"

• • •

Jim still handed down lore from time to time at meetings: "A quiz. What's wrong with drinking Listerine?" He answered with this story: Back in 1998 and '99, a series of deaths on the street had made headlines. The Department of Public Health had asked the Program to investigate. None of the victims had died from Listerine, but all except for one had drunk it regularly. "Bars and package stores were closed on Sundays then," Jim explained. "But Listerine you could always buy, or steal. The yellow kind is twenty-seven percent alcohol."

Listerine came up periodically, in reports on patients. A man had been admitted to the ER at 10:00 A.M., had been discharged at 1:00 P.M., then had come to see Katy, the nurse practitioner, at 3:30. He was inebriated, Katy told the team.

On what? Jim asked.

She smiled. "He smelled very fresh."

. . .

Back in the spring at the gala, Jim had shown the audience a giant photograph of Michael, the small Black man who had spent decades living outside and was being treated for metastatic cancer. Jim had said that Michael was soon to be housed, and in the fall the promise was finally fulfilled. The place Beckie had found for him was a one-bedroom studio in a well-appointed building. Jim and I visited him there. Michael already had a bowl of milk for his cat sitting on the kitchen floor and framed pictures on the apartment's freshly painted walls. "Going to the furniture bank with him was like the highlight of my year," Beckie had said.

Michael asked Jim and me to help him straighten out his rug. Three decades outside, and already he seemed domesticated. Jim took another picture of him there—Michael with his cat in his arms and wearing a huge grin.

On the way out, Jim said, "Pretty good, huh? There are gifts. And his prostate cancer's in remission."

3

~~~~~~~~~~~

The Hug

In midsummer, Jim was arraigned before the board for "unprofessional" gift-giving. It was a small humiliation, foretold on a Friday in June when, in Finagle a Bagel, a basso profundo had resounded over the chattering voices, the clashing tableware: "Is Dr. O'Connell here? Dr. O'Connell?"

A tall Black man stood in the center of the breakfast place, scanning the room.

"I'm Dr. O'Connell," said Jim.

The man strode up to our table. "I'm John Jones of the U.S. Army retired, and I need a few dollars to get back to Brockton."

Jim stared up at him, eyes narrowing, lips pursed. He didn't usually give money to strangers, and never on rounds or during van rides. But hadn't he treated this Mr. Jones a year or two ago, for extremely swollen feet? Mr. Jones confirmed it. Jim pulled a folded ten from his shirt pocket, handed it to the veteran, and told him to be mindful of his feet.

Mr. Jones thanked him, then offered some advice of his own. "Go the back way out, because they're all lined up." He meant that the people in Mousey Park were awaiting Jim and his donations.

The old soldier departed. John Cotrone lifted his eyebrows, smothered a grin, and said through his beard, "Hey, Jim, can I have your Platinum Card? So I can get home?"

Jim laughed. "Go away, John."

Later, recalling this incident, Jim said it was a sign that things had gotten out of hand in the park, and it was probably time to stop dispensing gifts of money there. In August, an employee who was leaving had complained to the board about Jim's largesse: Because Jim gave money to patients, many would vie angrily for the chance to be seen by him and not the other providers—and this had created a "hostile work environment" at Thursday Street Clinic.

The board investigated and cleared Jim of the charge. But they asked him to stop his long practice, even though some among them confessed that they, too, gave homeless people money. Jim understood their worry. He said he would stop, and he did. But even without the promise of cash, many patients at Thursday clinic still insisted on seeing Jim and no one else. And the clinic continued to run as always, just this side of chaos.

When Jim had told him about the prohibition, Tony had made up a story and spread it among the Mousey Park crew: "Some guy OD'd. Second time he OD'd was at Mass General. The doc there said, 'How can you OD two days in a row, where do you get the money?' And he said, 'Oh, I met Dr. Jim O'Connell, he threw money in my pocket,' and they had a big meetin', and they went back to Jim, and Jim felt disgraced. So Jim can't give out money anymore."

When Jim heard of this, he put his head in his hands. "Oh God."

But Tony was sure his strategy had worked. "So I set it up, and now it's not so many people askin' him for money when he walks through the park."

• • •

Soon after Christmas, before leaving for vacation, Jim went upstairs to McInnis House and conferred with Tony about patients—which ones to keep an eye on, which ones would need cheering up over the holiday. This seemed like normal procedure by now, leaving Tony in charge of the milieu when he was in his Dr. Jekyll phase in McInnis House. Jim wished him a Merry Christmas and offered his hand. Tony pulled him into a hug instead, something he'd never done before.

Then Tony headed to his room, and Jim started toward the elevators, but as often happened, he got waylaid by another patient, then another. On the way out at last, he remembered that he was supposed to give Tony a message about his prescriptions. The door to Tony's room was ajar. Jim looked in around the jamb and saw Tony in distress. The overhead lights were on. Tony sat on the edge of his bed, facing a quarter turn away from the door, head bowed over his knees, his shoulders heaving.

In the past, Tony's weeping fits had been mixed with alcohol, cocaine, and exhaustion, and they had been unrestrained. This was different. Emotion expressed privately always has the most authentic air. And this was clearly a scene that no one, Jim least of all, was supposed to witness. He backed out of the room.

• • •

McInnis House was mostly financed by Medicaid, which required that a patient's stay be medically justified. Although the Program had made a strict policy never to bill Medicaid improperly, it had long ago resolved that its respite would aim first to serve the needs of homeless people and worry about revenue afterward. Sometimes a patient no longer needed medical care but seemed too fragile to survive on the streets. Jim and others would search for an alternative, such as a nursing home, while the patient stayed on at McInnis House and the Program paid the costs. Some patients had stayed for six months, others

for a year. Three years was the record, set by an undocumented im-
migrant who had been paralyzed by a bullet wound.

Jim had managed to keep Tony at McInnis House for the first two
months of the previous winter. When he couldn't justify an extension,
he'd secured a room for Tony at the Program's "step-down" respite,
used mainly for patients in sub-acute condition, recovering from cancer or surgery. But the place didn't have enough social life for Tony to
direct. He turned down the room and went back to the streets.

One morning in March, I found Jim in his office at Seven-Eighty,
poring over Tony's medical record. It contained the history of all his
drug tests since he'd first appeared at the Street Team's door. Jim
paraphrased the findings aloud: "Cocaine in almost every urine he's
ever given. And often marijuana. Also Suboxone. Never street opiates.
His creatinine's consistently high, so are his kidneys under stress? His
thyroid is under, so his thyroid-stimulating hormone is high, consistently. Why is that? What am I missing? He got an MRI on his back
three months ago: 'A severe displacement of vertebrae in the lower
back.' So he has lots of reasons for being in pain." Jim looked away
from his computer screen and smiled. "It's terrible to say, but I'm kind
of thrilled about all these mysteries. So I can keep him inside."

More recently, Jim had remarked, "I think if Tony had a studio
apartment downtown, he'd be fine." This was optimistic even by Jim's
standards. Tony might well fail at housing. He was too gregarious; his
many friends would probably get him evicted. On the other hand,
more improbable candidates than Tony had gone into apartments
and thrived. Suppose Tony got housed and started taking Ritalin and
lithium faithfully, as he'd done during several stays at McInnis? He
might end up employable, maybe even a candidate for the official
position of New Milieu Director.

That was the stuff of daydreams, though. It would be enough if an
apartment allowed Tony to survive. But could housing be arranged?

4

The Law of Pariahs

L ike all fifty states and Washington, D.C., Massachusetts main-
tained a classification and registration system to track and control convicted sex offenders once they got out of jail. Lawsuits
challenging these measures had reached courts of every level. The
most recent Supreme Court case had tested the Alaska Sex Offender
Registration Act (ASORA), which required sex offenders to present
themselves regularly to the police after being released from prison.
Alaska's act also specified that certain information about offenders be
published on the internet. The central issue in the plaintiff's case was
Article 1, Section 9, Clause 3 of the U.S. Constitution, which states:
"No . . . ex post facto Law shall be passed." In the court's recent inter-
pretations, this clause forbade legislatures from adding punishments
for crimes already committed and adjudicated. The Alaska case

turned on what seemed like a simple question: Did Alaska's law prescribe a civil procedure to protect the public from sex offenders? Or
was it punitive in nature?

A majority of the court decided that ASORA didn't amount to
punishment and upheld the statute. The concurring opinion by Justice Clarence Thomas is hard to read without coming to the opposite
conclusion—that the statute was indeed punitive. Thomas wrote: "In
this case, ASORA does not specify a means of making registry information available to the public. It states only that '[i]nformation about
a sex offender . . . that is contained in the central registry . . . is confidential and not subject to public disclosure except as to the sex offender's . . . name, aliases, address, photograph, physical description,
description of motor vehicles, license numbers of motor vehicles, and
vehicle identification numbers of motor vehicles, place of employment, date of birth, crime for which convicted, date of conviction,
place and court of conviction, length and conditions of sentence, and
a statement as to whether the offender . . . is in compliance with requirements of AS 12.63 or cannot be located.'"

What was left to be *publicly disclosed*? Imposing ASORA's conditions
represented a nearly complete invasion of privacy. In her dissent from
the verdict, Justice Ruth Bader Ginsburg wrote: "Alaska's Act imposes
onerous and intrusive obligations on convicted sex offenders; and it
exposes registrants, through aggressive public notification of their
crimes, to profound humiliation and community-wide ostracism."

Massachusetts's registration law unquestionably inflicted punishment on Tony. He had served the full eighteen years of his sentence,
and when he got out, his photograph and the legal title of his crime
("attempted rape") had been published on the internet for anyone to
see, including every potential employer or landlord. He was also required to register with the Boston Police Department every month.
These requirements weren't imposed in his sentence, but the registration law had the effect, as Jim had said, of making Tony a pariah and
condemning him to homelessness. His status as a level-three sex offender
disqualified him from all federally subsidized housing opportunities

and job-training programs. Beckie could occasionally get a state-financed housing voucher for a level-three, but it would grant Tony only a rent subsidy that fell below the market rate for anything like a decent studio apartment in Boston. And a landlord could refuse him for any reason, including his level-three status.

At the moment, Tony didn't even qualify for a state voucher. He had entered the bureaucratic labyrinth of poor people's housing in Boston. Like BJ, he had fallen off the city's chronic list because he had spent more than a month of consecutive nights off the streets, inside McInnis House. He was also disqualified because he had outstanding arrest warrants for failing to register as a sex offender—not once, but off and on for several years, and recently for several months in a row.

These failures were indefensible but easy to understand. It is hard for anyone living on the streets to keep track of dates. When Tony missed one appointment for registering, he would usually miss the next, because he didn't dare go to the police station for fear of being arrested and sent back to jail. Potential penalties for failing to register were severe: Six months to a year in jail for a first offense and a minimum of five years for a subsequent offense. He'd had a taste of this, of course, when in his first months out of prison he had failed to register twice and was sent back to jail for nearly a year. Since then, he'd been arrested a few times for failing to register. The courts had continued the cases and let him go each time, once on bail and at others on his own recognizance. But court dates on the charges loomed. He lived in increasing danger of more years in jail, which would be more perilous for him now than in the past because his offense would be published and easily found by fellow inmates in the era of ubiquitous computers.

If Tony hadn't been homeless, he could have registered much more easily. A level-three who was housed had to report only once a year. But it was hard for a level-three to get housed in the first place, because he was a level-three. Massachusetts law allowed a person in Tony's position to apply for a reduction in his level, but this essentially required that he become a model citizen first—clean and sober, and "offense-free" for five years, among other things. Those were near-insuperable obstacles for many people living on the streets. Even if a rough sleeper didn't commit serious crimes, he couldn't avoid being cited for trespassing or, a common charge, public urination. To get his level reduced, Tony would probably have to get housed. That is, he'd have to be housed in order to get housed.

Tony didn't seem likely to commit a sex crime now. He hadn't sexually assaulted anyone in prison, at least not according to his old friend from Shirley Max. There was nothing in his record to suggest that he'd been charged with a sexual crime after prison. The only such crime recorded in his record was the charge of "attempted rape," for which he'd served eighteen years. His sentence might have been shorter if he'd been charged with second-degree murder. Certainly, he would have been better off now. Moreover, it was hard to see how it made the city safer to keep a former sex offender in a state of home-lessness and roaming the streets.

To have a chance of getting him into a studio apartment, Beckie had to obtain the special housing voucher for level-threes and then find a willing landlord. The first step was to get him back on the chronic list. This was easy to do and already under way—he'd just have to sleep outside at least one night a month and make sure the van saw him. Step two for getting the voucher would be much harder. He had to stop acquiring new arrest warrants, which meant he had to start going faithfully, every month, to the downtown police station, where he would declare himself a sex offender once again. Most dif-ficult of all, he had to clear away the arrest warrants he'd already ac-cumulated for failing to register.

Beckie and Jim divided the task. She'd work on the housing. Jim would try to get him right with the law.

5

In Boston Municipal Court

The campaign began in 2019. On a warm, sunny morning in April, Jim picked Tony up at Seven-Eighty and drove him to court. The traffic was thick. Tony stared out the windshield. He murmured, "I'm so nervous about today."

"I know, I know," said Jim. "We'll get through this."

Tony said he hoped his case would be continued.

"No! I want your warrants cleared *today*," Jim said. He'd make it clear to the judge that if Tony got sent to jail, he'd lose his chance at housing, the first chance he'd had in years. Jim made it sound as if housing lay much nearer than it did, and his tone had the intended effect.

Tony stared out the window silently for a while longer, then said,

"Jim, I get my apartment and stuff, I want to come and like clean for the building, McInnis."

"Okay."

"In the daytime. Keep me busy. For free."

Jim started to speak, but Tony went on, in an unusually soft voice, "Yeah, give me something to do. Get cleaned up. Stay away from all the stuff. I'm gonna try to get off everything. Even Suboxone. I'm down to two a day now." I had the impression he was talking to himself, from within a daydream. Then the courthouse hove into view.

The building was twenty years old, a contemporary-looking version of the American church of the law, expensive and imposing, made of marble and granite and extravagantly spacious—it had an atrium five stories tall. It asserted the grandeur of the law, a necessary message because the law's authority rests unsteadily on compliance, which rests on fear, on the belief that if one commits a crime, punishment inexorably follows.

Tony knew the courthouse well, the passage through the metal detector, the many uniforms accessorized with guns, the ranks of elevators, the rules. Get here on time. Take your hat off when you enter. When you find the courtroom you're assigned, claim a seat among the other defendants, and stand up when the judge comes in. Then sit down and wait, and wait some more, on the hard wooden benches with their right-angled backs, handsome-looking but painful to occupy. And don't complain.

Two months earlier, Tony had been arrested for failing to register and was brought to one of these courtrooms in handcuffs. But he got lucky with a judge who, upon hearing that Tony was a patient of Jim's, announced that Dr. O'Connell was a saint and released Tony on his own recognizance. Today's judge was just as promising. After she entered and everyone rose and sat again, Jim whispered to Tony, "We're old friends. She's tough as nails, but she has a heart."

When the clerk called his name and docket number, Tony limped slowly to the defendant's spot at the railing, where there was a microphone. He had arrived on time, but his lawyer wasn't there. She was in the next courtroom, the judge said. As soon as she came in, the judge would call Tony again. But when Tony's public defender appeared a while later—a middle-aged woman in a trench coat—another case was in progress. She merely nodded to Tony, then left again. And for the next two hours, you could see why Hamlet included "the law's delay" among good reasons for killing oneself. Other cases came and went. Defendants were called who hadn't shown up. ("A warrant will be issued," said the judge.) A man in shackles was brought in from a side door for dealing drugs in prison. A man on probation wanted permission to travel to Canada. People were numbered and named, a familiar litany of modern human failings intoned—drug trafficking; assault and battery with a dangerous weapon (to wit, a shod foot); possession of a Class B substance; driving without a license. Many cases were continued and a very few resolved.

A tower of manila folders sat on the prosecutor's desk, and the public defenders carried armloads of them—a problem on display. No one could properly handle those stacks and armloads of cases in a session. This court and others that dealt mainly with the problems of the poor were perhaps the only places in America where there weren't enough lawyers. A few defendants had hired their own lawyers, who didn't have four or five other cases spread among various courtrooms, and therefore were on hand when their clients were called. Sitting there waiting, it was hard not to feel that this was just one of many ways to put people like Tony in their place.

Waiting on that bench with nothing else to do, I wondered when Tony's case would be heard. I had managed to worry the question into suspenseful form. It was nearly lunchtime when Tony's lawyer's duties and the court's business finally coincided. Tony stood silently at the railing while the prosecutor and Tony's lawyer and the judge hashed things out. Early in their colloquy, the judge looked over the documents, saying, "So, I take it there are two matters on which the Commonwealth has filed a motion. Failure to register as a sex offender . . ." I was sitting beside Jim on the bench. I could sense him stiffening. He glanced at Tony, a doctor worried for his patient. Tony's salt-and-pepper beard was trimmed. He wore the usual casserole of extra-large clothing, freshly laundered, that Julie had found—blue hospital scrubs for pants, a hooded sweatshirt, a light camouflage hunting jacket. He looked about as well-groomed as everyone else who couldn't afford their own attorney. But standing at the rail before the judge, he looked smaller than usual, stooped, his injured right knee bent dramatically, eyes straight ahead.

"Please report whether Mr. Columbo is currently registered as a sex offender," said the judge to the prosecutor. I looked at Tony. I thought he must feel eyes on his back from the gallery and imagine people thinking, "Ohhh, one of *those*."

Up at the judge's bench, the worst outcome was averted. Instead of the case being bumped up to Superior Court, where he would have been tried for repeated offenses, Tony would have to face only one charge here in District Court. But not today. He would have to come back for a pretrial hearing and arraignment in a month. The long morning had amounted only to a half step in getting Tony a housing voucher.

But he seemed cheered up for now. On the way to the parking garage, he moved rather nimbly on his wounded knee—flooded, I imagined, with the analgesic of the fresh spring air, of relief from bruised buttocks and the boring, routine terror of the law.

• • •

Beckie had made progress. She'd negotiated the maze of housing regulations and had gotten Tony back on the city's chronic list so he would be eligible for a voucher once Jim got his warrants cleared away.

But then Tony fell into one of his troughs. Beckie had arranged for him to meet a housing agent, but Tony didn't show up. Doing his part, Jim tried to drive Tony to the police station to register, but Tony climbed into the car and begged Jim to take him to get a new ID instead, and after Jim did that, Tony refused to go through the ritual of registering. He also declared that he was infested with bugs again. Was he taking meth? The symptoms fit. Tony who had for so long said he hated meth, Tony who had vividly described how it turned people into monsters, Tony who had risked his life—or so he thought—to keep Deuce from selling the drug near Seven-Eighty.

A few days later, Jim was called to the Mass General ER, where he found Tony with minor abrasions on his forehead. He said he'd been hit last night by a woman wielding a cane. "She apologized after. She thought I was someone else."

Much worse than the cane, Tony had begun to suffer acute urinary retention—a liter and a half of fluid had been drained from his bladder. He seemed to have recovered and was discharged. But that same evening, Jim was summoned to the ER again, where he found Tony on a gurney, writhing and shouting. The staff had given him a bunch of pain meds, but he was still in agony. The attending physician said it must be psychosomatic. Jim replied, with elaborate politeness, that he had seen this before in several patients, during the crack cocaine epidemic of the 1990s—an anticholinergic response to the drug Tony must have taken, all his muscles in contraction, causing acute urinary retention and pain everywhere, "a total body charley horse." Jim told the attending, "It sounds crazy, but he needs Benadryl." The attending shrugged, as if to say, "He's your patient," and walked away, and—to the delight of Julie, who in her four years with Jim had never before seen him actually doctoring—Benadryl worked almost at once.

• • •

Tony was supposed to meet Jim at Mousey Park early on the morning of his next court appearance, in May. But driving down Cambridge Street, Jim spotted a figure on the other side of the road, across from the park—a man bending over a storm sewer at the mouth of a side street. He had a metal pole in his hands. A wheelchair laden with stuff sat behind him.

"That's not Tony, is it?"

Jim pulled a U-turn, peering out the windshield. "Oh my God, he's a mess."

It was a warm morning, but a heavy coat and a gray Pine Street blanket were draped over the wheelchair, which had TUFTS branded on its back, apparently the latest hospital on Tony's itinerary. The thing in his hands turned out to be the wheelchair's pole for holding pouches of intravenous fluid. Tony had removed it to use as a fishing pole. He was limping around the storm drain, staring down, then sticking the pole through the grate. In a calmer time, he had described his procedure: "I get a stick. A long stick. You put gum on the end, or you can put like tape inside out. But you'd be surprised. Hundred-dollar bills will drop down there."

In the car, Jim sat for a moment watching Tony circle the storm drain. Then he got out and greeted Tony as if nothing were wrong— "How are *you*?" Then he reminded Tony that he had to go to court today, if he didn't want to go to jail.

"Jim, puttin' me in jail would be a favor," Tony said. "But it's not gonna happen, because God knows that."

Tony was wearing the same clothes he'd been in all week, infused with that smell of hangover and fermentation. On the way to the courthouse, the wheelchair and cash-fishing pole jammed into the back of Jim's car, Tony darted among preoccupations, talking very fast. Everyone he got close to would die, and Jim might be next: "I love youse to death. Something will happen. Karma. I don't know." And also the self-pity that often erupted when he was in a manic state: "In five years I haven't fucking jaywalked. Worse, worse, worse. Not one good thing happened to me in the last month. I fall asleep and get robbed. A rainstorm, I got soaked. So I took my sneakers off. Four fucking hours later I wake up and my sneakers are gone. I'm predicting bad things." At the metal detector, it took him two tries to get his pockets emptied and make it past the security guards.

When he limped up to the courtroom door, a Black man in a wheelchair called to him. It was Isaac, his friend from prison, the man who had praised Tony's strength and generosity. He'd come to court to settle some old charge. He had a beatific face. He stared up at Tony and said, "Look me in the eye." Then: "The street's gonna kill you, Tony."

Tony murmured something about how all his urines had been clean. But he kept looking down and away from his old friend, who said gently, "Don't bullshit me, Tony."

When Tony left for the bathroom, Isaac said to Jim, "You know, he's a good guy. We spent a lot of time together."

Court was much the same as it had been back in April. A different judge, but the same long wait. In a scolding tone, the judge told Tony's lawyer, her arms full of case files, to talk to the prosecutor and get Tony's case resolved today. But to get the charges dropped, Tony's lawyer needed documents showing that he had been in McInnis House or Mass General at some of those times in the past when he had failed to register, and Jim didn't have those records, because he hadn't been asked for them. So the case was continued for two months—to the middle of July. Tony left relieved that he hadn't been arrested. Jim was overtly angry: "It's an arcane system. I can't understand it. Not *one thing* was resolved all morning. It's a colossal waste of everyone's time. In a medical system you would have the medical records. Here there are none of the necessary records. It's like running in place and getting nowhere."

6

Childhood

I didn't see Tony for a while that spring, but I got dispatches from Jim. On occasion his emails were gloomy. This seemed unusual, though maybe the shadows had been there all along, camouflaged by his cheery manner, by what he called "my never-ending journey to see the good side of things." One report was alarming: The Mass General lab had found fentanyl in Tony's most recent urine sample.

But soon afterward, Tony seemed to enter his revival stage. He showed up along with forty-three others at the annual memorial service, held as usual in Mousey Park, this year on the eve of summer. Half of the congregation were Street Team patients, including BJ in his electric wheelchair. Tony was still taking care of him most nights. Tony had told Jim once again that he couldn't help respecting BJ, because his tolerance for alcohol was superhuman. It was a morning of warm rain. Flowers surrounded the linden tree again, chrysanthemums this time, with seashells scattered among them. The death count was eighteen, far lower than the year before. Jim gave a short speech, a eulogy both for the dead and for the park itself, which was slated for demolition. "This sacred place," he said, "which is to vanish in the next two to four years, a casualty of Mass General's continuing expansion." Reverend Tina had moved on to another parish and had been replaced by Reverend Laura. Tony, solemn-faced, held an umbrella over her as she spoke, and when the recitation of the year's dead began, he bowed his head and offered up a name, but I couldn't make it out, his voice was so soft and the traffic noise so loud.

Soon afterward, still on the upswing, Tony kept an old promise and gave Jim a tour of the North End, a tour of his youth. It began with a stroll down Hanover Street to Prado park, Tony reciting the story of his first experience with murder: "This is where the dude got shot. Hey, the kid is against that wall, and he drops, just like a sacka patatahs. That's how he described it, the shooter. Jackie. That's what he said. I dropped the groceries and took off."

Jim made his eyes big. *"Wooo!"* he exclaimed.

"Hey, there's still—to this day, Jim—bodies in the cellars here."

American history was also on Tony's agenda. In the park, he stopped before a bronze Paul Revere mounted on a horse, the steeple of the lovely Old North Church rising over the hero's cocked hat: "The steeple wit the window in it? That's where he hung the lanterns. One if by land, two if by sea." And eventually a quiz: "That's where Paul Revere hung the lanterns. One if by land, two if by sea. Do you know what they did? Was it by land or by sea that they came?" He answered before Jim had a chance: "They came by sea."

At every stop, Jim let out his sincerest laugh, sudden and high-pitched. Attractions included Copp's Hill Burying Ground and the resealed mausoleums that Tony's friends had broken into with dynamite. The site of the Brinks robbery, memorialized in film. The rooftop from which, back in Tony's day, the body of a Peeping Tom was hung—a warning to pedophiles. Tony led the way to the top of his old street: "There'd be a hundred ladies leaning out the windows. So this would be like, there wouldn't be tourists and stuff, just us kids running in the street and if you did something wrong, your mother a street over, she'd know right away."

There were only a few figures in the windows now, among them an elderly woman leaning out just above street level, her forearms resting on a pillow that must have been custom-made to fit the sill. Tony called to her: "Do you remember the dog Verrazano? Remember, German shepherd Verrazano?" She nodded. He knew her name, she recognized his. Jim gazed from a little distance, watching, thinking: What a village this place must have been. Tony stood below the window, holding the old woman's hand. "I used to know your brother. Has he passed away, too? I remember Jeannette moved here, years and years ago. Yeah, wow. I'm looking atchya, I'm like, it's just like a fairy tale, yeah, we used to play cards, Christine's house on Sadday night, me, Connie, Josey, and their little brothers and stuff." It went on like this for maybe fifteen minutes, Tony asking after people from the neighborhood—Stevie and Peter and Phyllis, Twitchy and Richie D. As for her, she said she had grown up right here, three bedrooms for a family of eighteen. On the other side of the street, Tony's family of seven had made do with one bathroom and a kitchen stove for heat. Tony led the way there. It was a narrow street with alleyways like apertures between four- and five-story brick buildings, which seemed to lean inward toward one another. And here was Tony's former stoop.

Jim gaped at the door. "This was your house!"

"Second floor. Goes right through, all the way back and it's almost like a little park back there, it's all fire escapes."

"These little alleys. They're fabulous!"

Then, for a time, the day turned somber. Here was the corner where, down in the basement, behind these boarded-up windows, a local pederast had imprisoned Tony and two other boys. Or so Tony said. "There were three radiators, we were chained to one each. I would've been right about here." Tony pointed to a spot low on the plywood window.

Jim said, "This is a horrible story."

Tony didn't offer the graphic details. He simply shrugged. "It's history. You know, the crazy part."

He led the way to his former elementary school, now condominiums. He had liked the nuns, he said. But for some kids the school's basement was scary and worse. "Like if you raise your hand to go to the bathroom and you go down there, you'd see guys behind the boilers wit' some girl, screwing around or whatever." He went on for a while, as if the memories were unstoppable and had to get out. "There was this kid. Make a long story shawt, the other kids from down here stripped him to his underwear, took his clothes, went back to classes. He came up the stairs just in his briefs, crying and stuff, they robbed all his clothes." Tony stared at the schoolhouse door in silence for a few long moments.

The tour moved on, Tony leading the way past St. Leonard's church, saying, "This is where the priest supposedly molested the kids. I didn't see it, and I was around."

Jim began, "Was there any . . ."

Tony interrupted him. "Nah. Father Alan was the one they blamed here, but I didn't see it." Tony had been an altar boy. "I mean, we used to change right in the room, right in front of like Father Alan, change our clothes and stuff. I never seen him act funny wit' any of the kids, and a lot of kids came forward and said the same thing." I pressed Tony on the subject. Abuse by priests had been so prevalent in Boston in his childhood. Surely he knew of cases here. "No!" he said. He made a noise in his throat like a growl. "Listen. I know when I was in prison they came at me wit' a priest that me and my brother worked for. I can say honestly I never seen anything wrong with that priest. A lot of kids made up stories about priests to get money and stuff."

Ruminating afterward, Jim said he felt as if he could see Tony with his friends, breaking into the crypts and shooting their guns at night in the ancient cemetery. And Tony playing with friends on the

street of his infancy and youth, overseen by the mothers of the neighborhood, who couldn't save him and the two other boys from being
chained up to radiators in that basement and raped. And yet Tony's
account of that horror had seemed oddly offhand. Tony had mentioned it and then cast it aside, as if episodes like that were just part of
growing up in the neighborhood. What struck Jim most forcefully was
how vividly Tony had seemed to remember that story of the little kid
who was stripped by bullies in the basement of the grade school. Was
that Tony reimagining himself as a little boy, standing at the schoolhouse door, worrying he might be next?

. . .

We had a late lunch at a restaurant on Hanover Street. I said it was
high time for Tony to get off the streets.

He said, "You can't get the street off me, though. How do you say,
you bring a horse to water, you can't make it drink."

"Would you be okay in housing, though, do you think?" Jim asked.

Tony uttered a long guttural sound, like a door creaking open, followed by: "I think you wouldn't see me much."

"The hardest thing, at least from everybody I've talked to," said
Jim, "is how you manage all your friends."

"Yeah."

"You're too nice. You're gonna say yes to everybody, let 'em all
in."

"Nah."

Then Tony got distracted by clips of Mafia films that were being
beamed onto an adjacent wall in the restaurant. Before he turned to
them, though, he said he was going to call the housing agent tomorrow. She had found a place she wanted him to see.

7

A Free Man

Two weeks later, in court, everything fell apart. At every hearing during Jim's campaign to get Tony's warrants cleared, a different judge had presided. This one was male and tough, intolerant of cases that had lingered for months and of all irregularities. This judge—Tony called him "Hang-'em-high"—handed out default arrest warrants to everyone who was late, no matter the reason. He got exercised about a new charge on Tony's record—trespassing, for sleeping in a doorway downtown. A cop with any heart would never have written the citation. A judge with any imagination would have dismissed the charge.

Judge Hang-'em-high ordered Tony to stand trial for his failures to register, in a month and a half, at the end of August.

To Jim, the days spent with Tony in court felt like the bad old days of health care for homeless people in Boston—when the patients most in need of care rarely saw the same doctor twice. There had been no continuity to any of Tony's appearances, apart from the long delays and the uncomfortable seating—though, to be fair, the same lawyer had stayed with him throughout.

Leaving the courthouse, Tony said he knew, absolutely knew, that if he came back in August for a trial, they'd send him to jail. "Because that's what always happens."

But before that could happen, Tony once again appeared in the ER, this time with cuts and bruises and a fracture of his left orbital bone. Someone had hit him hard enough to break the bone of his left eye socket. Soon after he got out of the hospital, Tony collapsed in the lobby of Seven-Eighty, from an overdose of an opiate, almost certainly fentanyl. Mike Jellison revived him with the emergency antidote Narcan, now ubiquitous in the city. Mike and Kevin managed to get Tony into McInnis House afterward. Jim was off on his annual trip to Australia and received the news in an email from Julie on the other side of the day. Julie also wrote to tell him that the board member Joanne Guarino was very ill and in the ICU.

By the time Jim got home, Joanne was better and Tony worse. His descent had become precipitous. He seemed no longer capable of handling even McInnis House. He had called Julie from his room upstairs, saying in a husky whisper, "Julie, listen carefully! They don't want me here anymore. Heather's poisoning me." He had often told Julie that Heather was his favorite nurse.

Julie went upstairs at once to Tony's room. Heather came in, carrying a large plastic cup of water with a straw in it, saying, "Tony, you need to drink something."

Tony told Heather to leave, then whispered to Julie, "She's trying to poison me."

The drama ended when Jim arrived. He took Tony into the atrium and talked him into staying on for another night. Tony slept most of the weekend and emerged reborn again, for a while.

• • •

Tony had gone AMA from McInnis House two nights before his next hearing, telling Julie he'd meet me at the courthouse. He had stood me up on a few occasions, so I got there early and waited, convinced that he wouldn't appear. But he arrived only ten minutes later than he'd promised, saying with some indignation—preempting anything of the sort from me—that on his way over he'd come across BJ lying on pavement beside his capsized electric wheelchair, and he'd had to get BJ's chair upright and put him in it, then call 911 and wait for the ambulance, and besides it was only five to nine now, so he wasn't even late for court. When we walked into the courtroom, he smiled at me and said of his lawyer, "She ain't here yet."

Today "Hang-'em-high" was replaced by a woman judge with a kindlier disposition. She, too, scolded defendants who arrived late. She said she would fine them if they ever did it again. Tony's lawyer wasn't on hand when his name was called. Case after case followed, another mind-numbing, butt-numbing wait. The judge took a break, which gave Tony and me time to chat. I hadn't seen him in a while. "I stink," he said. It was true. He'd been outside for several days and clearly hadn't bathed. His face was tanned. On his left temple beside the eye, there was a very dark patch of skin, like a stain over the bone that had been fractured. I mentioned it. He said, "Two in the morning on State Street. Four guys, one of 'em wit' a baseball bat. I didn't see their faces. One had a mask on him. You don't know how bad I want revenge."

When his lawyer showed up, I told her that the judge's first call had come and gone, and she said that was okay, and I said, "Well, it's not okay for me and Mr. Columbo." And she said, with some heat, that she had a client who was in custody and therefore had priority.

Afterward Tony said to me, "You fired her up." He smiled. "But don't do it again."

I said it was an awful system. Tony said, "She's busy as hell, though."

He was sane again, the kind of well-mannered boy who surrenders his seat on the bus to the elderly.

Tony was right about his lawyer. She was lugging half a dozen different case files. She had stuck with him, and in the end, later that day, she made a passionate plea to the kindly judge, saying that the Boston Health Care for the Homeless Program had "wrapped their arms around Mr. Columbo." The judge said, "It's a great program," and ordered that the case be resolved that day. She sent the matter off to another courtroom, where after some delay the chief justice appeared and cleared Tony's warrants.

"So that's good," Tony said to his lawyer afterward. She said it was indeed, but he must not fail again to register, or he would surely go to jail. It was a reminder, oddly startling just then, that Tony was still a sex offender under the law, a public fact available online, which he would never be permitted to forget.

He had to wait for an official document a few floors below, in the Probation Department. I sat with him for a while. He mentioned a new problem with his ID, saying he wished he had a driver's license. I asked him if he'd ever driven a car. He said, "Sure," then added, "Not *legally*." When we ran out of small talk, he told me I didn't need to wait with him. "We're just gonna part ways anyhow, when we leave."

I stayed a little longer, though. Tony stared ahead at nothing, and I studied his face. In profile, it made me think of eagles. A declarative face. A smile passed across it. He was no longer a wanted man. I imagined he was thinking that he didn't have to worry for now about cops picking him up. I let myself imagine this was a new and not a recursive beginning. When I called Jim with the news that evening, he said, "I'm ecstatic!"

8

Confession

We should have known better. On a night soon afterward, Jim found Tony sleeping on concrete in a half-hidden nook near the Famine Memorial, the place he called the Circle. He asked Jim to send him to McInnis House. Jim arranged a bed for him the next day, but by then Tony had disappeared.

A week later, I got a call from a social worker at Mass General, where Tony was an inpatient again. She gave Tony the phone, and he began weeping—he had let Jim down, he had been drinking too much, he had tried to dry out for three days, but he couldn't. "I had a hard life," he said, his baritone in an upper register. "I had a hard life."

He went in and out of the hospital several times during the following week. On Thursday afternoon, he was back in Mousey Park, where Jim found him after Street Clinic—semidistraught, saying that his cohorts were all beating each other up. Jim suggested a rest at McInnis House. Tony said, "They need me right now. I'm the only one that can stop the fights." So he couldn't go to McInnis House. But could he have a word with Jim away from the people in the park?

Jim's car, a block away in the parking garage, was the nearest quiet place. Once inside, Tony began to talk about his childhood, in a tumult of words: "The priest in front of two other boys, he stripped me naked and beat me. Beat me, wit' a belt, I don't know if you remember the razor belt, the old razor strop. After that he used to molest me wit' a candle and stuff, and do other things and stuff. His name was Father Alan. And the other kids used to call me 'Shit Drawers' because my insides used to come out, I used to bleed, I always had blood in my shorts. So between my family and everything else, okay, I knew back then when I was a little kid, there's no such thing as God."

This was the priest whom Tony had mentioned during the tour of his old neighborhood, denying that the man had molested him, suggesting that allegations others made against this priest were false. In fact, the same priest—Father Alan E. Caparella—had been sued, posthumously and successfully, for sexually abusing a child back when Tony was in grade school. "I never told on him," Tony went on. "That he raped me wit' candles and stuff, and it was a hidden thing in the North End. Back then we didn't lock our doors. We were supposed to be so happy. Happy was being abused, hurt, raped."

Tony sat in the passenger seat and talked to Jim for most of an hour, in varying tones of distress. Jim listened, now and then murmuring softly, "Yeah," and wincing inwardly when Tony said "and stuff." The throwaway phrase seemed so clearly Tony's substitute for all the other things the priest had done to him. "And stuff." It seemed to carry in itself the force of a confession, and Tony's shame for a crime inflicted on him long ago.

Some of what Tony said was a catalog of early sorrows—not only the priest's assaults but also memories such as the day his cat was euthanized because the family was moving into a building that didn't allow pets. At one point, he veered into his recurrent dread that he had become a carrier of death. "I wonder sometimes if you're gonna drive home and get—I don't wanta sound stupid—and get crashed or killed or something because I'm *near* you. That's the type of luck I have."

"Stop it!" said Jim, and then more softly, "Stop it. It's not true."

"I want to be there for your kid," said Tony. "When your daughter grows up and they need help. I want to hold a sword for you. But I can't, I can't do it!"

Twice in his long monologue Tony spoke about his recent overdose and harsh rescue by Narcan: "I remember going to sleep and I remember waking up miserable, feeling cold and hurt and everything. The best feeling in my life, the best feeling, was going to sleep, the worst feeling was waking back up. To realize, first of all, that tomorrow there's no such thing as religion or God." He said, "I'm not suicidal or anything. It's just that I want to disappear. I don't wanta *be,* you know?"

Tony veered off into church history and the emperor Constantine—"He hadda find another way to control the world"—and then denouncing God—"Cruel, insane, sadistic God!"—all while seeming to say that he was so angry at God he wasn't going to believe in him anymore.

"Where do you see God, Jim? You took theology. Hadda believe in God. Because there's no way you're doing all this and you don't believe in God." This seemed at last like Tony's central, urgent question. "You been fortunate and lucky, but you worked *very* hard for it, Jim. But I believe you're doing it for us people, because you see what's going on and you see the truth in our world."

Jim had said very little during that hour in the car. Tony's story rocked him back on his heels. All the same, Jim was angry with himself. As Tony had remarked, Jim had studied theology. In his years of reading philosophy, he'd been exposed to some of the best that human beings had known and thought. As Tony spoke, Jim thought of words to offer him, but every idea emerged stillborn. He'd think of something to say and then think of the ways in which it could be just the wrong thing to tell Tony. Perhaps it was hopeless. At one point, he began to speak about the book of Job, a good man who suffered for no reason, but Tony rushed on in his unstoppable way, and in the end, Jim felt that all he had managed to offer was "insipid and monosyllabic interjections."

In the car, Jim checked quickly to see if any beds were available at McInnis House, but there were none. So he broke his promise to the board and gave Tony cash for a hotel—in Jim's view, not a gift but an emergency prescription.

Before he got out of the car, Tony said, "But just if you can, Jim, find me something to grasp on, please. Even if it's a verse in the Bible."

Jim said he would try to do that tomorrow.

• • •

When he found Tony the next morning in Mousey Park, Jim took him aside and told him that while he didn't feel he was on an errand from God, he found meaning and even joy in his job because of the people that both he and Tony tried to help. What "shone through down the years" for him, Jim said, was being able to sit with Tony and the others and try to deal with the bad things that happened to everyone all the time. A large group of friends got created that way, and Tony should know that even the people who had betrayed him appreciated everything he'd done. "You've enriched all our lives," Jim told him.

Tony listened but said little. It was hard to know if those words met his need. Several nights later, out on the van, Jim found him downtown near Pi Alley. They had another chat under streetlights. Among other things, Tony said: "I know there's goodness in the world." Jim had heard him use this phrase before, but that night it came out at crazy speed, with spittle flying, amid skeins of other pressured, wildly digressive talk, Tony saying in one mouthful that maybe he should go to McInnis House, but first he had to check on everybody out on Cambridge Street, and he'd bought fifteen Big Macs and given them to everyone, and yet he was still starving. Jim couldn't slow him down. He urged him to get his monthly registration done by tomorrow, which was the deadline, and then to come back to McInnis House. Jim rode off in the van, hoping for the best.

Jim had recently incurred medical problems of his own, in a cascading pattern that reminded him of his elderly patients. A shoulder surgery had led to the discovery of an anomaly in his heart's electrical conduction system, which would require a pacemaker. When the news reached Mousey Park, Jim had to answer questions there. He said it was nothing very serious, but when Julie ran into BJ, he told her, "Jim's a fucking liar." An accusation founded on worry, which spread to Tony, of course.

Jim got his pacemaker and afterward spent a night under observation in the ICU. Earlier, he'd learned that Tony was back inside the hospital. Jim tried to reach him by phone from his room, but Tony had already left AMA. Jim spent the night alone. The ICU rules were strict. Not even Jill was allowed in. When he woke up the next morning, however, a familiar voice asked, "How ya feelin'?"

A small, wiry man had pulled the visitor's chair over to the bedside. It took Jim a moment to realize this wasn't a doctor, but rather one of the old classics, a charter member of the Mousey Park crew, a patient of many years, Billy Bianchino.

Billy was smiling. "We've all been real worried aboutchya, Dr. Jim, and I thought I'd come and see ya."

Jim wanted to ask Billy how he'd managed to get in, but he didn't let himself. The rough sleepers' devious ways were more amusing and miraculous left unknown, like the mechanics of a magic trick. Jim often told the team how important it was to visit patients when they were languishing in the hospital, lonesome and afraid. Once the surprise wore off, he realized that he himself had been feeling lonely, and it was reassuring to see Billy sitting there.

9

~~~~~~~~

The Night Watchman

Elizabeth had been sleeping with Tony for several chilly late-October nights. Not sleeping with him for sex but for warmth and company. On the night of October 27, 2019, a Sunday, they shared the concrete floor of the alcove beside the Wyndham hotel on Blossom Street.

She had spent other nights with Tony over the past few years, usually when they happened to run into each other in places like Pi Alley. Almost always when she fell asleep—often having had far too much to drink—she would see that he was sitting upright, guarding their concrete camp, with his back against a wall or knapsack. She had been attacked many times, both before and after she became homeless. So Tony was a comfort to her, an antidote to terrifying memories and nighttime fears.

This night, though, the situation was reversed. Earlier that day, she had seen him lying on cardboard in Mousey Park, clutching his stomach, crying in pain. She knew he'd been in and out of the hospital, and she told him he should go back there. But he had refused. This made her worry that he didn't want to live anymore. And she felt doubly worried when she found him in the alcove that evening, lying flat on the concrete instead of sitting up as he had always done in her company.

There was another man sleeping there that night, a mutual friend. Elizabeth took the place on the other side of Tony. She had some extra blankets. She put several over Tony and lay close beside him to keep him warm, also holding both his hands, which felt cold. Around dawn, when she awoke, he seemed to be sleeping. But when she kissed his forehead, it felt as cold as his hands. Later, when Jim asked her what had happened, she said, "I think I kissed a dead man," and started to cry.

Later that morning, someone called 911, and routine asserted itself. As Tony's friends stood a little distance away, police cars pulled up, officers took down the names of his friends, confirmed that Tony was dead, taped off the alcove, and called the medical examiner's office, which dispatched a van and took the body back to the morgue on Albany Street, just down the block from Seven-Eighty.

. . .

Jim had been traveling during Tony's last week. He'd returned to Boston late Sunday night and heard the news of Tony's death at the Monday Street Team meeting. They were all astonished, collectively declaring, "What!" The news rippled out through Seven-Eighty. To the lobby and the receptionist, Joyce, who used to hold Tony's mail for him—she wept silently at her post. And upstairs into McInnis House, to Omar and others who had known him well, including Tony's favorite nurse, Heather, who also wept.

Late Monday afternoon, Jim went out to Mousey Park, where Elizabeth and a bunch of other Street Team patients had gathered.

Elizabeth told Jim the story of Tony's last night. Others said that Tony had made it a policy to stay awake and guard those who were sleeping and vulnerable, especially women. Of course, there had been nights when Tony could have used a guard himself, after passing out. But no one mentioned that. One of the women said, "We call him the Night Watchman."

Jim rode in the van that night. It was raining hard, streets and gutters streaming in the headlights, Mousey Park abandoned. Rain always put him in mind of the facts of life in that urban outdoors— dripping eaves and sodden pants and shirts and blankets, odors of wet socks. Long ago a patient had described rain as "water torture." A constant liquid assault. You couldn't get dry. Everything stuck to your skin and clothes. A rainy October night like this carried the risk of frostbite and hypothermia. The van ride was one of the most disheartening that Jim could remember. At every stop he would look up from pouring hot chocolate, half expecting to see Tony emerge from the rainy dark, in his splay-footed shambling gait.

A small group sat huddled on the concrete floor in the alcove on Blossom Street where Tony had died early that morning. The community of rough sleepers, usually so loose and informal, could sometimes seem as intimately connected as mycelium under a forest floor. At every van stop, rough sleepers had heard the news. And at each, the reaction was much the same. Someone would say, "Tony, he'd give you the shirt off his back," and someone else would put in, "You could see it coming. I should've done something." Jim asked the drivers to swing by all the spots where BJ usually hid from rain, but he was nowhere to be found. Who was going to take care of BJ now?

The next morning, Jim reviewed the record of Tony's last five days: Episodes of severe abdominal pain had taken him to the Mass General emergency department, where a startling amount of fluid had again been removed from his bladder and sent to the lab for a bacteria culture, which had grown staphylococcus, "a significant infection." Tony had been admitted to the hospital and spent the night receiving antibiotics intravenously, with a Foley catheter inserted to keep his bladder drained.

Julie had been on hand during Tony's last days. She relived some of that time for Jim in the library. Tony hadn't stayed long in the hospital, she said. "The next morning he left the hospital AMA, to the horror of the physician assistant." Julie added, "Tony pulled out his catheter."

Jim's eyes widened. "It must have hurt like *hell*! I can't believe he could do that!" A few patients had done the same in the past, but only in fits of rage or dementia.

Tony had gone into the ER three more times and had left AMA each time. Julie remembered his cycling between near euphoria and agony. At one point, during Thursday clinic, he had come in sweating profusely and saying, "Julie, I'm burning up, I'm burning up."

"*Was* he burning up?" asked Jim.

"He wouldn't let us take his temperature, but his forehead felt cool."

"I think he was probably between bacteremia and septic," said Jim. "With sepsis, fever comes and goes. When it goes down, you start to sweat."

A bladder full of liquid would have made a perfect home for bacteria. In Jim's hypothesis, while Tony languished in pain, his staph infection grew acute and led to sepsis, then to septic shock. The records showed that the hospital had given Tony oral antibiotics when he left AMA, but evidently he hadn't taken the pills. "I'm pretty sure this led to his death, and he was probably taking all sorts of drugs to dull his pain." Had Tony committed suicide? It seemed possible. "Going AMA when he was so sick, ripping out his Foley, not taking the antibiotics they gave him. In the car that time, he seemed to be saying he was giving up."

A month had passed since Tony had climbed into Jim's car and told the story of being abused by the priest. To Jim, that account loomed over all that had followed. It had seemed completely credible,

full of grief and anger and shame in the telling. Tony's other stories of
being sexually abused seemed flat by comparison. Could they have
been proxies for the thing itself? Jim said, "I *know* that something
really horrible happened to him."

Julie shared this impression. In his last few weeks, Tony had called
her almost every day, she said, and had delivered long and troubled
monologues. "I know that whatever it was, Tony's trauma was ex-
treme and it was resurfacing."

. . .

Jim opened the Thursday team meeting with the news that Frankie
had been evicted from his apartment and was terrified, imagining that
in his old age he faced life on the streets. "I decided we will make a
bed for him at McInnis House no matter what." Jim's voice sounded
unusually pugnacious. A pause followed. Then Jim said, "I suppose
we should talk about Tony."

Mainly, they exchanged news of how Tony's death was still reso-
nating: A patient downstairs in the waiting room had just been told
and was in tears. Omar, the manager, had been heard to say that
many patients at McInnis House were "frantically upset." And some
of the nursing staff there couldn't say Tony's name without bursting
into tears.

Jim told the team that he'd stopped by the medical examiner's office yesterday. When an autopsy of a street person turned up drugs,
the pathologists didn't usually look for other causes. Jim had asked
that they test for evidence of sepsis, too. "I read them into the history,
so they wouldn't just do toxins, so they'd look for urine retention."

An uncomfortable silence followed, as if everyone in the stuffy
little room was waiting for someone else to speak. Then Jim declared,
"All right. Let's get out of this. Please."

But there was no avoiding the subject. Jim's usual first patient,
John Cotrone, reported that everyone on the street was talking about
Tony and everyone was upset. The next patient was an old favorite,

named Kevin Blanchard. Jim greeted him with his usual "How are *you*?" Kevin replied, "I'm not in a good mood about Tony, man. It messed up my head, man."

Kevin wore jeans and a trucker jacket, both clean. He wasn't a big man, but he had a loud voice, a reputation as a brawler, and a colorful past that he'd often recounted for Jim—he'd done time in prison for robbing banks, among other things. He sat beside Jim in the patient's chair, looking glum.

"So, we don't know what happened. Tony was sick over the weekend."

"But why did he die on a sidewalk? Where?"

Jim described the location. "He was sleeping all night and then never woke up."

"He died in his sleep? At least he didn't feel no pain."

"That's what I'm thinking. That's the one bright side to this," said Jim. "So did you meet Tony before you saw him at McInnis?"

"I knew him in prison before that. Shirley Max. Yeah."

I said that Tony used to talk about helping a lot of other inmates there. Was it true?

"Tony, that's all he does is help people!" said Kevin. Tony's got something? He'll give his last dollar, he'll give it to you." Kevin went on, "Don't get me wrong, don't get him mad, bro. Don't take his kindness for weakness. Dude, he could *fight*."

Jim had brought out his stethoscope. Now he applied it. "Deep breath for me, Kevin, okay?"

"You can see I'm all hyper right now," Kevin said. He took the deep breath and then went back to praising Tony. "His biceps were the size of Jim's head. I'm not saying no wrong to your head, Jim. He had big hands, bro." Kevin stared across the room at nothing. "Can't believe he's dead." He turned back to Jim. "Died in his sleep, Jim, seriously?"

"Yeah. He just never woke up."

"At least he died peaceful, bro. I'm glad. I hate to say it, but I'm glad he died in his sleep."

Tony had a knack for inventing stories. Some were odd and apparently inconsequential. For instance, his claim that he was Jim's greatnephew. There was also the vague story he told about his prison sentence—that he'd been sent away for a crime he didn't commit. About a year after his death, I found the police report. It explained the basis of the charges that were leveled against him when he was twentysix. The document read:

> ON THE ABOVE DATE AND TIME [A YOUNG MAN] CAME
> TO THE STATION TO REPORT AN ASSAULT. THE FOLLOW-
> ING IS HIS STATEMENT GIVEN TO MYSELF AND P.O. [X] :
> ON 4-27-95 AT APPROX. 12:00 AM I WAS TAKING A
> SHORT CUT THROUGH THE FIELDS BEHIND PAUL REVERE
> SCHOOL PARK AFTER PLAYING BASKETBALL. I HEARD
> [TONY COLUMBO] CALL ME FROM BEHIND, HE TOLD ME
> TO WAIT UP AND SAID HE KNEW A QUICKER SHORT CUT
> TO BEACH ST.. AS I WAS GOING OVER THE FENCE TO JUMP
> IT, HE GRABBED ME FROM BEHIND BY THE NECK, AND
> PULLED ME DOWN. HE THEN HELD A KNIFE TO MY NECK
> AND SAID OVER AND OVER—I AM GOING TO KILL YOU.
> THEN HE PULLED MY TROUSER'S DOWN, THEN PULLED
> ME UP BY THE NECK. HE THEN PULLED HIS OWN PANTS
> DOWN TO HIS KNEES, HE EASED UP ON MY NECK. I
> GRABBED HIM BY THE TESTICLES TO GET AWAY HE THEN
> FELL BACK AND I RAN AWAY.
> HE ALSO REPEATED TO ME THAT HE HAD A GUN AND
> HE WAS GOING TO KILL ME.

The report probably fell into Barbara McInnis's category of history better left unknown. It told the sort of story that neither Jim nor I had wanted to imagine, partly because we had enjoyed Tony's company, and, speaking for myself, I'm not sure I would have enjoyed it as much if I had known those details of his past. Maybe this is true more

generally, a magnification of a common problem: If we knew everything that everyone had said and done, we might not enjoy anyone's
company.

Jim wondered if Tony had been gay and had punished himself for
it inwardly. Homophobia had been endemic in neighborhoods like
the North End and Southie, where, an old saying went, a young gay
man's only options were to become an actor, a priest, or a homeless
person. Had those patients been forced into assuming sham hetero-
sexual identities, and was that a part of what had made a mess of their
lives? Of Tony's life?

Tony had spent eighteen years in prison for an attempted rape.
The crime, as reported, was repulsive and the punishment was ex-
treme, if only because it was in effect everlasting. But there was another way to view Tony's past, the doctor's view. "Here's another twist
to this," Jim said. "There are some people on the street who do nasty
things to other people, and then I just have a hard time liking them. If
one of the men in our panel beats the shit out of one of the women,
it's really hard to look that man in the eye and still like him. But I don't
think we judge—at least I haven't—we don't judge people on what led
them here. It's what they do once they're here. And Tony was the
character on the stage who handled that best. He was nothing but—
99 percent of the time—nothing but gracious and living out his life as
best he could, given the circumstances. So there was nothing about
Tony that I could ever dislike. His condemnation was to be on the
street, but once he got there he really was a protector. He was just
what our folks say he was. I have to keep remembering that this is
what I really loved and admired about him, no matter what led him to
the street in the first place."

• • •

The autopsy report arrived months after Tony's death. It stated that
he had died from a drug overdose—from the combined effects of alcohol, cocaine, and fentanyl. It offended Jim to see that tests for sepsis
hadn't been performed. Autopsies matter for practical reasons, of

course. But to Jim, a thorough attempt to determine what had killed a body also said that there was value in the life it once contained.

The mandates he'd been taught in residency—be friendly but not a friend; forget the last patient and move on to the next room—were designed to help a doctor manage deaths like Tony's. In Jim's organizational philosophy, you replaced those defenses by creating a community of patients and providers, and they managed sorrows by sharing them, partly with ceremony. In the old days, the Street Team would hold a separate memorial service for each patient who died, but as time went on, the services grew so numerous that they'd begun to have one service for many. There was talk of holding a special event for Tony, but the idea foundered on issues of equity.

Stories were told that served as tributes, appropriate to the harsh world of rough sleepers. One was delivered in the Street Clinic waiting room, by Tony's friend Kim. She had spent a year in jail and by the time she got out her boyfriend had died. She'd latched on to Tony, just as other women had, as a guide and protector in the wilds of Boston. In her testimonial, she and Tony and another man were sharing a room at the other man's apartment. She woke up and found the guy trying to undress her. She yelled, and Tony woke up. His wrath was impressive: "So he like picked up the bed, flipped me out of the bed, picked up a hammer and a screwdriver." He was about to kill the other man, Kim thought. She jumped onto Tony's back. "Now, Tony was a strong guy. And he's big. So I'm holding on to Tony . . ." She managed to keep him from killing her would-be rapist, and they left the apartment together. When they got outside on the street, Tony started crying. "He just kind of broke down. I think in his head, he couldn't see anything bad happen to me." He told her the attempted rape had reminded him of violence done to his mother when he was a child.

On a cold February morning, passing through an empty Mousey Park, Jim happened on a tombstone of sorts. He made inquiries. One of the women patients had created it, the same woman to whom Tony had given five dollars to encourage her to continue her detox. On a concrete wall between the benches, a tidy drawing in black ink of a heart, and beside it:

TONY COLUMBO RIP

WE LOVE YOU.

Jim took a picture of the tribute, before winter storms and maintenance crews began to wear it away.

Patients and Jim and Julie continued to talk about Tony, but less frequently and in a reminiscent mood. One day, taking a break in the library, Jim delivered something like a eulogy.

"He died without warrants, Julie."

"He *did* have a court date coming," she said.

"Oh well, there was that trespassing thing," Jim replied, in a tone that said all charges were dismissed.

VIII

The Portrait Gallery

1

⌐∿∿∿∿⌐

A Pandemic Season

The first flood of Covid infections was sweeping and lethal in Boston, especially inside nursing homes and jails and among people in low-income neighborhoods who went out to work in dangerous, low-paying jobs and came home to crowded apartments. Everyone expected a similar catastrophe for the city's homeless people. But by the fall of 2020, when the virus's first wave had abated, the rough sleepers, the most vulnerable in normal times, had been spared. Perhaps outdoor living and their untouchable status had protected them. And while the virus did spread among 30 to 40 percent of the people sleeping inside the city's two largest homeless shelters, most of the illnesses had been mild.

Boston's response on behalf of homeless people was impressively collective—the city's hospitals, the city and state public health departments, the mayor's and governor's offices, the shelter organizations all collaborated. The Boston Health Care for the Homeless Program ran testing in the shelters, converted a floor of McInnis House into a special Covid isolation unit, equipped and staffed two medical tents that the city erected for quarantine and isolation, and later helped to run a five-hundred-bed wing of a thousand-bed field hospital in the city's convention center. Everyone on the Street Team pitched in. The team's younger doctor, Kevin, caught the virus but soon recovered and went back to work.

Jim was obliged to listen and watch from a distance. He had come down with yet another new ailment, an autoimmune disorder causing inflammation of the blood vessels. His colleagues at Mass General had put him on a long course of medications to inhibit certain immune responses, and when Covid arrived, they advised him to go into quarantine. He retreated to Newport with Jill and Gabriella and stayed there most of the summer, conferring by phone and computer with other senior managers. Mostly, he offered encouragement and told them not to worry about money. He called the Program's response to the crisis "extraordinary." But he didn't do any of the work or issue any orders, and the closest he got to the action was on a virtual tour of the field hospital via cellphone.

He spent a fair amount of time looking out to sea during that first season of Covid. We spoke often by phone. His voice always sounded cheerful, even when his thoughts had a melancholy cast. On one call he said, "I think of this as my rehearsal for complete irrelevance." And on another: "It's a little taste of what it's going to be like when it comes to an end. But I have Gabriella now. I swam in the ocean with her all this week." And on still another: "It's almost like Tony's death was the beginning of the end for me. Just the feeling: I can't do this anymore."

I began to think he really was about to retire. But when I suggested as much early that summer, he replied with exclamations: "Oh no! I'm coming back! I've got six more months of these damn shots and stuff, and then I'm coming back!"

I was reminded of the time, one of many, when Jim was musing

about the ups and downs of lives like Tony's, and how they could in-
sinuate themselves into the lives of the Street Team's members. He
had said: "We just have to enjoy the good days and accept the bad
days. It's sort of the theme of our work. Sisyphus. If you don't enjoy
rolling the rock up the hill, this is not the job for you."

Then he had paused and revised his interpretation of the myth:
"Or I guess you have to enjoy the walk down. I used to think that a
beer with Barbara McInnis at Doyle's on Friday night was the walk
down the hill."

· · ·

In November, a second season of Covid moved into Boston. Though
still obliged to take immune-suppressing drugs, Jim went back to the
Street Team in person, once a week on Thursdays, wearing a surgical
mask. There was still work for him to do. The team was in flux. They
had a new nurse and a new physician assistant. Kevin was leaving to
to work in homelessness medicine in Maine, so they needed a new
doctor and, eventually, a replacement for Jim. Before he left the team
for good, he wanted it stable and "fine-tuned." It was far from that
just then. During the meeting, some members sat together in the air-
less clinic waiting room while others joined via computer. Long si-
lences marked the discussions of patients, as did puzzled talk about
the problems of trying to run their clinic now, how their patients
couldn't be allowed to just show up and congregate inside and yet
couldn't be expected to make or keep appointments. Several times,
Jim began to speak, then stopped. I felt as though I could hear him
thinking.

"Our old classics are dying." Over the past two years, Jim had
made this a refrain. But when he went outside after the meeting, a few
of his classics were sitting around in Mousey Park, where the drinking
day had begun—Karl and BJ in their wheelchairs and a mixture of
other old regulars and new patients, most wearing masks and most
awaiting what were now cash-free audiences with Dr. Jim. Covid
made it too dangerous for the team to see patients inside, so Thursday,

formerly Street Clinic day, had become Jim's day for street rounds. Jen, the team's new physician assistant, went with him. Covid vaccinations weren't available yet but she carried a large knapsack, with equipment for flu shots.

Covid had departed the city's shelters during August and September but had recently returned, so far in small outbreaks. The Street Team's patients, meanwhile, remained almost entirely untouched by the virus, while still suffering the miseries and fatal afflictions common to rough sleepers everywhere. Downtown, a familiar mixture of new and old acquaintances were camped at their stemming spots, in doorways and beside streetlamps and mailboxes. Jim and Jen made many stops among them.

One bearded fellow with a beautifully lettered and colored sign— EVERYTHING HELPS GOD BLESS—politely refused a flu shot, saying he'd been out on the streets a long time and figured he'd caught and survived every bug there was.

Jim knew almost all the street people who were out. One he hadn't met before, a young woman much too well-groomed for the streets, said she'd heard all about him from Tony. She added, "I miss Tony. He was a *nice* guy." Watching Jim talk to her and the other street people, I was struck all over again by his conversational manner: saying little, but actively listening, tilting slightly forward, his eyes unwaveringly attentive, a suggestion in his face that he was about to break into a smile. And rarely ending a conversation himself, but rather allowing almost all of them to talk for as long as they wanted, as if he had all the time in the world.

2

The Portrait Gallery

The photographs in the hallway outside Jim's office are like an exhibition—Street Team history told in twenty-nine pictures of patients from all eras, a few still alive, most long dead. Jim took all but one of the photos himself, and chose these from among hundreds on an utterly subjective basis. "People that I really liked," he says. "Each cost nearly a hundred dollars to frame, so I've put them up little by little." They hang at eye level. I imagine their faces turning toward passersby.

"So this is the Judge." The photograph has the air of formal portraiture. The man sits in muted light, a globe on an end table beside him. He looks like a gentleman of late middle age, bald and clean-shaven, dressed in a dark suit and tie. Jim remembers an evening when he and the Judge and BJ were riding in the van toward the shelter and the Judge was expounding on some legal matter that had come before the state's Supreme Judicial Court. BJ told him to cut the crap. "You're not a judge." The Judge smiled and, turning to Jim, explained that BJ was angry at him. "I've had to send him to jail three times already, Dr. O'Connell."

Jim remembers that when the Judge consented to come into McInnis House, he had assumed a role a little like Tony's. "He was always telling us about problems that should be fixed. 'I'm a judge,' he'd say. 'And I know about these things.'"

The picture comes from near the end of the Judge's life, when after thirty years on Boston's streets he had been housed in a two-room apartment. He called the living room his "chambers." There, at his desk in the middle of the floor, he would expound on landmark cases in constitutional law. "He had probably been through some horrible experiences," says Jim. "We don't know what they were, we'll never know. And to continue living and to imagine himself doing good things, I think, he took on the persona of a judge and poured in invented memories. Maybe it's the delusion that keeps some people going and allows them to be functional, and if you take that away, they're left with nothing but sorrow and wounds. The lesson for us was: You just have to accept him and figure out what you can do, but not push too far."

Most of the faces are white, about one-third Black or brown. Here is Kay, who lived in the tunnel under Copley Square for years. And among the still living, Lena, with a smile so big it closes her eyes—"It was good seeing her the other day. We love Lena." The man in sunglasses and the tam-o'-shanter with a tartan blanket draped over his shoulder is James Smith, from Atlanta, who became "Liam O'Sullivan" and spoke with a plausible Irish brogue when he was panhandling in front of the Black Rose pub. "He'd sit there on an old toilet he'd found somewhere or other. He collected bags of money every night, he was so entertaining."

Jim stops in front of a fellow who wears a knowing smile while leaning against the doorway of his subsidized apartment—a stars-and-stripes bandanna wrapped around his forehead. "This is Jimmy Dagget. He was just *fun*. Fun and a charactah," says Jim, his voice returning for a moment again to the Rhode Island of his youth. "I have some letters from prison he would send. He was a fighter. He had a sign when he was stemming at Fenway Park: FOR ONE DOLLAR YOU CAN HIT ME AS HARD AS YOU WANT IN THE STOMACH. FIVE DOLLARS AS HARD AS YOU WANT IN THE FACE. And that was his shtick. And some people took him up on it. He said, 'I'm a Marine, I can handle this.'"

"Did you ever have to treat him for a broken jaw?"

"No. But facial trauma all the time. He was doing really well. Then one day he was cruising North Station and started getting bad chest pains after smoking some cocaine, and by the time they got him to the hospital he was dead, of a cocaine-induced heart attack."

This young-looking woman in a silk blouse and broad sun hat could be laughing with a gentleman at a garden party. "Oh my God, she was wonderful. She had all the tools, she's really smart, but she couldn't get out of being homeless . . . Alcohol." She had longed for a reunion with her family. When Jim called her parents, though, they said they knew this sounded harsh, but would he please not call again until she was gone. "It must have been a really painful thing for them."

Next, a man with black hair and tawny skin, looking out of the photo with heavy-lidded eyes. "This is a guy whose name is Jonah Daniel. He *said* he was a persecuted Christian born in Pakistan who went to sea as a merchant sailor and got off in America. Every nurse who knew him loved him, he was so sweet, but when he was outside drinking, he just became uncontrollable." He and the man in the next photo were a case for a textbook on medical miracles. Both were found outside on a very cold night in January 2011, Jonah on a sidewalk, the other man in a dumpster. Ambulances rushed both of them to Mass General, where they got warmed up and revived on the lung-bypass machine and recovered without any obvious cognitive impairment. Later, on another very cold night, Jonah arrived at Cambridge Hospital suffering from hypothermia. "And he left AMA, took all his stuff, went outside, and froze to death. It was really awful."

A gay couple smile out toward the hallway, from around the time they got married in a grand ceremony—amid balloons and confetti, in a now abandoned shelter. The tall man, Bob, claimed to have been a Green Beret. He used to tell Jim war stories that sounded plausible. The short fellow, Jack, was a meticulous person. He had AIDS, which lay dormant for a long time but then erupted. "And I said, 'The good news now is we have medicine, Jack. We can treat this. You can just take this one pill a day, and that'll take care of it.' And he looked at it for a minute. He said, 'I don't know if I want to take a pill like that, Doc.' He thought a diet of kale would cure him. And I was crushed because his death was totally preventable. Bob tried to help me convince him to take the medicine, but Bob couldn't get through to him either." Bob died six months after Jack. "I was pretty devastated, because these were people I had been taking care of for a long time. Bottom line, though, as I look at this story—they stayed together for thirty-two years. In many ways it's kind of a quiet love story, that I never quite appreciated until they had died."

Touring the picture gallery with Jim is like walking through a book, the annals of a practice, its sorrows and joys, oddities and lessons. This man sent Jim two bricks in the mail anonymously and later explained that he wanted to get even with Jim for calling him a Native American. "I'm an Indian, goddammit!"

This handsome man, Nat, looks like a famous musician but did his strumming and singing in Boston subway stations, where he also sometimes slept. Jim remembers getting a call from him, from jail. In Charlestown, where Nat grew up, stealing a car was a rite of passage, but he had stolen a car that belonged to the mayor's chief of staff. A luckless fellow, except that when he was dying, his ex-wife took him in, even though she didn't have enough money for groceries. Jim stares at Nat. "There was quite a love story with this one, too."

The woman in this portrait got clean and became a worker on the outreach vans—"I worked on the van with her for five years, and then she broke out, and was back on the streets. It was really painful. But everybody loved her."

This other young woman had a boyfriend who used to lock her in the closet whenever he left his apartment, but she didn't dare run away from him for fear of ending up on the streets. "And it was *awful*. And we couldn't do anything about it." In the photo she smiles radiantly—she has all her teeth—as she leans her cheek against the cheek of a young man. He was a childhood friend, Jim explains, not her dreadful boyfriend. "He used to say that he was going to kill her boyfriend, but he was not able to do that."

And here is a picture that someone else took: Dr. O'Connell when he had dark brown hair, half kneeling with a flashlight in his mouth, beside a pile of blankets in an industrial-looking doorway and ministering to a woman in a wool hat. She has vacant-looking eyes, a down-turned mouth. "And this is Dawn. She was sent to Framingham for stabbing her abusive husband to death. But then she was one of the women let out." She never got housed, but after some years on the street, she achieved the state known as clean and sober, found a kinder boyfriend, and lived with him for several years in a tent on Hilton Head Island.

Here is the Black woman, Phyllis, who said, when Jill took over as her provider—Jim laughs his high-pitched laugh as he recites the words—"I'm so glad to have you take care of me now. You know that guy who's got pink skin? I don't think I want him."

Here is a woman in bed with her newborn child, surrounded by her mother and grandmother. All three had been patients, three generations who endured homelessness at one time or another. "And the child, who's now been given up for adoption—we don't know where the child will go."

And this elderly man very neatly dressed, gently smiling. "This is Matthew. What's his last name? He was an older guy who used to come into the clinic, and no one besides us could tell he was homeless. He just always would come in. But he had been homeless for like thirty or forty years. And just faked everybody out. He died one day of a heart attack, and it just *crushed* us, that he was dead."

This grinning fellow lived for years under the Storrow Drive bridges and claimed all sorts of illnesses that he didn't have, and this very thin Black man was one of those finally housed after years and years of rough sleeping. He stands in the bedroom of his newfound apartment, leaning with his elbow on a dresser beside a framed sampler: HOME SWEET HOME. "But he was one of those guys who was always sick, but he never let you know. He always came in upbeat, but his blood sugar would be out of control, his HIV stuff would be out of control. But he would just not, not let you worry about it."

Near the end of the hallway, Jim stops and gazes. "And this photograph I cherish." The two ex–college professors are on the way to one of those luncheons Jim hosted every month. Luncheons at which he would listen as the professors—"the two smartest people I ever knew"—debated matters of philosophy and art. The elder, Harrison, leans on the handlebars of a walker, wearing the downturned, grumpy look that gravity and collagen loss tend to inflict on eighty-year-olds. The younger former professor, David, stands beside him. He is tall, white-haired, very thin. Behind them rises the sign of the Union Oyster House, America's oldest restaurant, once the haunt of Daniel Webster. "David lived outside for the longest time and then the team found him an apartment on Beacon Hill. He came down with leukemia. He had always said that he was being pursued by electronic zappers, which would give him cancer. So he died more convinced than ever. I miss him."

· · ·

Jim had stored at least a thousand photographs of patients on his computer. Someday, he said, he'd create another gallery, upstairs in the atrium of McInnis House. Tony's photo was already framed.

The first patient photo that Jim took, in some ways the most notable, didn't hang in the hallway gallery. It's a picture of a woman named Gretel. Years of hard drinking had left her with end-stage cirrhosis. Jim and his colleagues pled her case with the specialists. They agreed to consider her for a liver transplant if she could achieve six months of proven sobriety. She went into McInnis House and quit alcohol for good. A few days before the surgery, she asked Jim to take her picture. She had lived on the streets for decades. Out on the van at night, he used to find her on the stoop of an abandoned building, surrounded by foul-smelling stuff—spoiled milk, rotten eggs—which she assembled to fend off nocturnal human predators. When she was living outside, he never saw her dressed in anything but filthy rags. But when she appeared for the picture taking, she was transformed. She had put on a dress, and mascara, lipstick, and nail polish. In the photo, she looks weathered in the face but elegant—fashionably thin, proudly erect. On the table beside her she has placed a bunch of cut flowers in a Styrofoam coffee cup.

Jim remembers wondering what all this meant. Was she afraid she would die in surgery? She laughed at him. She reminded him that she had been a *woman* living on the streets for decades, in danger of dying every night. "And then she explained to me that she had two kids, two daughters, and one had been three years old, I think, and the other had been six years old, when she last saw them. And that was about twenty-five years ago. And she was worried that, should they ever go looking to see who their mother was or what happened to their mother, there wouldn't be a picture of someone they could at least be proud of."

Until Gretel, Jim had refrained from photographing patients. He thought they might feel embarrassed or exploited. But the day after he took her picture, twenty-two others came to him, asking that he take their pictures, too. He was surprised, but thought he understood. "They wanted something to show they passed this way," he says. "I started to think that loneliness is really what drives much of what goes on in our world. Trying to fill that emptiness can be a real challenge."

Gretel survived the transplant. She lived for another five years, quite happily. At almost every lecture, Jim shows the photograph for which she'd gotten all dressed up more than twenty years ago. And he tells the audience her story, in the hope that one of her daughters might be sitting out there. He had the portrait printed and framed, but he has set it aside ever since for safekeeping.

"I never put it on the wall here, because I'm holding it for her daughters. I don't know if they're ever going to come looking for her or not."

Acknowledgments

I have worked with two editors for the past half century. The first was Richard Todd, who edited me and my writing for forty-seven years. I have dedicated this book to his memory. My other editor is Kate Medina, who joined Dick Todd and me in 1996. She has stuck by me ever since, and I owe her special thanks for her support, counsel, and friendship.

Many writer friends helped me with this book, foremost among them Jonathan Harr, who labored over many revisions with great good humor. Frances Kidder helped me beyond measure. For their literary counsel, I am also grateful to Dr. Alice Bukhman, James Conaway, Ophelia Dahl, Stuart Dybek, Miriam Feurle, Pacifique Irankunda,

Jon A. Jackson, Alex Kotlowitz, Luke Mitchell, Asvelt Nduwumwami, Sarah Toland, William Whitworth. The writer and copy editor Christine Jerome helped me all the way to the end. My thanks to John Graiff, who spent hundreds of hours conducting research for me, and thanks also to David Hoose and David Reid. I am immeasurably grateful to Judge Mark Wolf, Ed Davis, and Joe Lawless.

Thanks to Georges Borchardt, my friend and agent of more than forty years. And thanks to all my friends at Random House, especially Evan Camfield, London King, and Noa Shapiro. Matthew Martin and James Kilbreth all helped untangle legal issues.

In my attempts to fathom the complexities of homelessness in America and in Boston, I received gracious help from Travis Baggett, Don Berwick, Brett Feldman, Rosanne Haggerty, Jeff Olivet, Pat Perri, Jill Roncarati, Megan Sandel, Sam Tsemberis.

I am deeply indebted to all the people who worked with the Street Team at one time or another during the years I spent with the group, including Yvonne Bauer, Julie Bogdanski, Jim Bonnar, Joanne Callahan, Ross Chauvin, Davis Droll, Carlos Echeverria, Christine Hamilton, Mike Jellison, Cary Anne Kane, Katie Koh, Brandon Leung, Carolyn Matheson, Dave Munson, Rich Nickerson, Jen Nunes, Erin O'Neill, Lynnie Potter, Eileen Reilly, Kevin Sullivan, Katy Swanson, Beckie Tachick.

Thanks also to Larry Adams (now deceased), Michael Andrick, Suzanne Armstrong, Ari Barbanell, John Baynard, Heather Berrien, Poojah Bhalla, Jen Brody, Bruce Bullen, Sarah Ciambrone, Jason Clemons, Nicole Collymore, Denise De Las Nueces, Jessie Gaeta, Barbara Giles, Joanne Guarino, Cassis Henry, Joyce Jackson, Cheryl Kane, Pam Klein, Omar Marrero, Aura Obando, Linda Wood O'Connor, Sara Pacelle, Phillip Pulaski, Sara Reid, Lexi Schneider, Derri Shtasel, Sonja Spears, Georgia Thomas, Dirk Williams, Derek Winbush. I owe special thanks also to Barry Bock for tolerating my presence with great good humor, and to Mala Rafik for helping me with some of my research and for piloting me through the shoals of the law known as HIPAA.

Paul English and Robyn Glaser first introduced me to Jim O'Connell. Rick Schlegel put me up at his home and gave me a long tour of Jim O'Connell's past. I was tutored in the history of Boston's attempts to bring health care to homeless people by Governor Charlie Baker, John Bernardo, Barbara Blakeney, Barry Bock, Bruce Bullen, Dr. Roman DeSanctis, former mayor Ray Flynn, Stefan Kertesz, Alison May, Dr. John Potts, and Bob Taube. Rick Miller, Eileen Reilly, and Ben Tousley shared recollections of Barbara McInnis. Alicia Ianiere gave me a tour of the Pine Street Inn, and Lyndia Downie explained some of its history and current programs and policies. Margaret Boles Fitzgerald, Mary Ann Ponti, and John Unni helped me find my way around Boston, as did those who drove and staffed the outreach van: Nelson Bennett, Leroy Bush, Jason Clemente, Cesar Sandoval. Thanks also to Nick and Maddie Bukhman for their hospitality.

To Ellen Bubrick, Gene Bukhman, John Chi, Sarajune Dagan, Rose Du, Julie Ferragamo, Hanno Muellner, John O'Sullivan, Dan Solomon: Thank you for making it possible for me to finish this book.

Finally, my thanks to Jim O'Connell and the many patients whom I met while spending time with the Boston Health Care for the Homeless Program.

Sources

~~~~~~~~~~~~~~

Foot Soaking

Lenehan, G. P., B. N. McInnis, D. O'Donnell, and M. Hennessey. "A Nurses' Clinic for the Homeless." *American Journal of Nursing* 85, no. 11 (November 1985), 1237–41.

Reilly, E., and B. N. McInnis. "Boston, Massachusetts: The Pine Street Inn Nurses' Clinic and Tuberculosis Program." In P. W. Brickner, M.D., et al., eds. *Health Care of Homeless People.* New York: Springer Publishing, 1985.

Interview with Barbara Blakeney.

Disaster Medicine

The "scholarly study" used or misused by the Reagan administration:
Bassuk, E. L., L. Rubin, and A. Lauriat. "Is Homelessness a Mental Health Problem?" *American Journal of Psychiatry* 141, no. 2 (December 1984): 1546–50.

Numbers

It is commonly asserted that the new era of homelessness began in the 1980s. Here is one of many examples:

Spar, K. "The Homeless: Overview of the Problem and the Federal Response." Washington, D.C.: Congressional Research Service, Library of Congress, September 14, 1984. digital.library.unt.edu/ark:/67531 /metacrs8869. The following quotation from this article seems worth reproducing here: "A prolonged period of historically high unemployment and the resulting 'new poor' are calling attention to a problem which is not new in many large cities; that is, the number of people without permanent homes who are living in cars, tents or on the street. Unlike the skid row 'derelicts' who comprised the typical homeless population of the 1960s, today's street people represent many diverse groups including: the mentally ill, evicted families, the aged, alcoholics, drug addicts, abused spouses, abused young people, and cast-off children. The Department of Housing and Urban Development (HUD) noted in a recent report that the most commonly cited estimate of the number of homeless people is more than 2 million nationwide, based on information gathered by advocacy organizations for the homeless. However, HUD's own estimate of the number of homeless people nationwide is between 250,000 and 350,000."

For my account of how homelessness grew in Boston, I relied in part on the following:

CHAPA. "The Case for Preserving and Creating Single Room Occupancy Housing in Massachusetts." Boston: Citizens' Housing and Planning Association, 1990.

The following articles describe President Reagan's TV interview near the end of his presidency with quotations from him on homelessness:

Roberts, S. V. "Reagan on Homelessness: Many Choose to Live in the Streets." *New York Times*, December 23, 1988.

Cannon, L. "Reagan Cites 'Choice' by Homeless." *Washington Post*, December 23, 1988.

The role of the Reagan administration in the rise of homelessness is a disputed piece of recent American history. The following is a sampling of views:

Beirne, K. J. "America's Homeless: A Manageable Problem and Solution." *Backgrounder* 44. Washington, D.C.: The Heritage Foundation, May 4, 1987.

heritage.org/welfare/report/americas-homeless-manageable-problem-and
-solution.

Congressional Research Service. "Overview of Federal Housing Assistance
Programs and Policy." Updated March 27, 2019. crsreports.congress.gov
/product/pdf/RL/RL34591.

Danziger, S., and R. Haveman. "The Reagan Administration's Budget Cuts:
Their Impact on the Poor." irp.wisc.edu/publications/focus/pdfs/foc52b
.pdf.

Drier, P. "Reagan's Legacy: Homelessness in America." Shelterforce.org,
May 1, 2004. https://shelterforce.org/2004/05/01/reagans-legacy-home
lessness-in-america/.

Jones, M. M. "Creating A Science of Homelessness During the Reagan
Era." *Milbank Quarterly* 93, no. 1 (March 2015): 139–78. ncbi.nlm.nih.gov
/pmc/articles/PMC4364434/.

Kondratas, S. A. "A Strategy for Helping America's Homeless." *Backgrounder*
431. Washington, D.C.: The Heritage Foundation, May 6, 1985. heritage
.org/welfare/report/americas-homeless-manageable-problem-and-solution.

Pear, R. "U.S. Seen Curbing Help for Homeless." *New York Times,* June 12,
1983. nytimes.com/1983/06/12/us/us-seen-curbing-help-for-homeless
.html.

Rosenbaum, D. E. "First Major Cuts in Social Security Proposed in Detailed
Reagan Plan." *New York Times,* May 13, 1981. nytimes.com/1981/05/13/us
/first-major-cuts-in-social-security-proposed-in-detailed-reagan-plan.html.

Rubin, Beth A., James D. Wright, and Joel A. Devine. "Unhousing the
Urban Poor: The Reagan Legacy." *Journal of Sociology and Social Welfare* 19,
no. 1 (March 1992).

Tucker, W. "The Source of America's Housing Problem: Look in Your Own
Back Yard." Cato Institute Policy Analysis no. 127, February 6, 1990.
Washington, D.C.: The Cato Institute. cato.org/policy-analysis/source
-americas-housing-problem-look-own-back-yard#.

Western Regional Advocacy Project, San Francisco. "History of Slashing
HUD Budget: Sources." weap.org/uploads/fact%20sheets/WRAP-History
ofSlashingHUDBudgetFactSheet-Final.pdf.

The Reagan administration laid out its housing policy in this report:
"The Report of The President's Commission on Housing." Washington,
D.C.: The President's Commission on Housing, 1982.

This report contains an evaluation of the state of low-income housing at the end of the Reagan administration:
"A Decent Place to Live: The National Housing Task Force." Washington, D.C.: U.S. Department of Housing and Urban Development, March 1988. huduser.gov/portal/publications/affhsg/Task_Force_1988.html.

The following book contains a detailed account of what the Reagan administration hoped to do and actually did in regard to affordable housing. I found it both temperate and persuasive:
Hays, R. A. *The Federal Government and Urban Housing: Ideology and Change in Public Policy.* Albany: State University of New York Press, 1995.

The following is a useful history of deinstitutionalization, with citations:
Yohanna, D. "Deinstitutionalization of People with Mental Illness: Causes and Consequences." *American Medical Association Journal of Ethics* 15, no. 10 (October 2013): 886–91.

This report, aired on radio, describes Reagan's own involvement in deinstitutionalization as the governor of California:
Placzek, J. "Did the Emptying of Mental Hospitals Contribute to Homelessness?" KQED, December 8, 2016.

The figures on international homelessness come from:
FEANTSA and The Foundation Abbé Pierre. "Fifth Overview of Housing Exclusion in Europe." Brussels and Paris, July 2020. feantsa.org/en/news/2020/07/23/fifth-overview-of-housing-exclusion-in-europe-2020.

Institute of Global Homelessness. "State of Homelessness in Countries with Developed Economies." Chicago: Ruff Institute of Global Homelessness, 2019. ighhub.org/resource/state-homelessness-countries-developed-economies.

OECD, Social Policy Division, Directorate of Employment, Labour and Social Affairs, HC3.1. "Homeless Population." Paris: Organisation for Economic Cooperation and Development, 2021. oecd.org/els/family/HC3-1-Homeless-population.pdf.

United Nations Department of Economic and Social Affairs. "First-Ever United Nations Resolution on Homelessness." New York, March 9, 2020. un.org/development/desa/dspd/2020/03/resolution-homelessness/.

Sources for the discussion of numbers of homeless people:
National Center for Homeless Education. "Federal Data Summary School Years 2016–17 Through 2018–19: Education for Homeless Children and Youth." Greensboro: University of North Carolina, April 2021.

New York Times Editorial Board. "How Many Americans Are Homeless? No One Knows." *New York Times,* January 28, 2021.

The point-in-time count for 2020 comes from:
U.S. Department of Housing and Urban Development. "The 2020 Annual Homeless Assessment Report (AHAR) to Congress. Part 1: Point-in-Time Estimates of Homelessness in the United States." Washington, D.C., January 2021.

Estimate of total numbers sheltered at any time during 2018:
U.S. Department of Housing and Urban Development. "The 2018 Annual Homeless Assessment Report (AHAR) to Congress. Part 2: Estimates of Homelessness in the United States." Washington, D.C., September 2020.

This is the original source of the 3.5 million figure used in hundreds of other homelessness studies:
Burt, M. R., L. Y. Aron, E. Lee, and J. Valente. "How Many Homeless People Are There? Helping America's Homeless: Emergency Shelter or Affordable Housing." Washington, D.C.: Urban Institute (2001): 23–54.

Another approach to quantifying homelessness is described in the following:
Link, B. G., E. Susser, A. Stueve, J. Phelan, R. E. Moore, and E. Struening. "Lifetime and Five-Year Prevalence of Homelessness in the United States." *American Journal of Public Health* 84 (1994): 1907–12.

The cited estimate of housing insecurity comes from:
National Alliance to End Homelessness. "State of Homelessness." 2021 edition. endhomelessness.org/homelessness-in-america/homelessness-statistics/state-of-homelessness-2021/.

Definitions of housing insecurity vary. The following article illuminates the issues and suggests that the estimate cited above is low:
Leopold, J., M. Cunningham, L. Posey, and T. Manuel. "Improving Measures of Housing Insecurity: A Path Forward." Washington, D.C.: Urban Institute, November 23, 2016.

The principal source for what I call the "taxonomy" of homelessness:

Kuhn, R., and D. P. Culhane. "Applying Cluster Analysis to Test a Typology of Homelessness by Pattern of Shelter Utilization: Results from the Analysis of Administrative Data." *American Journal of Community Psychology* 26 (1998): 207–32.

The following are also useful:

Byrne, T., and D. P. Culhane. "Testing Alternative Definitions of Chronic Homelessness." *Psychiatric Services* 66, no. 5 (2015). works.bepress.com /dennis_culhane/146/.

Culhane, D. P., and R. Kuhn. "Patterns and Determinants of Public Shelter Utilization Among Homeless Adults in New York City and Philadelphia." *Journal of Policy Analysis and Management* 17, no. 1 (1998): 23–43.

Estimated percentages of chronically homeless who are unsheltered in Boston and nationally:

U.S. Department of Housing and Urban Development. "The 2018 Annual Homeless Assessment Report (AHAR) to Congress. Part 1: PIT Estimates of Homelessness in the United States." Washington, D.C., September 2020.

These are my sources on death rates of homeless people in Boston:

Baggett, T. P., S. W. Hwang, J. J. O'Connell, B. C. Porneala, E. J. Stringfellow, E. J. Orav, D. E. Singer, and N. A. Rigotti. "Mortality Among Homeless Adults in Boston: Shifts in Causes of Death over a 15-Year Period." *JAMA Internal Medicine* 173, no. 3 (February 11, 2013): 189–95.

Roncarati, J. S., T. P. Baggett, J. J. O'Connell, S. W. Hwang, E. F. Cook, N. Krieger, and G. Sorensen. "Mortality Among Unsheltered Homeless Adults in Boston, Massachusetts, 2000–2009." *JAMA Internal Medicine* 178, no. 9 (2018): 1242–48.

Upside-Down Medicine

Starr, P. *The Social Transformation of American Medicine: The Rise of a Sovereign Profession and the Making of a Vast Industry.* New York: Basic Books, 1982.

Death by Housing

Kuhn, R., and D. P. Culhane. "Applying Cluster Analysis to Test a Typology of Homelessness by Pattern of Shelter Utilization: Results from the Analysis of Administrative Data." *American Journal of Community Psychology* 26, no. 2 (1998): 207–32.

Mr. Culhane is the principal author of a number of other important studies bearing on issues of homelessness. Here are some of those:
Culhane, D. P., and R. Kuhn. "Patterns and Determinants of Public Shelter Utilization Among Homeless Adults in New York City and Philadelphia." *Journal of Policy Analysis and Management* 17, no. 1 (Winter 1998): 23–43.

Culhane, D. P. "The Quandaries of Shelter Reform: An Appraisal of Efforts to 'Manage' Homelessness." *Social Service Review* 66, no. 3 (September 1992): 428–40. repository.upenn.edu/spp_papers/120/.

Culhane, D. P. "Shelters Lead Nowhere." *New York Times,* December 19, 1993.

Culhane, D. P., E. F. Dejowski, J. Ibañez, E. Needham, and I. Macchia. "Public Shelter Admission Rates in Philadelphia and New York City: The Implications of Turnover for Sheltered Population Counts." *Housing Policy Debate* 5, no. 2 (1994): 107–40. repository.upenn.edu/spp_papers/62.

Culhane, D. P., C. Lee, and S. M. Wachter. "Where the Homeless Come From: A Study of the Prior Address Distribution of Families Admitted to Public Shelters in New York City and Philadelphia." *Housing Policy Debate* 7, no. 2 (1996): 327–65. repository.upenn.edu/spp_papers/63.

Culhane, D. P., S. Metraux, and S. M. Wachter. "Homelessness and Public Shelter Provision in New York City." *Housing and Community Development in New York City: Facing the Future.* Albany: State University of New York Press, 1999.

Culhane, D. P. "Five Myths About America's Homeless." *Washington Post,* July 11, 2010.

Culhane, D. P., S. Metraux, and T. Hadley. "Public Service Reductions Associated with Placement of Homeless Persons with Severe Mental Illness in Supportive Housing." *Housing Policy Debate* 13, no. 1 (2002): 107–63. repository.upenn.edu/spp_papers/65/.

Culhane, D. P. "A First-Class Solution: Review of Deborah K. Padgett, Benjamin F. Henwood, and Sam J. Tsemberis, *Ending Homelessness, Transforming Systems, and Changing Lives.*" *Stanford Social Innovation Review* 14, no. 2 (2016).

On the PSH model program:
Tsemberis, S., and S. Asmussen. "From Streets to Homes: The Pathways to Housing Consumer Preference Supported Housing Model." *Alcoholism Treatment Quarterly* 17, no. 2 (1999): 113–31. doi.org/10.1300/J020v17 n01_07.

On costs of ACT teams generally:
"Assertive Community Treatment." *Harvard Mental Health Letter* 23, no. 5 (2006): 4–5.

On the nature of ACT teams:
Menzies Munthe-Kaas, H., R. C. Berg, and N. Blaasvaer. "Effectiveness of Interventions to Reduce Homelessness: A Systematic Review and Meta-Analysis." *Campbell Systematic Reviews* 14 (February 28, 2018): 1–281.

Jill Roncarati's study:
Roncarati, J. S., H. Tiemeier, R. Tachick, T. J. VandeerWeele, and J. J. O'Connell. "Housing Boston's Chronically Homeless Unsheltered Population: 14 Years Later." *Medical Care* 59, no. 4, suppl. 2. (April 2021). pubmed.ncbi.nlm.nih.gov/33710091/.

The following study attempts to evaluate the evidence that housing homeless people saves money and improves health outcomes:
National Academies of Sciences, Engineering, and Medicine: Health and Medicine Division; Board on Population Health and Public Health Practice, and Policy and Global Affairs Division; Science and Technology for Sustainability Program. "Permanent Supportive Housing: Evaluating the Evidence for Improving Health Outcomes Among People Experiencing Chronic Homelessness." Washington, D.C.: National Academies Press, July 11, 2018.

The following represent a small range of criticisms of Housing First:
Eide, S. "Housing First and Homelessness: The Rhetoric and the Reality." New York: Manhattan Institute, April 2020. media4.manhattan-institute. org/sites/default/files/housing-first-and-homelessness-SE.pdf.

Kertesz, S. G., T. P. Baggett, J. J. O'Connell, D. S. Buck, and M. B. Kushel. "Permanent Supportive Housing for Homeless People—Reframing the Debate." *New England Journal of Medicine* 375, no. 22 (December 1, 2016): 2115–17.

Eulogies for Barbara

The lyrics to "A Song for Barbara" come from the album *Open the Gates,* Ben Tousley, Whole World Music (BMI), 1998.

A History of Tony

My sources for questioning the assumption that most male victims of childhood sexual abuse become abusers themselves:

Carey, B "Preying on Children: The Emerging Psychology of Pedophiles." *New York Times*, September 29, 2019, p. 27. nytimes.com/2019/09/29/us /pedophiles-online-sex-abuse.html.

Leach, C., A. Stewart, and S. Smallbone. "Testing the Sexually Abused– Sexual Abuser Hypothesis: A Prospective Longitudinal Birth Cohort Study." *Child Abuse and Neglect* 15 (2016): 144–53. sciencedirect.com/science/article /abs/pii/S0145213415003828.

Hall, R.C.W., and R.C.W. Hall. "A Profile of Pedophilia: Definition, Characteristics of Offenders, Recidivism, Treatment Outcomes, and Forensic Issues." *Mayo Clinic Proceedings* 82, no.4 (April 1, 2007): 457–71. mayoclinicproceedings.org/article/S0025-6196(11)61074-4/fulltext.

The Social Director

The study in which Jim participated:
National Academies of Sciences, Engineering, and Medicine. "Permanent Supportive Housing." Op. cit.

Success

Joanne's pamphlet:
Prepared by Joanne Guarino on behalf of the Consumer Advisory Board of Boston Health Care for the Homeless. *Housing Guide: Tips and Tools for a Successful Housing Experience.* Undated. The pamphlet has four parts: *Housing Basics:* "How to Settle In," "How to Stay Safe," "How to Keep Rooms Clean," "How to Buy Groceries and Do Laundry," "Weekly Meal Planner Template." *Staying Organized:* "How to Keep Track of Appointments and Bills," "How to Keep a Weekly Schedule." *Finances:* "How to Budget and Open a Bank Account," "How to Write a Check." *Everyday Life:* "How to Stay Connected to Family and Friends," "How to Get a Photo ID," "How to Get a Library Card," "How to Make the Internet Work for You," "How to be Informed About Your Record."

The Prism

A brief summary of Jim O'Connell's view on homelessness and its possible cures:
O'Connell, J.J., M.D. "Zones of Excess Mortality for Homeless Adults in the US—A Half Century Later." *JAMA Internal Medicine* (August 29, 2022). jamanetwork.com/journals/jamainternalmedicine/article-abstract /2795478.

Statistics on poverty in 2018 come from:
U.S. Department of Health and Human Services. "Annual Update of the
HHS Poverty Guidelines." Washington, D.C., 2018. federalregister.gov
/documents/2018/01/18/2018-00814/annual-update-of-the-hhs-poverty
-guidelines.

U.S. Census Bureau. "Income and Poverty in the United States, 2020."
Washington, D.C., September 14, 2021. census.gov/library/publications
/2021/demo/p60-273.html.

On rents in Boston:
Acitelli, T. "Boston Apartment Rents: Jumps This Winter in West Roxbury,
South End; Dips in Mattapan, Hyde Park." *Curbed Boston.* May 22, 2018.
boston.curbed.com/2018/5/22/17378336/boston-apartment-rents-spring
-2018.

**The estimate of homelessness among Black Americans comes
from:**
U.S. Department of Housing and Urban Development. "HUD Releases 2020
Annual Homelessness Assessment Report, Part 1." Washington, D.C., March
18, 2021. hud.gov/press/press_releases_media_advisories/hud_no_21_041.

Variations in life expectancies in Boston come from this study:
Zimmerman, E., B. F. Evans, S. H. Wolf, and A. D. Haley. "Social Capital
and Health Outcomes in Boston." Technical Report, Center on Human
Needs. Richmond: Virginia Commonwealth University, 2012.

The study concerning housing insecurity and diabetic emergencies:
Berkowitz, S. A., S. Kalkhoran, S. T. Edwards, U. R. Essien, T. P. Baggett.
"Unstable Housing and Diabetes-Related Emergency Department Visits and
Hospitalization: A Nationally Representative Study of Safety-Net Clinic
Patients." *Diabetes Care* 41 (2018): 933–39.

For data on the housing projects in Denver, see:
Colorado Coalition for the Homeless. "Milestones." Denver: Colorado
Coalition for the Homeless. Accessed 2021 at coloradocoalition.org
/milestones.

For data on the housing projects in San Francisco, see:
Office of the Controller, City Services Auditor. "Human Services Agency:
Care Not Cash Is Achieving Its Goals." City and County of San Francisco,
April 30, 2008.

San Francisco Human Services Agency. "San Francisco's Ten Year Plan to End Chronic Homelessness: Anniversary Report Covering 2004 to 2014." City and County of San Francisco, June 2014.

San Francisco Human Services Agency. "Care Not Cash—Overview and Progress Report." Prepared for San Francisco Ten Year Plan Implementation Council. Department of Human Services/Department of Aging and Adult Services, February 9, 2005.

For context on the situation in Los Angeles:
I relied in part on interviews with Brett Feldman, director of the Division of Street Medicine, assistant professor of family medicine, Keck School of Medicine, University of Southern California.

For the data on Skid Row:
Los Angeles Homeless Services Authority, "2020 Greater Los Angeles Homeless Count—Skid Row." July 30, 2020.

For official data on homelessness in Greater Los Angeles:
Los Angeles Homeless Services Authority. "Greater Los Angeles Homeless Count—2020." lahsa.org/documents?id=4558-2020-greater-los-angeles -homeless-count-presentation.pdf.

For the data on the multibillion-dollar attempt to solve the housing problem in Los Angeles:
Council of the City of Los Angeles. "Final Resolution for Proposition HHH." Council of the City of Los Angeles. June 29, 2016. clkrep.lacity.org /election/final%20homelessness%20hhh%20for%20web.pdf.

Galperin, R. "Re: The High Cost of Homeless Housing: Review of Proposition HHH." Office of L.A. Controller, October 8, 2019.

Galperin, R. "Meeting the Moment: An Action Plan to Advance Prop. HHH." Office of L.A. Controller, September 9, 2020.

Galperin, R. "Re: The Problems and Progress of Prop. HHH." Office of L.A. Controller, February 23, 2022.

Klein, E. "The Way Los Angeles Is Trying to Solve Homelessness Is 'Absolutely Insane.'" *The New York Times,* October 23, 2022. nytimes.com /2022/10/23/opinion/los-angeles-homelessness-affordable-housing.html.

KPCC (Southern California Public Radio). "10 Things You Need to Know About Measure HHH." KPCC, November 4, 2016. kpcc.org/show/take -two/2016-11-04/10-things-you-need-to-know-about-measure-hhh.

Los Angeles County Registrar-Recorder/County Clerk. "LA County Election Results." November 8, 2016. results.lavote.gov/#year=2016&election =3496.

Mihalik, L., A. Pesce, and B. Welsh. "California 2016 Election Results." *Los Angeles Times,* November 9, 2016. graphics.latimes.com/la-na-pol-2016 -election-results-california/.

Shelley, S. "After Squandering HHH Funds, a New Effort to Waste More Money Emerges." *Los Angeles Daily News,* March 8, 2022. dailynews.com /2022/03/02/after-squandering-hhh-funds-a-new-effort-to-waste-more -money-emerges/.

Smith, D. "County Voters to Decide on Quarter-Cent Sales Tax for Homelessness Programs." *Los Angeles Times,* February 14, 2017. latimes.com /local/lanow/la-me-ln-county-measure-h-campaign-20170214-story.html.

The Times Editorial Board. "Editorial: The Only Way Out of Homelessness Is Permanent Housing. That's Why We Need the HHH Program." *Los Angeles Times,* March 8, 2022. latimes.com/opinion/story/2022-03-08 /hhh-homeless-permanent-housing.

Vives, R., and D. Smith. "L.A. Paying Up to $837,000 per Unit for Homeless Housing. Audit Raises Red Flags." *Los Angeles Times,* February 23, 2022. yahoo.com/lifestyle/l-1-2-billion-bond-182220416.html.

During the early months of Covid, Los Angeles moved a number of homeless people into motels, a temporary partial solution that has become permanent:

Weber, C. "California Spending Billions to House Homeless in Hotels." Associated Press, August 21, 2021. apnews.com/article/lifestyle-business -health-california-coronavirus-pandemic-835c2091c63c199d397346a497e 7ae49.

Confession

Sources on Father Alan E. Caparella:

"Assignment Record—Rev. Alan E. Caparella, o.f.m." Waltham, Mass.: Bishop-Accountability.org. October 2, 2013. bishopaccountability.org/assign /Caparella_Alan_E_ofm.htm.

"Franciscan Friars—OFM—185 Accused in This Religious Order." Waltham, Mass: Bishop-Accountability.org. February 27, 2021. bishop -accountability.org/religious_orders/ofm-franciscan-friars-0520/.

Garabedian Law. "Results for Victims and Survivors." April 8, 2022. Boston: Law Offices of Mitchell Garabedian. garabedianlaw.com/results-list.

"Group Wants Further Disclosure of Priests Accused of Sexual Abuse." 90.5 WESA, Pittsburgh, Penn. September 12, 2013. wesa.fm/identity-justice /2013-09-12/group-wants-further-disclosure-of-priests-accused-of-sexual -abuse.

Lindsay, J. "Boston Lawyer Clergy Sex Abuse Victims Releases New List of Alleged Abusers." Waltham, Mass.: Bishop-Acountability.org. September 4, 2013. bishop-accountability.org/news2013/09_10/2013_09_04_Lindsay _BostonLawyer.htm.

"PA—Victims 'Out' Two Abusive Catholic Priests." Chicago: Survivors Network of Those Abused by Priests (SNAP). September 12, 2013. snapnetwork.org/pa_victims_out_two_abusive_catholic_priests.

Here are books I found useful regarding Boston and homelessness:

Flynn, Nick. *Another Bullshit Night in Suck City.* New York: W. W. Norton, 2004.

Hirsch, Kathleen. *Songs from the Alley.* Boston: Ticknor & Fields, 1989.

Lukas, J. Anthony. *Common Ground: A Turbulent Decade in the Lives of Three American Families.* New York: A. A. Knopf, 1985.

MacDonald, Michael Patrick. *All Souls: A Family Story from Southie.* Boston: Beacon Press, 1999.

O'Connell, James J. *Stories from the Shadows: Reflections of a Street Doctor.* Boston: Boston Health Care for the Homeless, 2015.

PHOTO CREDIT: FRAN KIDDER

TRACY KIDDER graduated from Harvard and the University of Iowa. He has won the Pulitzer Prize, the National Book Award, the Robert F. Kennedy Award, and many other literary prizes. He is the author of *A Truck Full of Money*, *Good Prose* (with Richard Todd), *Strength in What Remains*, *My Detachment*, *Mountains Beyond Mountains*, *Home Town*, *Old Friends*, *Among Schoolchildren*, *House*, and *The Soul of a New Machine*.

About the Type

This book was set in Baskerville, a typeface designed by John Baskerville (1706–75), an amateur printer and type-founder, and cut for him by John Handy in 1750. The type became popular again when the Lanston Monotype Corporation of London revived the classic roman face in 1923. The Mergenthaler Linotype Company in England and the United States cut a version of Baskerville in 1931, making it one of the most widely used typefaces today.